T0212684

Lecture Notes in Computer Science   9417

Commenced Publication in 1973
Founding and Former Series Editors:
Gerhard Goos, Juris Hartmanis, and Jan van Leeuwen

Editorial Board

More information about this series at http://www.springer.com/series/7410

Sonja Buchegger · Mads Dam (Eds.)

Secure IT Systems

20th Nordic Conference, NordSec 2015
Stockholm, Sweden, October 19–21, 2015
Proceedings

 Springer

Editors
Sonja Buchegger
KTH Royal Institute of Technology
Stockholm
Sweden

Mads Dam
KTH Royal Institute of Technology
Stockholm
Sweden

ISSN 0302-9743   ISSN 1611-3349 (electronic)
Lecture Notes in Computer Science
ISBN 978-3-319-26501-8   ISBN 978-3-319-26502-5 (eBook)
DOI 10.1007/978-3-319-26502-5

Library of Congress Control Number: 2015954347

LNCS Sublibrary: SL4 – Security and Cryptology

Springer Cham Heidelberg New York Dordrecht London
© Springer International Publishing Switzerland 2015

Printed on acid-free paper

Springer International Publishing AG Switzerland is part of Springer Science+Business Media
(www.springer.com)

Preface

This volume contains the papers from NordSec 2015, the 20th Nordic Conference on Secure IT Systems. The conference was held during October 19–21, 2015, at KTH Royal Institute of Technology in Stockholm, Sweden.

The NordSec conferences were started in 1996 with the aim of bringing together researchers and practitioners within computer security in the Nordic countries, thereby establishing a forum for discussions and cooperation between universities, industry, and computer societies. NordSec addresses a broad range of topics within IT security and privacy.

NordSec 2015 received 38 submissions, with all 28 valid submissions receiving three reviews by Program Committee (PC) members. After reviewing, a discussion phase, and some shepherding, 16 papers were accepted, five thereof as short papers. They are all included in these proceedings.

This year, NordSec was flanked by two co-located security events. During October 18–19, COINS, the Norwegian Research School of Computer and Information Security, held their annual meeting in coordination with NordSec in Stockholm. During October 21–23, CySeP, the Cybersecurity and Privacy winter school held at KTH, took place for the second time. NordSec also held a poster session by students of Nord-SecMob, the Master's Program in Security and Mobile Computing that spans several Nordic universities. There were three invited keynote speakers, combining experience from academia, public policy making, and industry. Eugene H. Spafford from Purdue University gave a keynote on "Rethinking Cyber Security," Marit Hansen from the German Data Protection Commissioner in Schleswig-Holstein on "Protection Goals for Privacy Auditing and Engineering," and N. Asokan from Aalto University in Finland on "Technology Transfer from Security Research Projects: A Personal Perspective."

We thank all authors and presenters who contributed to the NordSec program. Moreover, we are very grateful to the PC members and additional reviewers who submitted thorough reviews, actively participated in the discussions, and especially those PC members who took on the role of shepherd to help improve the final versions of accepted papers. We also would like to express our gratitude to the VR ACCESS Linnaeus Center, the School of Computer Science and Communication, and the Department of Theoretical Computer Science at KTH Royal Institute of Technology for sponsoring the conference. Special thanks go to Sandhya Elise Hagelin and Ann Seares for their excellent administrative support in the local organization.

October 2015

Sonja Buchegger
Mads Dam

Organization

NordSec 2015 was organized at KTH Royal Institute of Technology, Stockholm, Sweden.

Program Committee

Conference Chair

Sonja Buchegger   KTH Royal Institute of Technology, SE

Program Chairs

Sonja Buchegger   KTH Royal Institute of Technology, SE
Mads Dam   KTH Royal Institute of Technology, SE

Reviewers

Ben Smeets	Magnus Almgren
Bengt Carlsson	Martin Hell
Christian Damsgaard Jensen	Panagiotis Papadimitratos
Christian Rohner	Peeter Laud
Dieter Gollmann	Rose-Mharie Åhlfeldt
Einar Snekkenes	Simin Nadjm-Tehrani
Hanno Langweg	Simone Fischer-Hübner
Ivan Damgaard	Stewart Kowalski
Jakob Illeborg	Tomas Olovsson
Karin Bernsmed	Tuomas Aura
Katerina Mitrokotsa	Vicenç Torra

Additional Reviewers

Thanh Bui	Peter Sebastian Nordholt
Rajat Kandoi	Mohit Sethi
Berit Skjernaa	Gert Læssøe Mikkelsen

Sponsoring Institutions

VR ACCESS Linnaeus Center
School of Computer Science and Communication, KTH Royal Institute of Technology
Department of Theoretical Computer Science, KTH Royal Institute of Technology

Contents

Cyber-Physical Systems Security

A Conceptual Nationwide Cyber Situational Awareness Framework for Critical Infrastructures

Hayretdin Bahşi(✉) and Olaf Manuel Maennel

Centre for Digital Forensics and Cyber Security,
Tallinn University of Technology, Akadeemia tee 15a, 12618 Tallinn, Estonia
{hayretdin.bahsi,olaf.maennel}@ttu.ee

Abstract. Protection of critical infrastructures against cyber threats is perceived as an important aspect of national security by many countries. These perceptions have extended the technical and organizational aspects of cyber security domain. However, decision makers still suffer from the lack of appropriate decision support systems. This position paper presents a conceptual framework for a nationwide system that monitors the national critical infrastructures and provides cyber situational awareness knowledge to organizational and national level decision makers. A research agenda is proposed for the implementation of this framework.

Keywords: Cyber situational awareness · Critical infrastructure

1 Introduction

Ensuring the security of the growing complexity in cyberspace is becoming the one of the major challenges in the world. This complexity is based on the fact that effective security solutions have to embrace the technical, organizational and national aspects. Technical aspect has been dealt with since the beginning of the cyber space era. Organizational cyber security efforts have been improved by the release of security policies, establishment of organizational structures and involvement of the top management in the subject matter. The links between national security and cyber security are empowered mostly due to cyber threats to critical infrastructures (CIs). Consequently, national cyber security strategies are prepared and high level decision making bodies are established. However, appropriate decision support tools have not been developed yet.

Cyber threats to critical infrastructures are one of the dangerous threats due to detrimental effects on human lives, assets and national economy. The dependencies between critical infrastructures make the problem more complicated so that cascading effects of a cyber attack may cause many subsequent disruptions. Situational awareness (SA) is defined as 'the perception of the elements in the environment within a volume of time and space, the comprehension of

© Springer International Publishing Switzerland 2015
S. Buchegger and M. Dam (Eds.): NordSec 2015, LNCS 9417, pp. 3–10, 2015.
DOI: 10.1007/978-3-319-26502-5_1

their meaning and the projection of their status in the near future'[1]. In order to identify and assess the aforementioned cyber threats to national CIs and provide relevant decision support, having the nation-wide knowledge is highly required.

This position paper proposes a conceptual framework for a nation-wide cyber security situational awareness system and identifies a research agenda for the implementation of such framework. The main purposes of framework are twofold: (1) Providing decision support to national policy makers and decision makers of CI organizations at all levels, (2) Detecting coordinated cyber attacks to various CIs and evaluating the effect of a cyber threat occurred in one CI to other CIs.

The scope of this paper is limited to presentation of building blocks of a conceptual framework which outlines main functions of subsystems, major information flows between them and targeted decision making hierarchy. Discussions of technical design and implementation details such as system architecture, communication protocols etc. are beyond the scope of this paper.

2   Related Work

National CERT organizations are evolving to more complex and bigger organizations such as national cyber security operations centers. Responsibilities regarding the national situational awareness knowledge is assigned to these organizations by the national strategies. This task is described with the term 'perception and action prospects' in the activity list of Dutch national operational center[1]. The collection of relevant data and sharing it with the appropriate partners across business is among the action priorities in the UK strategy 2011 [2]. US-CERT implements 'Enhance Shared Situational Awareness Initiative' in order to provide real time sharing of situational data between US Federal Cyber Centers and US critical infrastructure owners[2]. US-CERT runs EINSTEIN which is an intrusion detection system for monitoring the network traffic of US federal government networks[3]. National Cyber Security Center of the Netherlands runs BEITA which consists of honeypots and sensors deployed at government organizations[4]. FP7 funded project, European Control System Security Incident Analysis Network (ECOSSIAN), aims to provide a prototype of a multi-tiered system that runs at operator, national, EU levels and targets mostly operational level decision makers [3].

---

[1] Dutch National Cyber Security Centre web site, https://www.ncsc.nl/english/organisation, accessed date: 6 Aug 2015

[2] US-CERT web site, https://www.us-cert.gov/essa, accessed date: 6 Aug 2015

[3] US-CERT web site, https://www.us-cert.gov/government-users/tools-and-programs, accessed date: 6 Aug 2015

[4] Dutch National Cyber Security Center web site, https://www.ncsc.nl/english/Incident+Response/monitoring/beita.html, accessed date: 6 Aug 2015

3 Decision Making Hierarchy and Risk Management Perspective

Critical infrastructures are assumed to be national assets so that security of them does not only create concerns for their owners but for the national policy makers as well. Thus, complete decision making hierarchy includes national layer beside the CI organizational layers. A decision making pyramid is given for the nation-wide cyber security management [4].

The framework provides situational awareness information to decision makers of the hierarchy consisting of four layers: (1) National, (2) Strategic, (3) Tactical, (4) Operational. National layer, addresses national security policy makers such as disaster management authorities, regulatory bodies and members of national cyber security councils. The ones who align IT related activities with the long-term objectives of organizations form the strategic level. Managers of IT and core business units are considered at tactical level and technical operators who conduct the day-to-day cyber security operations stay at the operational level.

Security decision-making is mainly based on the risk management which is actually a vertical process among the national, strategic, tactical, operational decision levels [5] and requires the exact understanding of the situation [6] in terms of threats and vulnerabilities. Existing early warning and monitoring systems cannot provide sufficient situational awareness to risk management processes since they do not offer decision support to all levels and do not deal with threat and vulnerability information together. The proposed framework is designed to eliminate these weaknesses of existing implementations.

4 High Level System Entities

This framework is mainly comprised of subsystems which are classified into three categories, organizational cyber situational awareness (CSA), national CSA and CI Honeynets as shown in Fig. 1. Organizational CSA is responsible for providing decision support to CI organizations. National CSA is the component that detects the coordinated cyber attacks, conducts dependency analysis and gives decision support to national policy makers. CI Honeynets are the components that supply cyber threat intelligence to national CSA. Subsystems are detailed in the following subsections.

4.1 Organizational CSA Subsystem

Each critical infrastructure involved in the framework deploys this subsystem. In organizational context, subsystem provides results to decision makers of operational, tactical and strategic levels in CIs. It also conveys the relevant data and analysis results to national CSA subsystem. The inputs/outputs and analysis methods used in an organizational CSA subsystem are all shown in Fig. 2.

Organizational CSA system gathers data from the security products of current technology which are grouped into 11 different security automation

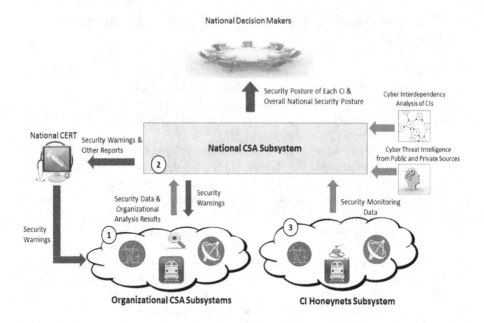

Fig. 1. High level system entities of the proposed framework.

domains [7]. The proposed framework obtains and correlates data from the domains of asset, event, vulnerability, configuration/network and incident management in order to provide situational awareness for the risk based security decisions. System data related with the safety functions of industrial control systems is another data source which may assist in conducting link analysis between cyber threats and industrial control process failures. The huge amount of data collected by the component requires the utilization of big data analytic methods. Organizational security posture analysis, which deals with the possible effects of cyber threats on business, constitutes the core of decision support for the strategic level decision makers such as CEOs, CIOs, heads of auditing departments. Framework objective for the tactical level decision makers is the identification of possible negative impacts of threats on resource management and services. Thus, data about the relationships between business, resources and IT processes are particularly required for the strategic and tactical level analysis tasks. Asset, service and organization based security posture analysis are conducted by the application of aggregation methods. Data visualization is utilized in the presentation of analysis results to all decision levels.

4.2   National CSA Subsytem

This subsystem correlates data coming from different CIs with respect to interdependency analysis of CIs in order to deduce the overall security posture of critical infrastructures and the actual impacts of cyber threats on national security.

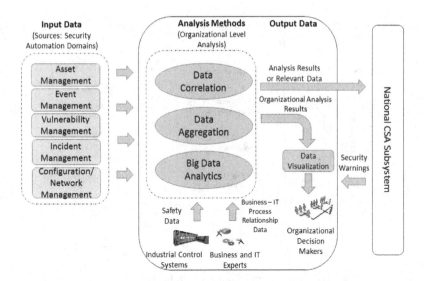

Fig. 2. Organizational CSA subsytem.

National CSA subsystem obtains input data from organizational CSA and CI Honeynets subsystems and it uses the interdependency analysis of CIs as an external input as shown in Fig. 3. Types of dependencies between CIs are classified into four categories, physical, cyber, geographic and logical [8]. The framework uses only cyber dependencies during the analysis. If interdependency analysis demonstrates that other CIs can be affected by a particular event or incident, relevant security warnings are sent to the national CERT and the other effected CIs. This subsystem also correlates event information of a CI with the similar events of others in order to detect systematic cyber attacks against various national CIs. The subsystem provides nation based, sector based and organizational based security posture results and cyber threat intelligence to members of cyber security council, regulatory bodies and disaster management authorities.

4.3 CI Honeynets Subsytem

Honeynet system constitutes an important platform that enable the defenders to deeply analyse the cyber threats and obtain information about their profiles without risking actual systems. Since honeynets simulate the production environment, administrators can freely alter them. The framework extracts cyber threat intelligence out of the collected data and send them to relevant national and organizational decision makers.

5   Research Agenda

Actual implementation of the conceptual framework requires to address important research problems including interdisciplinary ones. The overall research

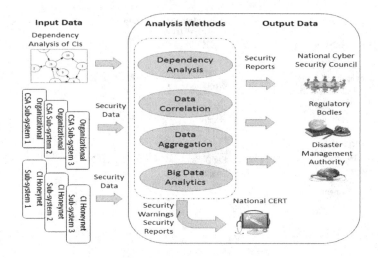

Fig. 3. National CSA Subsytem.

agenda is given in this section.

Ontology Development: Ontologies are appropriate tools for the formalization of complex problem domains such as situational awareness [9]. As the proposed framework addresses the same problem domain in a very dynamic environment, the development of an ontology can be the first step of agenda in order to create a common dictionary and formalize the relationships between different terms.

Socio-Technical Model: Due to the various national and organizational issues addressed by decision making hierarchy, the realization of the proposed framework can be achieved by socio-technical approaches which embraces technology and people aspects together. Socio-technical approaches have been studied in a general risk management model so that government, regulators and different decision making levels of organizations are all the parties of the model [10]. Especially business and legal aspects may cause harder obstacles than the technical aspects. For example, national policy making approach may differ when the critical infrastructures are owned by public or private companies. Similar problems can be solved with an interdisciplinary study involving management, political science, law and technical disciplines. A socio-technical method that determines the social and technical complexity levels of attacks was proposed for a global security warning system [11]. Similar approaches can be utilized in the determination of attack levels within the framework.

Data Correlation: Data correlation is accepted as an important defense mechanism by the cyber security community of critical infrastructures [12]. Correlation based security monitoring studies in the area of critical infrastructure security focus on mostly event data [13]. Proposed framework correlates various types of data about event, incident, vulnerability thus requires effective correlation methods. Collaborative intrusion detection systems have been developed for the identification of coordinated attacks, such as large-scale stealthy scans, worm attacks and distributed denial of service (ddos) attacks, against multiple administrative network domains [14]. Our framework requires to conduct research about how to use dependency analysis for the collaborative detection of cyber attacks in CI environments. The detection capability has to be improved beyond the identification of simple attack types since some of the attacks to critical infrastructures may use sophisticated techniques. Identification of the similarities and differences between safety and security related engineering practices has been studied [15]. Development of the correlation methods for the safety and security related data constitutes an important research problem.

Cyber Threat Intelligence with Honeypots: Honeypots are important instruments for the understanding of capabilities, behaviors, methods, tools and techniques of attackers. They have been improved to detect new cyber threats and integrated to other security mechanisms such as intrusion detection systems [16]. The outputs of systems are utilized for the improvement of situational awareness [17]. An important research area is the simulation of the critical infrastructures with honeypots and the analysis of attacks addressing them.

Privacy Preservation: Privacy concerns of critical infrastructure owners and other individuals accessing the critical services are among the main obstacles. Privacy preserved data analysis methods have been studied by the research community [18]. Adaptation of the existing methods according to the requirements of the framework is one of the challenges in the research agenda.

Data Visualization: Human is always the key actor in the all levels of decision making process of cyber security environment. Data visualization assists in presentation of complex situations to the humans. Investigation of data visualization techniques in providing situational awareness knowledge to each decision making level is among the research agenda.

6   Conclusion

Protection of critical infrastructures against cyber threats has strong technical, organizational and national aspects. Supporting the all levels of decision makers with the appropriate situational awareness knowledge poses a significant challenge in this problem domain. This position paper introduces a conceptual framework for a nation-wide cyber situational awareness system and presents a research agenda based on the proposed framework.

Acknowledgements. We thank our shepherd, Prof. Stewart J. Kowalski, for his insightful feedback and suggestions, also we are grateful to anonymous reviewers for their valuable comments.

References

1. Endsley, M.: Situation awareness global assessment technique (sagat). In: Proceedings of the IEEE 1988 National Aerospace and Electronics Conference, NAECON 1988, vol. 3, pp. 789–795 (1988)
2. Office, U.C.: The UK Cyber Security Strategy, protecting and promoting the UK in a digital world (2011)
3. Kaufmann, H., Hutter, R., Skopik, F., Mantere, M.: A structural design for a pan-european early warning system for critical infrastructures. e & i. Elektrotechnik und Informationstechnik **132**, 117–121 (2015)
4. Klimburg, A.: National cyber security framework manual. NATO Cooperative Cyber Defense Center of Excellence (2012)
5. Kowalski, S.: IT insecurity: a multi-disciplinary inquiry. Univ. (1994)
6. McLucas, A.C.: Decision making: risk management, systems thinking and situation awareness. Argos Press P/L (2003)
7. NIST: Information Security Continuous Monitoring (ISCM) for Federal Information Systems and Organizations (2011)
8. Rinaldi, S.M., Peerenboom, J.P., Kelly, T.K.: Identifying, understanding, and analyzing critical infrastructure interdependencies. IEEE Control Systems **21**, 11–25 (2001)
9. Kokar, M.M., Matheus, C.J., Baclawski, K.: Ontology-based situation awareness. Information Fusion **10**, 83–98 (2009)
10. Rasmussen, J.: Risk management in a dynamic society: A modelling problem. Safety Science **27**, 183–213 (1997)
11. Alsabbagh, B., Kowalski, S.: A cultural adaption model for global cyber security warning systems. In: 5th International Conference on Communications, Networking and Information Technology Dubai, UAE, pp. 16–18 (2011)
12. Egozcue, E., Rodrguez, D.H., Ortiz, J.A., Villar, V.F., Luis, T.: Smart grid security: Recommendations for Europe and member states (2012)
13. Skopik, F., Friedberg, I., Fiedler, R.: Dealing with advanced persistent threats in smart grid ict networks. In: 2014 IEEE PES Innovative Smart Grid Technologies Conference (ISGT), pp. 1–5. IEEE (2014)
14. Zhou, C.V., Leckie, C., Karunasekera, S.: A survey of coordinated attacks and collaborative intrusion detection. Computers & Security **29**, 124–140 (2010)
15. Paulitsch, M., Reiger, R., Strigini, L., Bloomfield, R.: Evidence-based security in aerospace: From safety to security and back again. In: 2012 IEEE 23rd International Symposium on Software Reliability Engineering Workshops (ISSREW), pp. 21–22. IEEE (2012)
16. Bringer, M.L., Chelmecki, C.A., Fujinoki, H.: A survey: Recent advances and future trends in honeypot research. International Journal **4** (2012)
17. Yegneswaran, V., Barford, P., Paxson, V.: Using honeynets for internet situational awareness. In: Proceedings of the Fourth Workshop on Hot Topics in Networks (HotNets IV), Citeseer, pp. 17–22 (2005)
18. Aggarwal, C.C., Philip, S.Y.: A general survey of privacy-preserving data mining models and algorithms. Springer (2008)

A Survey of Industrial Control System Testbeds

Hannes Holm[(⊠)], Martin Karresand, Arne Vidström, and Erik Westring

Swedish Defence Research Agency (FOI), Olaus Magnus väg 42, Linköping, Sweden
{hannes.holm,martin.karresand,arne.vidstrom,erik.westring}@foi.se

Abstract. Conducting security tests such as vulnerability discovery within Industrial Control Systems (ICS) help reduce their vulnerability to cyber attacks. Unfortunately, the extreme availability requirements on ICS in operation make it difficult to conduct security tests in practice. For this reason, researchers and practitioners turn to testbeds that mimic real ICS. This study surveys ICS testbeds that have been proposed for scientific research. A total of 30 testbeds are identified. Most of these aim to facilitate vulnerability analysis, education and tests of defense mechanisms. Testbed components are typically implemented as simulation models. Testbed fidelity is rarely addressed, and at best briefly discussed.

Keywords: Industrial Control Systems · Testbed · IT security · Cyber security · Systematic literature review

1 Introduction

Our society depends on various critical services such as electricity, water purification and transportation to properly function. Not long ago, the Industrial Control Systems (ICS) that supervised and controlled most of these critical services were realized by specially constructed isolated devices. Along with the rest of our society, ICS have evolved and are now often delivered by complex interconnected IT solutions including commercial-off-the-shelf (COTS) technologies that in one way or another are connected to the Internet. The main reasons behind this evolution are increased functionality and increased effectiveness, as well as reduced costs. For example, IP-based remote control of railroad signaling and interlocking systems has increased the level of control of the railroad system. The benefits of using IT for critical infrastructure applications are thus clear.

However, the trend of interconnectivity and COTS has also brought about problems. Issues that are common in regular IT architectures, such as malware and misconfigurations, do now occur in ICS systems as well. Reduced availability due to such issues might be acceptable in regular IT architectures, but are generally completely unacceptable for IT that supports critical infrastructure services. For instance:

- Computers along railway tracks in Sweden send continuous data regarding the state of the track to remote railway operators. If there are more than 15 seconds between two points of data for a device, the corresponding track is considered faulty and all trains designated to traverse it are blocked [37].

© Springer International Publishing Switzerland 2015
S. Buchegger and M. Dam (Eds.): NordSec 2015, LNCS 9417, pp. 11–26, 2015.
DOI: 10.1007/978-3-319-26502-5_2

– In the Energy Sector, digital protective relays are used to trip circuit breakers when power faults are detected – an event that can cause significant product damage and personnel harm. This function needs to be executed within a few milliseconds of the power fault to be of use.

To understand and manage the complexity of an IT architecture, e.g., to discover and mitigate security vulnerabilities within it, technical audits such as penetration tests are carried out. While technical audits often are considered an effective security solution, they can disrupt system services when they are conducted. This is particularly evident for ICS IT solutions – these are often not able to withstand even the most basic scanning tools. For example, a study involving Programmable Logic Controllers (PLC) and the vulnerability scanner Nessus showed that the 18% of the tested PLCs crashed as a result of a scan [32]. As a consequence, technical audits are generally thought of as (at best) difficult for IT architectures that support critical infrastructure services.

To study the vulnerability of IT architectures that are difficult to technically audit without compromising their reliability and performance, many researchers attempt to copy them in isolated environments, also called testbeds, where experiments safely can be performed. Creating a test bed however comes with various challenges, in particular: (i) it can be difficult to obtain a realistic test bed scale, and (ii) it can be difficult to achieve a realistic test bed configuration.

There are a number of approaches that can be used to implement components and configurations in testbeds. The most obvious approach is to include real hardware and software configured as they are configured in practice. This naturally provides a very high degree of fidelity. However, it is difficult to reconfigure and maintain real hardware and software in a testbed, especially given the presence of software exploits that have the potential to damage systems; not to mention reach a valid testbed scale due to the costs involved. An alternative is to employ simulation, to develop a new application or model that operate similarly to a desired solution [39][46]. Simulation models are generally easy to reconfigure, maintain and can provide an extensive testbed scale. However, it is difficult to obtain high fidelity from simulation models, especially when software exploits need be considered as these often only work given a specific code-base and configuration.

A third more attractive means of obtaining a large-scale realistic testbed is through virtualization. Virtualization is a technology which concerns isolating computer software in a means that enables layers of abstraction, both between different software and between software and hardware. For example, a virtual private network adds a layer on top of a computer network that isolates its users from others on the network; the Comodo antivirus uses operating system-level virtualization to create a sandbox for isolated web browsing; VMware and VirtualBox use hardware virtualization to enable guest operating systems to interface with software and hardware; the Quick Emulator (QEMU) use instruction set virtualization to provide a complete emulation of computer hardware in software. Virtualizing a testbed is attractive for several reasons, for example:

- It enables running multiple systems in parallel on single computer hardware.
- It enables quickly reconfiguring systems and networks using software scripts.
- It enables isolating the activity in the testbed from the physical systems as well as external systems.
- It enables using actual software and protocols rather than simulated equivalents.

In other words, virtualization can potentially allow low-cost, replicable and safe security studies of IT architectures that have configurations valid to those of real ICSs. An overview of virtualization approaches is given by Nanda and Chiueh [38]. Of the approaches discussed by the authors, hardware virtualization is especially attractive for testbeds as it enables high-performance execution of real applications in virtual containers. Emulation also enables execution of real applications, but is generally slower than virtualization as all instructions need to be trapped by the emulator.

1.1 Research Questions

This study surveys existing ICS testbeds that have been proposed for scientific research and tries to answer the following four research questions (RQs):

- *RQ1*: Which ICS testbeds have been proposed for scientific research?
- *RQ2*: Which research objectives do current ICS testbeds support?
- *RQ3*: How are ICS components implemented in current ICS testbeds?
- *RQ4*: How do existing ICS testbeds manage requirements?

These RQs are addressed to gain an understanding of how previously constructed ICS testbeds for scientific research have been designed.

1.2 Outline

This paper is structured as follows. Section 2 describes related work. Section 3 describes the method of the systematic literature review. Section 4 describes the outcome of the systematic review. Finally, Section 5 concludes the paper and presents possible future research directions.

2 Related Work

To the authors' knowledge, there are as of yet no articles that focus on surveying ICS testbeds. That said, most articles that describe specific testbeds also briefly compare these testbeds to a few others that are deemed similar in scope. A recent such example is the article by Siaterlis and Genge [50], who compare the testbed EPIC to eight other current ICS testbeds. They use a loosely defined scale from one to three to compare the testbeds according to six main criteria (fidelity, repeatability, measurement accuracy, safety, cost effectiveness and multiple critical infrastructures) and two sub-criteria (cyber and physical).

There are however articles that focus on surveying network and software testbeds for other domains than critical infrastructures and ICSs. This section describes such surveys. Harwell and Gore [25] provide an overview of cyber ranges (a type of network and software testbed) and their usage and note that there are more than 100 active in the United States alone.

Davis et al. [13] present a survey of cyber ranges and categorize these in three categories: (i) modelling and simulation (where models of each component exist), (ii) ad-hoc or overlay (running tests on production network hardware with some level of test isolation provided by a software overlay) and (iii) emulation (mapping a desired experimental network topology and software configuration onto a physical infrastructure). In addition to these categories, they discuss capture the flag competitions such as DefCon, which use their own cyber ranges for their events. The authors also categorize the cyber ranges according to their supporting sector: academic, military or commercial. They found that the objective of most cyber ranges was training, and that most cyber ranges used either simulation or emulation.

Gluhak et al. [19] provide a survey on testbeds for experimental internet of things (IoT) research and identify a total of 23 testbeds. These testbeds have a different scope than the cyber ranges surveyed by Davis et al. [13] in the sense that they focus on specific networking technologies such as Wireless Sensor Networks. This scope in effect requires that the testbeds to a greater extent employ real hardware in front of virtualization.

Leblanc et al. [31] provide a snapshot of different tools and testbeds for simulating and modeling cyber attacks as well as defensive responses to those. The authors note that there is a considerable interest in the topic and that significant progress have been made; however, they also observe that there appears to be very little coordination and cooperation behind this progress.

3   Review Protocol

The RQs were investigated using the standard systematic literature review approach described by Kitchenham [29]. The review began with unstructured searches related to the topic with the purpose of identifying relevant keywords for systematic searches. A set of preliminary keywords were then used to query Scopus[1] for articles published between January 2010 and the 20th of November 2014 with the chosen keywords within their titles, keywords or abstracts, yielding a total of 123 matches. The result of this query was deemed too narrow; thus, the keywords were extended to be more inclusive. During the 18th of December 2014, a final set of keywords[2] was used to query Scopus. This query identified 1335 articles.

---

[1] A database that contains conference and journal articles from all major publishers, including IEEE, ACM, Springer, Elsevier and Wiley.

[2] (scada OR ics OR mtu OR plc OR rtu OR io OR "embedded device" OR "embedded system") AND ((virtuali* OR simulat* OR emulat* OR hypervi* OR vmm OR "virtual machine" OR "dynamic recompilation") OR (testbed OR "test bed" OR "cyber range")).

The relevance of a subset of the 1335 articles (the 123 articles identified during the pre-study) was independently judged based on titles and abstracts by randomly chosen pairs of researchers. Redundant judgments were used to enable measuring the group's internal agreement with the statistical metric Cohen's Kappa [10]. The results showed strong agreement (a Kappa of 0.88 on a scale from 0 [no agreement] to 1 [complete agreement]), which is a sign that the group shares the same view on the project scope. Due to the strong agreement, each of the remaining 1212 articles was read by no more than one researcher. Out of the 1335 articles, 63 were judged as relevant and read in detail. Of these articles, 40 both concerned ICS testbeds and were deemed relevant after the more detailed review. The results from this literature review are presented in the following sections.

To answer the RQs, the following data were extracted from each article: (i) the objectives of the testbed, (ii) the configuration choices of the testbed and (iii) how the testbeds fidelity is ensured.

4   Results

The systematic literature review identified a total of 40 articles. These concerned 30 ICS testbeds that were planned or currently operational at the time of the present study. An overview of these testbeds is described by Table 1.

As can be seen, almost half of the identified testbeds were located in the USA. Five testbeds were only planned ([8], [15], [18], [28] and [58]), while the remaining 25 were claimed to be operational to an extent that facilitated technical studies related to their stated purposes. It should be mentioned that there are various other testbeds, such as DETER [5] and the U.S. National SCADA testbed, that were not directly identified by the systematic review. There are two explanations behind this: (i) they had either not published their results in forums indexed by Scopus or (ii) did not specifically concern ICS. The U.S. National SCADA testbed corresponds to the first explanation; DETER is not a testbed that has been designed for the purpose of ICS tests and thus corresponds to the second explanation. The testbeds that employ DETER, such as the testbed at the Technical Assessment Research Lab in China [17], view DETER as a tool that help realize an ICS testbed (similar to Matlab, OPNET or VirtualBox). The present study views DETER and other similar testbeds (e.g., Emulab, GENI and PlanetLab) in the same fashion as the ICS testbeds that use them.

4.1   Objectives of ICS Testbeds

An overview of the objectives that the creators of the testbeds present is given in Table 2. The most commonly mentioned objective is to use a testbed for vulnerability analysis, with education and tests of defense mechanisms on a split second place. These objectives highlight the fact that most testbeds focus on cyber security rather than, for instance, performance issues due to UDP packet loss.

Table 1. Overview of ICS testbeds.

ID	University/Organization	Country	References
1	American University of Sharjah	Abu Dhabi	[11]
2	Queensland University of Technology	Australia	[30]
3	RMIT University	Australia	[2],[40]
4	Research Institute of Information Technology and Communication	China	[58]
5	Technical Assessment Research Lab	China	[17]
6	Tsinghua University of Beijing	China	[9]
7	University of Zagreb	Croatia	[28]
8	Queen's University Belfast	Ireland	[61]
9	University College Dublin	Ireland	[51]
10	European Commission Joint Research Centre	Italy	[20],[50]
11	European Commission Joint Research Centre	Italy	[16]
12	Ricerca sul Sistema Energetico	Italy	[14]
13	American University of Beirut	Lebanon	[44]
14	University Kuala Lumpur	Malaysia	[47],[48]
15	TNO	Netherlands	[8]
16	ITER Korea	South Korea	[54]
17	Case Western Reserve University	USA	[34]
18	Iowa State University	USA	[22],[23]
19	ITESM Campus Monterrey	USA	[43]
20	Lewis Research Center	USA	[4]
21	Mississippi State University	USA	[35],[36],[41], [42],[57]
22	Ohio State University	USA	[21]
23	Pacific Northwest National Laboratory	USA	[15]
24	Sandia National Laboratories	USA	[56]
25	Tennessee Technological University	USA	[52]
26	The University of Tulsa	USA	[24]
27	UC Berkeley	USA	[18]
28	University of Arizona	USA	[33]
29	University of Illinois at Urbana-Champaign	USA	[6],[7],[12]
30	University of Louisville	USA	[26]

These objectives are in general described on a very superficial level. For example, the type of vulnerability analysis that is proposed is typically described with generic statements such as *"It is imperative to analyze the risk to SCADA systems in terms of vulnerabilities, threats and potential impact"* [8] and *"An evaluation of the security of SCADA systems is important"* [2]. However, as stated by Davis et al. [12], the complex hardware and software interactions that must be considered makes vulnerability analysis a difficult task. Thus, there is a need to break it down into more tangible topics in order to yield useful testbed requirements. The same reasoning applies for other objectives, such as education and tests of defense mechanisms.

Table 2. Objectives of testbeds.

Objective	Testbeds
Vulnerability analysis	16
Education	9
Tests of defense mechanisms	9
Power system control tests	4
Performance analysis	1
Creation of standards	1
Honeynet	1
Impact analysis	1
Test robustness	1
Tests in general	1
Threat analysis	1

4.2 Implementation of ICS Testbed Components

Based on NIST 800-82 [53], an ICS testbed should consider four general areas: the control center, the communication architecture, the field devices and the physical process itself. This section describes how components concerning these areas are implemented in the 30 surveyed testbeds. An overview of the results is described by Table 3. More detailed descriptions are provided in the following sections.

Table 3. Number of articles assessing different areas and methods of implementation (virtualization, emulation, simulation and hardware).

Area	Covered	Virtualization	Simulation	Emulation	Hardware
Control center	20	4	9	1	11
Communication architecture	22	6	10	3	11
Fields devices	23	0	14	0	14
Physical process	12	0	12	0	0

The Control Center concerns the servers and operator stations that are used to remotely observe and control field devices, such as MTUs and data historians. Approximately two thirds of all testbeds contain descriptions regarding how their control center components are incorporated. Of these, most utilize simulations (30%) and/or hardware (37%). It is interesting that so few (13%) testbeds choose to virtualize the control system components, something which to a large extent is possible as they typically involve COTS operating systems such as Windows and Linux. The virtualization solutions that are mentioned concern DETER,

Emulab, GENI, PlanetLab and VirtualBox. Simulation-based approaches concern LabVIEW, Mathworks Simulink, HoneyD in combination with IMUNES (FreeBSD jails), the RINSE network simulator and custom Python scripts. The emulation approach involves RINSE (it combines emulation and simulation). Hardware concerns standard x86-based computers such as CitectSCADA 6.1 on Windows XP (used as OPC server and HMI).

The Communication Architecture involves components that realize communication within ICS, for instance, routers, switches and modems. 73% of all testbeds contain descriptions regarding how their communication architecture is incorporated. Of these, most utilize simulations (33%) and/or hardware (37%). As for control systems, many kinds of communication architectures are possible to easily virtualize. For example, Ethernet is commonly used within ICS and is easily virtualized through e.g. VirtualBox. Thus, it is interesting that few testbeds (20%) choose to do so. Virtualization is proposed using DETER, GENI, Emulab or Virtualbox. Simulation is proposed using OPNET, SITL communication network simulator, Iperf (for background traffic), RINSE, OMNET++, PowerWorld simulator, Mathworks Simulink, the Inet framework, NS-2, Networksim, the c2windtunnel framework, IMUNES, and custom Python scripts. Emulation is proposed using CORE (in combination with OpenVZ) and RINSE. Hardware generally involves Ethernet devices such as routers and switches.

Field Devices concern the components that link the physical world to the digital world, for instance, a PLC or an RTU. 77% of the testbeds contain descriptions on how field devices are incorporated – a higher number than for the control system, the communication architecture or the process. None of the testbeds contain virtualized or emulated field devices. An explanation for this result is that ICS field devices generally are based on specialized, sometimes proprietary, hardware and software that are unsupported by common virtualization and emulation tools. Simulation (47% of all testbeds) and hardware (47% of all testbeds) are used instead. Used simulation tools include STEP7 (of Siemens S7 PLCs), RSEmulate (by Allen-Bradley), LabVIEW, Scadapack LP PLC, Modbus Rsim, Soft-PLC, Python scripts with CORE, OpenVZ, PowerWorld server, and HoneyD in combination with IMUNES (FreeBSD jails). Hardware includes, for example, Allen Bradley Control Logix PLC, National Instruments NI-PXI, Omron PLC CJ1M-CPU11-ETN, CompactRIO from National Instruments, ABB 800F, Siemens OpenPMC, Siemens S7 PLC, Emerson Ctrl MD, and GE FANUC Rx3i.

The Physical Process concerns the physical reality that the ICS observe and control. Less than half of the testbeds describe how the process is implemented. In all cases, implementation builds on simulation models (rather than actual physical processes). The simulation approaches build on Matlab, Mathworks Simulink, Power Hardware-in-the-Loop (OPAL-RT), LabVIEW, PowerWorld, AnyLogic and EZJCOM, ANSYS, real time digital simulators, an Abacus solar array simulator, a library file (.dll) for EPANET, OMNET, and a custom application written in Java.

Various Components and Protocols on different levels of abstraction are mentioned in the articles describing the 30 analyzed testbeds. The most commonly mentioned types of components are RTU (mentioned by 12 testbeds), MTU (8 testbeds), PLC (8 testbeds), HMI (7 testbeds) and IED (4 testbeds). Other product types that are mentioned by a single testbed each are DAQ, Data aggregator, HDBMS, OPC server/client, PDC, PMU, Relay and SCADA server/client. 13 testbeds do not mention any product types. It is worth mentioning that these definitions are rather vague, especially to practitioners. For example, the Swedish railroad has Siemens S7 PLCs that are connected to switchgear. The purpose of these PLCs is to package/unpackage the proprietary data that the switchgear sends and receives by the MTU. For this reason, the Siemens S7 PLCs are denoted as RTUs by operators of the Swedish railroad (as they have a specific purpose).

There are several components in NIST 800-82 [53] that are not explicitly mentioned for any testbed. In particular, the data historian, IO server and control server are not mentioned. The articles do not describe why this is the case. An explanation could however be that these components are thought of as integrated with the MTU.

Of the communication protocols described for the testbeds, Modbus (Modbus ASCII, Modbus TCP or Modbus RTU, mentioned by 13 testbeds) and DNP3 (12 testbeds) are by far the most commonly mentioned. OPC (5 testbeds), IEC 60870 (4 testbeds, including e.g. IEC 104), IEC 61850 (3 testbeds) and Profibus (2 testbeds) are also mentioned for more than one testbed. Fieldbus, FINS, GOOSE, ICCP, IEEE C37.118, CIP, RJ45, DeviceNet and Genius are mentioned for a single testbed each. Nine testbeds do not discuss any communication protocols. According to the American Gas Association's AGA-12 standard [1], there are between 150 and 200 SCADA protocols. There are thus a plethora of protocols that are not covered by current testbeds. How common these protocols are in practice is however unknown to the authors of this article.

4.3 Managing Testbed Requirements

Siaterlis et al. [49] describe four overall requirements that cyber security testbeds should fulfill:

- *Fidelity*: Reproduce as accurately as possible the real system under study.
- *Repeatability*: Repeating tests produces the same or statistically consistent results.
- *Measurement accuracy*: Observing tests should not interfere with their outcome.
- *Safe execution of tests*: Cyber security tests often involve adversaries that exploit systems using malicious software. As it can be difficult to know the

outcome of these activities beforehand, tests must ensure that the activity within the testbed is isolated.

Of these requirements, repeatability and measurement accuracy generally depend on activities outside of the technical scope of a testbed. For example, it is difficult to ensure that adversaries act in the same way during consecutive tests. For this reason, repeatability and measurement accuracy are excluded from the scope of the present pre-study. Safe execution of tests has been a focus area for most testbeds for cyber security analyses; for this purpose, it is arguably less interesting to study than fidelity.

Ensuring testbed fidelity, i.e., that a testbed accurately reflects the desired real environment(s), is a critical task as the quality of any data produced from interaction with the testbed otherwise is uncertain. More than half (63%) of the testbeds are not discussed at all regarding fidelity (see Table 4). The remaining testbeds are analyzed in respect to fidelity in two different means: practical experiences and/or standards. The fidelity of 23% of the testbeds is argued based on real data gathered by the authors: either from quantitative data gathered from ICS systems in operation and/or from qualitative personal experiences or discussions with ICS manufacturers, providers and operators. For instance, *"Based on discussions with some industry partners and on our own experience"* [2] and *"In order to capture real image of the power network, a small part of power network was taken"* [11]. The remaining 13% that discuss fidelity base their testbed designs on standards developed by NIST (e.g., the NIST 800-82), ISA (e.g., the ISA-99) or IEC (e.g., the IEC Smart Grid Standardization Roadmap).

Table 4. Testbed fidelity.

Fidelity	Testbeds
Not covered	19
Study of real systems	7
Based on standards	4

Of the testbeds that are discussed in terms of fidelity, two provide specific metrics that can be used to replicate their results with some degree of accuracy. The first is Reaves and Morris [41] (a testbed at the Mississippi State University), who describe 11 metrics involving Modbus traffic (e.g., byte throughput, master-to-slave inter-arrival time, error count and packet size). These metrics were chosen based on the rule sets of model-based intrusion detection systems. The authors also compare the result from attacks against testbed components (which in this case are simulated) to attacks against real components. The second is Siaterlis and Genge [50], who compare the execution time of their testbed to the required execution time of seven physical processes. Their results show that they fulfill the execution time for everything but the IEEE 118 bus model (the testbed has an execution time of 155ms and the IEEE bus system has a requirement of 24ms).

An important aspect of testbed fidelity concerns what data should be collected in order to recreate a valid testbed design. For example, how a network topology or machine configuration best should be captured. Of all testbeds, the Iowa State University testbed is the only one that discusses this topic [22]. Hahn and Govindarasu [22] discuss how different data collection tools are able to fulfill the NIST 800-115 [45] methodology and the NERC critical infrastructure protection requirements. They used Wireshark to analyze network traffic, The Open Vulnerability Assessment Language (OVAL) Interpreter for analyzing machine configurations, Nmap and Sandia's Antfarm for network and service discovery, Firewalk and the access policy tool (APT) for firewall rule set discovery, and Nessus for vulnerability scanning. The results showed that these tools overall had excellent support for regular IT solutions such as Windows operating systems, but poor support for ICS specific components such as PLCs. For instance, *"there appeared to be numerous communications employing proprietary protocols which Wireshark was unable to identify"* and *"Nmap was not able to identify 53 out of 157 the open ports utilized in the network. This occurrence is a result of the heavy utilization of proprietary and SCADA specific protocols which are not recognized by Nmap"*. The analysis by Hahn and Govindarasu [22] is also limited as it does not study the potential to collect configuration data through agent based software, which is a common ICS industry practice.

5 Conclusions and Future Work

This study examined what ICS testbeds currently exist (RQ1), what ICS objectives these propose (RQ2), how ICS components are implemented within them (RQ3) and how they manage testbed requirements (RQ4).

The study identified 30 different ICS testbeds. The most common objectives of these testbeds are to facilitate vulnerability analysis, education and tests of defense mechanisms. These three objectives are described on a very superficial level for all existing testbeds. In order to be able to relate these objectives to actual testbed design decisions, there is a need to break them down and make them more tangible. One means to make them more tangible is to employ taxonomies, e.g., the taxonomy for ICS vulnerability assessment which is presented by NIST 800-82 [53]. This taxonomy employs three topics (policy and procedure vulnerabilities, platform vulnerabilities and network vulnerabilities) containing a total of 71 more concrete types of vulnerability assessments that can be used to create better requirements for ICS testbeds. For instance, if one wishes to analyze the presence of the platform vulnerability buffer overflow, there is a need for real software to be in place. This would preferably involve hardware, and at worst virtualization or emulation - simulation simply would not be sufficient as the software codebase would differ.

ICS components within the control center and communication architecture should generally be possible to virtualize without too many technical issues but are still typically simulated by the testbeds. The technical difficulty of implementing field devices (e.g., a PLC or an RTU) depends on the kind of device that is considered. Modern field devices are often based on architectures and firmware that have current virtualization and/or emulation support. The same applies for field devices that manufacturers have created emulation software for (it is however not certain that manufacturers would want to share such technology). Older or proprietary field devices (such as the Siemens S7 series) are however not supported by any current virtualization or emulation approach. As a field device can be used for up to 40 years [55], there is bound to be a plethora of such devices in operation. Thus, it would be beneficial to construct emulators for these old and/or properietary devices. There have been some research regarding virtualization of embedded systems [62][60][3][63]. Unfortunately, these works deal with performance issues such as the resource scheduling in hypervizors rather than how to virtualize specific existing field devices such as Siemens S7-1200. We are aware of but a single research project concerning this topic: an ongoing study by Idaho National Laboratory [27] proposes using the emulator QEMU in combination with the compiler LLVM to emulate field devices. This is a non-trivial task due to the extensive undocumented functionality in these devices. An example of the difficulty of reversing undocumented PLC code is given by Vidström [59], who present the results from reversing models in the Siemens S7 series. Due to this difficulty, a reasonable solution for field devices that are unsupported by current virtualization and emulation technologies could be simulation or implemention using real hardware. Of these two approaches, simulators are sufficient for most testbed purposes, with the exception of software and hardware vulnerability discovery.

What fidelity requirements that are posed on testbeds, and how these requirements are fulfilled, are rarely addressed by the studied articles. This is troublesome given the difficulty of validating cyber security results in general: if the validity of the testbed that facilitates tests of cyber security solutions is uncertain, any results produced by it are uncertain as well. To sum up, to accommodate high-fidelity security analyses, future ICS testbeds should:

- Clearly state the objectives of the testbed and relate these objectives to the configuration of the testbed.
- Employ virtualization or emulation in front of simulation and hardware approaches.
- Provide empirical results describing how the testbed fulfills its stated requirements.

For the third task, there is a need for a comprehensive evaluation framework that can be used to compare the fidelity of a testbed over time as well as compare it to other testbeds. As there currently is no "gold standard" available for this purpose, future work should focus on creating a standard framework for fidelity analyses of ICS testbeds.

Finally, there are various limitations to this work. First, the chosen search criteria have likely left out testbeds. Second, the data extraction formulary was iteratively developed based on the results from a pre-study and the opinion by the group researchers. Even though the group was shown to share the same general mindset, a different set of researchers would certainly have amounted to different results.

References

1. (AGA), A.G.A.: Cryptographic protection of scada communications - retrofittingserial communications. Tech. rep., American Gas Association (AGA) (2006)
2. Almalawi, A., Tari, Z., Khalil, I., Fahad, A.: Scadavt-a framework for scada security testbed based on virtualization technology. In: 2013 IEEE 38th Conference on Local Computer Networks (LCN), pp. 639–646. IEEE (2013)
3. Åsberg, M., Forsberg, N., Nolte, T., Kato, S.: Towards real-time scheduling of virtual machines without kernel modifications. In: 2011 IEEE 16th Conference on Emerging Technologies & Factory Automation (ETFA), pp. 1–4. IEEE (2011)
4. Beach, R., Kimnach, G., Jett, T., Trash, L.: Evaluation of power control concepts using the pmad systems test bed. In: Proceedings of the 24th Intersociety Energy Conversion Engineering Conference, IECEC 1989, pp. 327–332. IEEE (1989)
5. Benzel, T.: The science of cyber security experimentation: the deter project. In: Proceedings of the 27th Annual Computer Security Applications Conference, pp. 137–148. ACM (2011)
6. Bergman, D.C.: Power grid simulation, evaluation, and test framework (2010)
7. Bergman, D.C., Jin, D.K., Nicol, D.M., Yardley, T.: The virtual power system testbed and inter-testbed integration. In: CSET (2009)
8. Christiansson, H., Luiijf, E.: Creating a european scada security testbed. In: Goetz, E., Shenoi, S. (eds.) Critical Infrastructure Protecti. IFIP, vol. 253, pp. 237–247. Springer, Boston (2008)
9. Chunlei, W., Lan, F., Yiqi, D.: A simulation environment for scada security analysis and assessment. In: 2010 International Conference on Measuring Technology and Mechatronics Automation (ICMTMA), vol. 1, pp. 342–347. IEEE (2010)
10. Cohen, J.: Weighted kappa: Nominal scale agreement provision for scaled disagreement or partial credit. Psychological Bulletin **70**(4), 213 (1968)
11. Darwish, K.W., Dhaouadi, R., et al.: Virtual scada simulation system for power substation. In: 4th International Conference on Innovations in Information Technology, IIT 2007, pp. 322–326. IEEE (2007)
12. Davis, C., Tate, J., Okhravi, H., Grier, C., Overbye, T., Nicol, D.: Scada cyber security testbed development. In: Proceedings of the 38th North American power symposium (NAPS 2006), pp. 483–488 (2006)
13. Davis, J., Magrath, S.: A survey of cyber ranges and testbeds. Tech. rep, DTIC Document (2013)
14. Dondossola, G., Garrone, F., Szanto, J.: Cyber risk assessment of power control systems-a metrics weighed by attack experiments. In: 2011 IEEE Power and Energy Society General Meeting, pp. 1–9. IEEE (2011)
15. Edgar, T., Manz, D., Carroll, T.: Towards an experimental testbed facility for cyber-physical security research. In: Proceedings of the Seventh Annual Workshop on Cyber Security and Information Intelligence Research, p. 53. ACM (2011)
16. Fovino, I.N., Masera, M., Guidi, L., Carpi, G.: 2010 3rd Conference on An experimental platform for assessing scada vulnerabilities and countermeasures in power plants. In: Human System Interactions (HSI), pp. 679–686. IEEE (2010)

17. Gao, H., Peng, Y., Dai, Z., Wang, T., Jia, K.: The design of ics testbed based on emulation, physical, and simulation (eps-ics testbed). In: 2013 Ninth International Conference on Intelligent Information Hiding and Multimedia Signal Processing, pp. 420–423. IEEE (2013)
18. Giani, A., Karsai, G., Roosta, T., Shah, A., Sinopoli, B., Wiley, J.: A testbed for secure and robust scada systems. ACM SIGBED Review 5(2), 4 (2008)
19. Gluhak, A., Krco, S., Nati, M., Pfisterer, D., Mitton, N., Razafindralambo, T.: A survey on facilities for experimental internet of things research. IEEE Communications Magazine 49(11), 58–67 (2011)
20. Guglielmi, M., Nai, I., Perez-Garcia, A., Siaterlis, C.: A preliminary study of a wireless process control network using emulation testbeds. In: Chatzimisios, P., Verikoukis, C., Santamaría, I., Laddomada, M., Hoffmann, O. (eds.) MOBILIGHT 2010. LNICST, vol. 45, pp. 268–279. Springer, Heidelberg (2010)
21. Guo, F., Herrera, L., Alsolami, M., Li, H., Xu, P., Lu, X., Lang, A., Wang, J., Long, Z.: Design and development of a reconfigurable hybrid microgrid testbed. In: 2013 IEEE Energy Conversion Congress and Exposition (ECCE), pp. 1350–1356. IEEE (2013)
22. Hahn, A., Govindarasu, M.: An evaluation of cybersecurity assessment tools on a scada environment. In: 2011 IEEE Power and Energy Society General Meeting, pp. 1–6. IEEE (2011)
23. Hahn, A., Kregel, B., Govindarasu, M., Fitzpatrick, J., Adnan, R., Sridhar, S., Higdon, M.: Development of the powercyber scada security testbed. In: Proceedings of the Sixth Annual Workshop on cyber Security and Information Intelligence Research, p. 21. ACM (2010)
24. Haney, M., Papa, M.: A framework for the design and deployment of a scada honeynet. In: Proceedings of the 9th Annual Cyber and Information Security Research Conference, pp. 121–124. ACM (2014)
25. Harwell, S.D., Gore, C.M.: Synthetic cyber environments for training and exercising cyberspace operations. M&S Journal, 36–48 (2013)
26. Hieb, J., Graham, J., Patel, S.: Security enhancements for distributed control systems. In: Goetz, E., Shenoi, S. (eds.) Critical Infrastructure Protection. IFIP, vol. 253, pp. 133–146. Springer, Boston (2008)
27. (INL), I.N.L.: Control system automated vulnerability assessment study. Tech. rep., Idaho National Laboratory (INL) (2013)
28. Jurisic, B., Holjevac, N., Morvaj, B.: Framework for designing a smart grid testbed. In: 2013 36th International Convention on Information & Communication Technology Electronics & Microelectronics (MIPRO), pp. 1247–1252. IEEE (2013)
29. Kitchenham, B.: Procedures for performing systematic reviews. Keele, UK, Keele University 33(2004), 1–26 (2004)
30. Kush, N., Clark, A.J., Foo, E.: Smart grid test bed design and implementation (2010)
31. Leblanc, S.P., Partington, A., Chapman, I., Bernier, M.: An overview of cyber attack and computer network operations simulation. In: Proceedings of the 2011 Military Modeling & Simulation Symposium, pp. 92–100. Society for Computer Simulation International (2011)
32. Lüders, S.: Cern tests reveal security flaws with industrial network devices. The Industrial Ethernet Book 35(CERN-OPEN-2006-074), pp. 12–23 (2006)
33. Mallouhi, M., Al-Nashif, Y., Cox, D., Chadaga, T., Hariri, S.: A testbed for analyzing security of scada control systems (tasscs). In: 2011 IEEE PES Innovative Smart Grid Technologies (ISGT), pp. 1–7. IEEE (2011)

34. Moore, D., Murray, J., Maturana, F., Wendel, T., Loparo, K., et al.: Agent-based control of a dc microgrid. In: 2013 IEEE Energytech, pp. 1–6. IEEE (2013)
35. Morris, T., Srivastava, A., Reaves, B., Gao, W., Pavurapu, K., Reddi, R.: A control system testbed to validate critical infrastructure protection concepts. International Journal of Critical Infrastructure Protection 4(2), 88–103 (2011)
36. Morris, T., Vaughn, R., Dandass, Y.S.: A testbed for scada control system cybersecurity research and pedagogy. In: Proceedings of the Seventh Annual Workshop on Cyber Security and Information Intelligence Research, p. 27. ACM (2011)
37. Mossberg Sonnek, K., Holm, H., Lindgren, J., Lindgren, F., Westring, E.: Foi-r-4029-se, ncs3 - informations- och styrsystem inom spårbunden trafik, en kartläggning. Tech. rep., Swedish Defence Research Agency (FOI) (2014)
38. Nanda, T.C., Chiueh, S.: A survey on virtualization technologies. RPE Report, pp. 1–42 (2005)
39. Pegden, C.D., Sadowski, R.P., Shannon, R.E.: Introduction to simulation using SIMAN. McGraw-Hill, Inc. (1995)
40. Queiroz, C., Mahmood, A., Tari, Z.: Scadasim-a framework for building scada simulations. IEEE Transactions on Smart Grid 2(4), 589–597 (2011)
41. Reaves, B., Morris, T.: An open virtual testbed for industrial control system security research. International Journal of Information Security 11(4), 215–229 (2012)
42. Reddi, R.M., Srivastava, A.K.: Real time test bed development for power system operation, control and cyber security. In: 2010 North American Power Symposium (NAPS), pp. 1–6. IEEE (2010)
43. Salazar, E., Macías, M.E., et al.: Virtual 3d controllable machine models for implementation of automations laboratories. In: 39th IEEE Frontiers in Education Conference, FIE 2009, pp. 1–5. IEEE (2009)
44. Sayegh, N., Chehab, A., Elhajj, I.H., Kayssi, A.: Internal security attacks on scada systems. In: 2013 Third International Conference on Communications and Information Technology (ICCIT), pp. 22–27. IEEE (2013)
45. Scarfone, K.A., Souppaya, M.P., Cody, A., Orebaugh, A.D.: Sp 800–115. technical guide to information security testing and assessment (2008)
46. Schriber, T.J.: Introduction to simulation. In: Proceedings of the 9th Conference on Winter Simulation, vol. 1, p. 23. Winter Simulation Conference (1977)
47. Shahzad, A., Musa, S., Aborujilah, A., Irfan, M.: A new cloud based supervisory control and data acquisition implementation to enhance the level of security using testbed. Journal of Computer Science 10(4), 652 (2014)
48. Shahzad, A., Musa, S., Aborujilah, A., Irfan, M.: Secure cryptography testbed implementation for scada protocols security. In: 2013 International Conference on Advanced Computer Science Applications and Technologies (ACSAT), pp. 315–320. IEEE (2013)
49. Siaterlis, C., Garcia, A.P., Genge, B.: On the use of emulab testbeds for scientifically rigorous experiments. IEEE Communications Surveys & Tutorials 15(2), 929–942 (2013)
50. Siaterlis, C., Genge, B.: Cyber-physical testbeds. Communications of the ACM 57(6), 64–73 (2014)
51. Stefanov, A., Liu, C.C.: Cyber-power system security in a smart grid environment. In: 2012 IEEE PES Innovative Smart Grid Technologies (ISGT), pp. 1–3. IEEE (2012)
52. Stites, J., Siraj, A., Brown, E.L.: Smart grid security educational trainingwith thundercloud: A virtual security test bed. In: Proceedings of the 2013 on InfoSecCD 2013: Information Security Curriculum Development Conference, p. 105. ACM (2013)

53. Stouffer, K., Falco, J., Scarfone, K.: Guide to industrial control systems (ics) security. NIST Special Publication **800**(82), 16–16 (2007)
54. Suh, J., Oh, J., Choi, J., Goff, J., Tao, J., Song, E., Fu, P., Lee, G., Eom, K.: Korean r&d on the converter controller for iter ac/dc converters. In: 2011 IEEE/NPSS 24th Symposium on Fusion Engineering (SOFE), pp. 1–5. IEEE (2011)
55. Sun, Y., Ma, T., Huang, B., Xu, W., Yu, B., Zhu, Y.: Risk assessment of power system secondary devices for power grid operation. In: 2012 China International Conference on Electricity Distribution (CICED), pp. 1–5. IEEE (2012)
56. Urias, V., Van Leeuwen, B., Richardson, B.: Supervisory command and data acquisition (scada) system cyber security analysis using a live, virtual, and constructive (lvc) testbed. In: Military Communications Conference, MILCOM 2012, pp. 1–8. IEEE (2012)
57. Vaughn, R.B., Morris, T., Sitnikova, E.: Development & expansion of an industrial control system security laboratory and an international research collaboration. In: Proceedings of the Eighth Annual Cyber Security and Information Intelligence Research Workshop, p. 18. ACM (2013)
58. Wang, Y.F., Zhang, T., Ma, Y.Y., Zhang, B.: An information security assessments framework for power control systems. In: Advanced Materials Research, vol. 805, pp. 980–984. Trans. Tech. Publ. (2013)
59. Widström, A.: Foi-r-4029-se, möjligheter och problem vid analys av fientlig kod riktad mot siemens s7-serie. Tech. rep, Swedish Defence Research Agency (FOI) (2012)
60. Xi, S., Xu, M., Lu, C., Phan, L.T., Gill, C., Sokolsky, O., Lee, I.: Real-time multi-core virtual machine scheduling in xen. In: 2014 International Conference on Embedded Software (EMSOFT), pp. 1–10. IEEE (2014)
61. Yang, Y., McLaughlin, K., Sezer, S., Littler, T., Im, E.G., Pranggono, B., Wang, H.: Multiattribute scada-specific intrusion detection system for power networks. IEEE Transactions on Power Delivery **29**(3), 1092–1102 (2014)
62. Yoo, S., Park, M., Yoo, C.: A step to support real-time in virtual machine. In: 6th IEEE Consumer Communications and Networking Conference, CCNC 2009, pp. 1–7. IEEE (2009)
63. Zamorano, J., De La Puente, J., et al.: Design and implementation of real-time distributed systems with the assert virtual machine. In: 2010 IEEE Conference on Emerging Technologies and Factory Automation (ETFA), pp. 1–7. IEEE (2010)

The Timed Decentralised Label Model

Martin Leth Pedersen[1], Michael Hedegaard Sørensen[1], Daniel Lux[2],
Ulrik Nyman[1], and René Rydhof Hansen[1]([⊠])

[1] Department of Computer Science, Aalborg University, Aalborg, Denmark
{mped10,mhso10}@student.aau.dk, {ulrik,rrh}@cs.aau.dk
[2] Seluxit, Aalborg, Denmark
daniel@seluxit.com

1 Introduction

By some estimates, the number of devices connected through the so-called *Internet of Things* (IoT) will reach the 50 billion mark in 2020[1]. While forecasting such numbers is not an exact science, it seems clear that in the near future, a very large number of Internet connected devices will be deployed everywhere, not least in our homes, e.g., in the form of smart meters, refrigerators, and other household appliances, facilitating the "smart home" of the future. However, filling our homes with sensors and devices able to measure, monitor, and report on all activities, immediately raises questions about how security and privacy can be handled satisfactorily.

Of particular importance for security is the fundamental question of how to model the security (and privacy) policies such a system must comply with: the highly distributed and decentralised nature of the underlying system does not fit well with the classic policy models, such as Bell-LaPadula [5] or Clark-Wilson [8], nor with traditional MAC/DAC access control models. This is further complicated by the fact that security and privacy policies in IoT systems must be able to cope with *time dependent* elements, e.g., a smart meter may only send (aggregate) measurements every 15 minutes in order to preserve privacy. None of the classical models mentioned above incorporate timing constraints and although a number of temporal aspects, in various security models, are discussed in [17], focus is *information release* and they only indirectly deal with real-time constraints on security policies. One possible solution would be to encode temporal constraints/policies into the highly flexible formalism of *Flow Locks* [6, 7]. However, based on our experience in modelling, analysing, and verifying the safety of systems that incorporate real-time timing constraints, we have found that safety- and security-properties involving real-time clocks and constraints are often subtle and counter-intuitive. We therefore believe it is important that time is represented *explicitly* in security models for IoT.

In this paper we propose the *Timed Decentralised Label Model* (TDLM) as a step towards a modelling formalism for IoT security policies and illustrate this for a non-trivial smart meter system. As the name suggests, the TDLM is an extension of the decentralised label model (DLM) with a time component [13,14],

---

[1] http://www.brookings.edu/blogs/techtank/posts/2015/06/9-future-of-iot-part-2

© Springer International Publishing Switzerland 2015
S. Buchegger and M. Dam (Eds.): NordSec 2015, LNCS 9417, pp. 27–43, 2015.
DOI: 10.1007/978-3-319-26502-5_3

formalised here by *timed automata* [1]. Given the decentralised structure of typical IoT systems, as noted above, the DLM seems like a natural match with its emphasis on local (decentralised) control; similarly timed automata have a long history of modelling systems with time components. It bears mentioning, that instead of the DLM, we could instead have extended the Flow Locks formalism mentioned above with timed automata, potentially yielding a more flexible approach. We leave this for future work.

To illustrate the features of the TDLM, we have chosen a *smart meter* use case. Smart meters were chosen because the relevant security policies are quite complex with a non-trivial time component. Furthermore, smart meters are being introduced on a massive scale throughout the European Union and are expected to replace "dumb" meters in the coming years. A smart meter is a device responsible for monitoring power consumption in households and reporting this to electrical companies in order to ensure correct billing and to enable "smart" use of power, e.g., by (automatically) postponing certain power consuming tasks to a time of day when prices are low, e.g., doing the laundry at night. There are many security and privacy aspects to take into account when designing and implementing a smart meter system: a major privacy concern, which is also the main focus of this paper, is that power companies can build highly detailed power consumption profiles for individual homes. To prevent this, power companies are only allowed to access the measured power consumption at certain time intervals [11]. For further smart meter security issues, see [2,3].

The work reported on in this paper, is a simplified and summarised version of the work done in the master's thesis of the two first authors [16].

2   Preliminaries

In this section we briefly review the main theories underlying the work in this paper: the decentralised label model (DLM) and timed automata.

2.1   The Decentralised Label Model

The fundamental idea of the DLM, is that every *principal* that contributes information to a system, should be allowed to define a security policy for how the contributed data can be used (in that system) [15]. Principals are the authority entities, or actors, in a system, e.g., users, groups, or roles, between which data can flow (through data channels).

In order to capture common access control idioms, such as individuals acting for a group or vice versa, principals in the DLM are ordered into a hierarchy, the so-called *principal hierarchy*, through the *act-for* relation. A principal a allowed to *act-for* another principal b, denoted $a \succeq b$, intuitively inherits all the privileges of b, i.e., can access the same data as b. In practice, the *act-for* relation can be specialised to more specific privilieges, e.g., reading a specific file. The *act-for* relation is taken to be reflexive and transitive; an example principal hierarchy is shown in Figure 1.

Fig. 1. Example principal hierarchy: $a \succeq a'$, $a' \succeq a''$, and $a' \succeq b$.

In the DLM, data (or rather data sources, sinks, and channels) can be annotated with *labels* expressing the (security) policies that should hold for that data. A label is composed of a set of *security policies*, where each security policy comprises an *owner* and a corresponding set of *readers* the owner wishes to permit access to the labelled data. Formally:

$$\mathsf{Label} = \mathcal{P}(\mathsf{SecPol}) \qquad \mathsf{SecPol} = \mathsf{Owner} \times \mathcal{P}(\mathsf{Reader})$$

In keeping with tradition, we write $o\colon R$ for $(o, R) \in \mathsf{SecPol}$. Intuitively, only readers that are permitted by all owners (of a particular label) are permitted to access data with that label. This set of readers is called the *effective set of readers* and is formalised as follows (for $L \in \mathsf{Label}$)

$$effectiveReaders(L) = \bigcap_{o \in owners(L)} readers_{\succeq}(readers(L, o))$$

where $owners(L) = \{o \mid (o, R) \in L\}$, $readers(L, o) = \{r \mid (o, R) \in L, r \in R\}$, and $readers_{\succeq}(R) = \{p \mid \exists p' \in R \colon p \succeq p'\}$. A policy with no owner and an empty reader set is equivalent to allowing all principals in the system access [15].

In order to facilitate and reason about the flow of labelled data through a system with varying labels, data can be *relabelled* either by *restriction* or *declassification*. The latter is an intended and deliberate "leak" of data, while the former allows data to flow to actors with a more strict security policy. A relabelling from a label L_1 to another label L_2 is called *safe*, denoted $L_1 \sqsubseteq L_2$ if the relabelling is a *restriction*, i.e., if L_2 is at least as restrictive as L_1, intuitively that means L_2 has fewer readers and/or more owners. Taking the principal hierarchy into account, we can formalise safe relabelling as follows

Definition 1 (Safe Relabelling). *Let* $L_1, L_2 \in \mathsf{Label}$ *and* $I_1, I_2 \in \mathsf{SecPol}$ *and define safe relabelling:*

$$L_1 \sqsubseteq L_2 \equiv \forall I_1 \in L_1 \colon \exists I_2 \in L_2 \colon I_1 \sqsubseteq I_2$$

where $I_1 \sqsubseteq I_2$ *iff* $o_2 \succeq o_1$ *and* $readers_{\succeq}(R_2) \subseteq readers_{\succeq}(R_1)$ *for* $I_1 = (o_1, R_1)$ *and* $I_2 = (o_2, R_2)$.

The above definition corresponds to the complete relabelling rule in [15]. For a proof that the complete relabeling rule is both sound and complete with respect to the formal semantics see [12]; meaning that the rule only allows safe relabelings and allows all safe relabelings.

When executing a program within a system, values are often derived from other values, for example a new value may be derived by multiplying two other values. In the DLM a derived value v must have a label that enforces the policies of the values used to derive v meaning that the label of v must be at least as restrictive as the combined label of the operands. Formally if we have two operands labeled with the labels L_1 and L_2 respectively the label for a derived value would be a join of these two which in terms is the union of the labels joined, as described in Definition 2.

Definition 2 (Label Join). *Let* $L_1, L_2, \in$ Label *define* label join:

$$L_1 \sqcup L_2 = L_1 \cup L_2$$

Intuitively, the label join produces the *least* label that restricts both L_1 and L_2.

The security policies mentioned so far have all been *confidentiality* policies that only considers who can observe data. However, the DLM can also specify *integrity* policies which considers who are able to modify the data protected by the policies. The integrity policies are quality guarantees provided by the owners of the policies that only the specified writers have modified the data. The syntactical notation is similar to the notation for confidentiality policies but instead of a reader set, a writer set is associated with the policies. An integrity policy can also be relabelled in a manner similar to that of a confidentiality policy [15]. We do not go into further details with integrity policies or the DLM here, but refer instead to [12,15].

2.2 Timed Automata

Finite automata are well known theoretical computation models used for describing logical program behavior based on transitions and states that a program can be in. An extension of the finite automata formalism with time is called a *timed automaton*, which adds a finite set of real-valued clocks to the finite automaton [1]. The clocks are increased at the same rate and can be reset during a transition if need be. The primary use of the clocks is to set up guards that can prevent transitions from being executed or prevent the program from being in a certain state.

A timed automaton is a tuple $T = (\Sigma, L, L_0, C, E)$ consisting of the following components:

- Σ is the input alphabet accepted by the automaton.
- L is the set of possible finite locations that the automaton can be in.
- L_0 is the set of start locations which is a subset of L; $L_0 \subseteq L$
- C is a finite set of clocks

 – E is the set of possible transitions in the automaton, formally defined as
 $$E \subseteq L \times L \times [\Sigma \cup \{\epsilon\}] \times 2^C \times \Phi(C)$$

An edge in the timed automaton is then defined as $\langle s, s', \sigma, \lambda, \delta \rangle$, which represents a transition from a program location s to another program location s' on the input σ. λ is then the set of clocks that will be reset with the transition, and δ is the enabling condition (the guard). The automaton starts in one of the start locations with all clocks set to zero. The clocks then increase to reflect time elapsed and a transition may be taken when the guards of an edge is satisfied.

An example of a system that is ideally modelled with a timed automaton is a simple smart meter system consisting of a smart meter and a power company. The power company must be restricted to only being able to read the smart meter data at certain time intervals. In Figure 2 this scenario is presented with a timed automaton constructed in the UPPAAL model checker [4][2] UPPAAL is used to verify timed automata models, such as the model presented in Figure 2. The automaton consists of two locations smd and ec, where smd is the smart meter data and ec is the power company. The system can take the transition from ec to ec nondeterministically while waiting for the clock x to be larger than 90 (days). When the clock x is larger than or equal to 90, the transition guarded by the expression $x >= 90$ can be taken thus modelling a read of smart meter data by going to the location smd, where the only transition that can be taken resets the clock variable to zero and leads back to ec. This simple example models an electrical company that can read smart meter data of a single customer every 90 days.

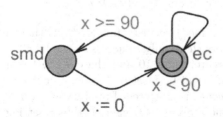

Fig. 2. Simple smart meter example where an electrical company reads smart meter data every 90 days. The location with the double circle is a start location.

However, the simple model also reveals some of the non-trivial issues encountered when formalising access control policies with a time element, e.g., for how long time is access allowed (when can/does the timed automaton leave state smd). In a later section, we show how the UPPAAL model checker can be used to answer such questions and validate the model.

---

[2] http://uppaal.org

3 The Timed Decentralised Label Model

In the following we define and describe the *timed decentralised label model*. The main idea is to extend DLM policies with *time constraints* formulated over *clock variables* associated with underlying timed automata (see Section 2.2). In this work we assume that clocks used by the system are controlled by the system; this is similar to the assumption in "normal" DLM that the principal hierarchy is under control by the system.

Note that this sidesteps the well-known thorny issue of how to synchronise (real-time) clocks in a distributed system. In fact the TDLM, as explained later, does not necessarily require clocks to be synchronised, but can in fact be used to model systems with several (local) clocks. We leave it for future work to investigate the consequences of this modelling assumption.

We start by discussing the new label constructs added to DLM and follow that by a formalisation and semantics of the new constructs in terms of a network of timed automata.

3.1 TDLM Constructs

To clarify the constructs TDLM adds to the DLM, an explanation of the individual constructs is presented to give an intuitive understanding of the security policies that can be expressed with these. We start with an example of of a (timed) security policy, illustrating all the new constructs by extending a basic DLM security '$o: r$':

$$o(x[15; ?event; 1] > 10 \,\&\&\, y < 5): r[!event]$$

Informally, the above (timed) security policy states that the policy owner, o, allows any stated readers (here only r) access to the labelled data whenever the clock x has a value greater than 10 and the clock y has a value less than 5. Furthermore, the clock x will be reset to 1, whenever it reaches the value of 15 or an event, named '*event*', is triggered. Finally, whenever the reader r accesses the data, an event named '*event*' is triggered (thus resetting the x clock). Note that, in order to be able to reason about time, e.g., how long is there between any two reads of a variable, we have introduced events. This is a departure from other formalisations of secure information flow where the exact time of a read is implicit (or rather: irrelevant). In future work, we will investigate if it is possible to move towards the more traditional approach.

We now discuss the individual constructs in more detail:

- **Declaring clock variables.** Clock variables are used to restrict access to data based on time (x and y in the above example) and are declared within a set of parentheses which is placed after a principal (owner or reader) to restrict that principal's access. If a clock is placed on an owner of a policy then all readers associated with this owner are restricted by the clock, however if a clock is placed on a reader then only that specific reader is restricted by it. A clock variable is identified by its unique name which can be any combination of alphabetic characters and the value of a clock variable can be any positive integer.

- **Comparing clock values.** Clock variables can be compared to other clock variables and constant integers with the use of the usual binary comparison operators. If that comparison evaluates to true then the clock variables allows access to the entity it is associated with. The comparison is defined within the parenthesis along with the declaration of the clock variable for example $(x > 10)$. The value the clock variable is compared to is called the comparison value.
- **Multiple comparisons.** Multiple clock comparisons can be performed within the same parenthesis by separating them with the logical && and || operators, which evaluates as expected for example $(x > 10 \ \&\& \ x < 15)$ would evaluate to true when x is between ten and 15. A statement of clock comparisons placed within a single set of parenthesis is called a clock expression and must evaluate to true before the associated principal(s) can gain access to the data.
- **Parameterised clock variables.** Clock variables can be parameterised with the use of square parentheses placed after the name of the clock variable. However, if no parameters are defined on a clock variable then the square parentheses may be omitted. Within the square parenthesis three optional parameters can be declared. Parameters are separated with a semicolon and are identified in the order: upper limit, event, and reset value. If only one parameter is declared and that parameter's identifier starts with a question mark then it is an event otherwise it would be an upper limit. A parameterized clock variable would then be defined as $(x[15; ?event; 1] > 10)$.
- **Upper limit.** An upper limit is a constant used to define when a clock variable should be reset. Upon reaching the upper limit the value of the clock variable will instantly get reset.
- **Reset value.** The reset value is a constant used to define the value of a clock variable when it resets. If omitted from a clock variable the reset value is always zero.
- **Events.** Events are defined by a unique alphabetic name starting with a question mark and can be placed as a parameter on a clock variable, which indicates that when the event is triggered then the value of the clock variable is reset.
- **Event trigger.** An event trigger can be specified on any principal, and is placed immediately after a principal's identifier. An event trigger starts with the symbol ! followed by the name of the event to be triggered when the corresponding principal successfully reads data. Several event triggers can be placed on the same principal in the same security policy by separating the event triggers with a comma, for example $p[!event1, !event2]$ would trigger *event1* and *event2* when p reads the data. An event can only be triggered from within the system by those principals that have an event trigger defined on them in a given security policy.

We now proceed to the formal definition of timed security policies and timed labels.

3.2   Formal Definition

In the following, we assume without further specification, the existence of countably infinite sets of *clock variables* ClockVar and events (or rather event names) Event. Clock declarations are then defined to have the following form:

$$\Upsilon ::= c \mid c[\alpha; ?\beta; \gamma]$$

where $c \in$ ClockVar, $\alpha, \gamma \in$ ClockVal, and $\beta \in$ Event. As discussed above, we allow clock declarations to omit any and all of α, β, and γ in the above, indicating that default values should be used (for α and γ) or that no reset events are defined (for β). We can now define *clock expressions* as combinations of clock declarations. A clock expression is of the form:

$$\Phi ::= \Upsilon \mid \Upsilon \bowtie \Upsilon \mid \Phi \&\& \Phi \mid \Phi \| \Phi$$

with $\bowtie \in \{<, \leq, ==, !=, \geq, >\}$ representing the standard comparators. As mentioned above, clock expressions Φ can be placed on any principal in a security policy.

Finally, by extending DLM security policies and labels with clock expressions, we are able to give the formal definition of TDLM security policies and labels (again using $\perp$ to denote optional values):

$$\mathsf{SecPol}_T = \mathsf{Owner} \times \Phi_\perp \times \mathsf{Event}_\perp \times \mathcal{P}(\mathsf{Reader} \times \Phi_\perp \times \mathsf{Event}_\perp)$$

Which leads to the following obvious definition of TDLM labels:

$$\mathsf{Label}_T = \mathcal{P}(\mathsf{SecPol}_T)$$

Having defined these, we next turn to the semantics of TDLM labels (and security policies).

3.3   From Policies to Timed Automata

In the following we define the semantics of TDLM labels and security policies by translating them into a network of timed automata. In essence, TDLM security policies describe which principals can access protected data and when.

The behavior of security policies can be expressed via one or more timed automata where each principal present in the security policy is associated to a timed automaton describing their access restrictions. However if several principals are allowed to access the data under the same conditions then a single timed automaton might describe the access restrictions for multiple principals. A timed automaton that describes the access restriction for a principal has its start location labeled with the name of the principal that the automaton describes as depicted in Figure 3, where rw_i is the principal that the timed automaton depicts the access possibility of. The location named *data* is used to describe that when the timed automaton is in this location, the principal is allowed to observe the data. Note however, that the location is *committed* (denoted with a C) indicating that an edge going away from this location *must be taken immediately* to enforce the access restriction. The access restriction must be placed on an ingoing edge to the *data* location thus modeling that the data is protected by some time constraints Φ. If a policy contains events β that should be triggered by certain principals then the timed automaton that describes the access behavior of these principals must trigger the event on the edge going away from the *data* location thus modeling reset only on successful read/write.

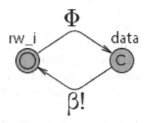

Fig. 3. General timed automaton that describes the access restrictions for the principal rw_i restricted by the clock expression Φ and triggering the event β on successful read/writes.

In addition to this, for each clock variable in a security policy, a timed automaton is used to describe how this clock variable is incremented and who can increment it. A timed automaton that describes a clock variable consists of one location with up to three cyclic edges that describe incrementing the value of the clock c, resetting the clock value upon reaching an upper limit α, and resetting the clock value when an event β is triggered. Note that we use UPPAAL channels as a natural fit for modelling for events. The clock value is reset to the reset value γ when an event is triggered or an upper limit is reached. When an upper limit is present on a clock variable then a guard on the incrementation edge must be placed to force a reset when reaching the upper limit. Figure 4 depicts a timed automaton that describes the behavior of the clock c which can be incremented by the principal co.

As an example consider the following TDLM security policy:

$$\{o\,(x[20;\,?reset;\,5] > 10 \,\&\&\, y > 15) : r[!reset]\} \tag{1}$$

The timed automata in Figure 5 formalises this policy. The first timed automaton labelled 1. describes the access restrictions for the owner o which is restricted by the guard placed on the edge from the initial location to the *data* location

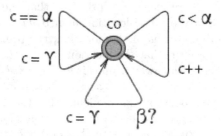

Fig. 4. General timed automaton that describes a clock c that can be incremented by the principal *co*.

meaning that the owner o may only observe the data when the conditions for x and y are met. When o has successfully gained access to the data (the timed automaton is in the location named *data*) the timed automaton immediately goes to the initial location such that the restrictions placed on the data can be enforced correctly.

Since o and r are restricted by the same clocks they should be modelled by the same timed automata, however r triggers an event when successfully reading the data and thus the access behavior for r must be modelled by a different timed automaton. The timed automaton labeled 2. models the access behavior of r and is equivalent to the timed automaton modeling o except for the event (*reset!*) that is triggered when r has successfully gained access to the data. Events are expressed by channel synchronization meaning that when a timed automaton takes an edge marked with an event trigger such as *reset!* then all[3] the corresponding timed automata in the system take any available matching edges marked with the same event name such as *reset?*.

The timed automaton labeled 3. models the behavior of the clock variable x, which can be incremented by the principal o (indicated by the name of the start location) when the value of x is below 20 but upon reaching the value 20, o must reset the clock to five before the clock can be incremented again thus modeling the upper limit and reset value of x described by the policy. The edge marked with *reset?* models the event that is triggered by r and resets the clock to its reset value when the event is triggered.

The timed automaton labeled 4. models the behavior of the clock variable y which also can be incremented by the principal o but this timed automaton contains only one edge as there is no upper limit, reset value or event associated with y.

---

[3] This is the case as we use UPPAAL's *broadcast channels* in these models.

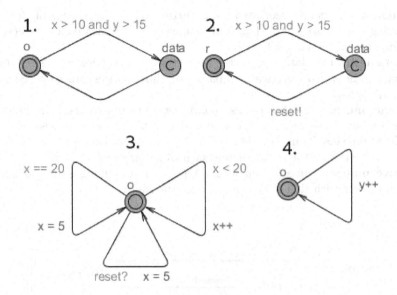

Fig. 5. Timed automata describing the security policy $\{o(x[20; ?reset; 5] > 10 \&\& y > 15) : r[!reset]\}$

4 Smart Meters: A Case Study

To explore and illustrate the capabilities and expressiveness of the TDLM, a case study of a real world scenario is presented here in some detail. The case study involves a smart meter system which consists of multiple users (household owners and residents), smart meters, power companies, distribution companies, smart meter manufactures, third parties, a data hub and a government entity as depicted in Figure 6. A definition of each entity in the smart meter system is as follows:

- **Users.** Two types of users exist in the smart meter system - household owners and residents. Household owners own one or more households, which each have a smart meter installed, and may also be residents in the households they own. Residents are permitted to live in a household by the household owner.
- **Smart meters.** A smart meter is responsible for collecting electricity consumption data for the household it is installed in. Furthermore, it also serves as a platform for other devices to connect to and communicate with for example for doing home automation.
- **Power companies.** A power company is responsible for delivering electricity to one or more customers and billing the customers according to their electricity consumption.
- **Distribution companies.** A distribution company is responsible for maintaining the power distribution grid and keeping track of which electrical

companies users are associated with. Furthermore, it is responsible for processing raw smart meter data and making this data available to electrical companies via a data hub.

- **Data hub.** The data hub serves as a storage center for processed smart meter data which electrical companies or third parties can gain access to when appropriate.
- **Smart meter manufacturers.** Smart meter manufacturers are responsible for producing the smart meters and updating the firmware if need be.
- **Third parties.** Third parties are entities that might have an interest in the data collected by the smart meters such as research companies.
- **Government.** The government is interested in obtaining power consumption reports such that they can optimize the smart grid.

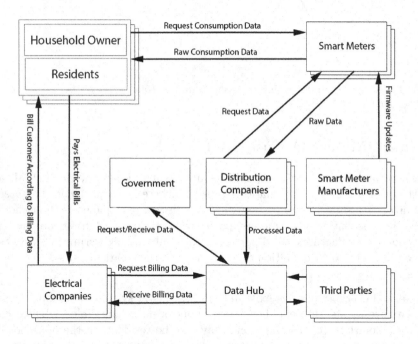

Fig. 6. Overview of the smart meter system with communication channels outlined.

The users can monitor their own power consumption by directly communicating with the smart meter in their household, in order to identify how power can be saved. However, the household owner is capable of granting and revoking access to the smart meter, e.g., for residents living in the household. The distribution companies request data from the smart meters they are associated with and perform necessary processing of the data in order to protect the privacy of the users. The processed data is delivered to a data hub which enforces which entities that can gain access to the data, when they can gain access to the data, for how long they may access the data, and the granularity of the data that may be accessed. The government and potential third parties can access the data they need through the data hub, however the permissions of each entity may vary for example a research company may be able to access more fine-grained data than the government. The power companies deliver electricity to the users and bill them according to billing data obtained from the data hub and as such an electrical company is implicitly associated with one or more smart meters/users. Note that power companies are not able (or allowed) to access the detailed usage statistics for a single household; depending on the particular setup, such information may or may not be available to distribution companies.

4.1   Smart Meter Privacy Concerns and Access Rights

A smart meter system makes it possible to observe fine-grained electricity consumption data of users associated with a smart meter. The system allows users to observe their own power consumption down to the minute which opens up the possibility of optimizing their usage patterns to lower overall power consumption [11]. In addition to this, the smart meter system provides users with a platform for home automation which can further lower their power consumption by automatically turning off unused devices or starting devices based on electricity prices [3]. However, the possibility of reading fine-grained power consumption data also posses several privacy issues due to the possibility of deriving personal behavior patterns from the power consumption data, for example it is possible to figure out if a person is home during their sick leave or if they left late for work by observing when they consume power [11]. As such it would be favorable to regulate whom that has access to this data and in how fine a granularity the data can be extracted in relation to the entity that wants to observe the data.

As there are several privacy and security issues in regards to smart meters, it should *not* be possible for all entities in- and outside the system to obtain data collected by smart meters or data transferred internally between entities. The smart meter collects data about the user's electrical consumption and as such the data collected by the smart meter are directly related to the user, meaning that there is no need to restrict the user's access to the data in any form. The user is able to observe and analyze the data collected by the smart meter at any time via for example a web interface.

4.2   Smart Meter System Modelled with the TDLM

The smart meter system cannot be described by the DLM alone as this model lacks the possibility of defining time-based security policies, which are crucial in regards to modeling smart meter security. However, the TDLM extends the DLM with the required components for describing a smart meter system in regards to secure information flow and access control.

The principal hierarchy in the smart meter system consists of all the users (u), the smart meters (s) associated with those users, the power companies (e)

associated with users, distribution companies (d) associated with smart meters, the data hub (dh), smart meter manufactures (m) and the government (g). The acts-for relationship between these principals is then given as $d \succeq s$ and $s \succeq u$.

The smart meter data can be divided into three segments; the first containing the personal information about the user that is associated with the smart meter at the current time, the second containing the real-time electrical readings recorded by the smart meter, and the third being the smart meter firmware which controls how the smart meter behaves. The first part of the data is owned by the user as it is sensitive information about them, but the electrical company that is associated with the user at the current time is allowed to read the data for billing purposes: $\{u_i : e_j\}$. In addition to this, the data should have an integrity policy which expresses that the user is the owner of the data but trusts the electrical company to change the data if needed. However, in this paper we are only concerned with confidentiality properties and refer to [16] for the full case study.

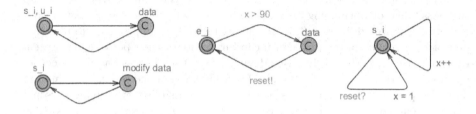

Fig. 7. The smart meter security policies modelled with four timed automata.

The second part of the smart meter data comprises the actual power consumption readings saved by the smart meter every minute. Since this data could reveal a user's private behaviourl pattern, it should only be accessible to the power company in aggregate form. To enforce this, the TDLM introduces time-based security policies formalising that the power company only should have access to the data once in a while, e.g., every quarter, which is the requirement for quarterly billing. Formally, this is captured by the following TDLM policy:

$$\{s_i : u_i, e_j(x[?reset : 1] > 90)[!reset]\} \qquad (2)$$

The semantics of this security label is depicted by the four timed automata shown in Figure 7.

Figure 8 gives an overview of the TDLM annotations needed for the entire system. For lack of space we are unable to go into further details with the case study here, but refer to [16] for the full case study. From the above discussion, it seems that the TDLM is a good fit for modelling many of the security properties relevant for smart meters, in particular those involving timing elements.

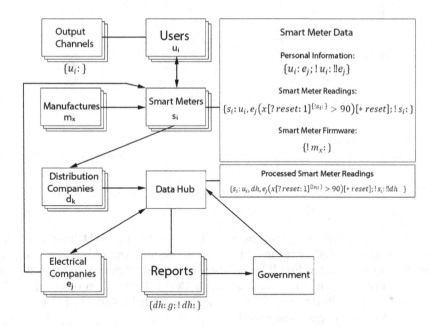

Fig. 8. Smart meter system with security labels as per the definition of TDLM. Arrows depict information flow.

5   Automated Verification of Security Goals

A problem common to all security policy formalism is that once the policies reaches a certain level of complexity, it becomes very difficult, if not impossible, to verify that the security policies actually capture the relevant security properties. Since the TDLM is rooted in timed automata, it is possible to leverage the strong tool support for verifying properties of models using timed automata, mainly through [4] model checking. In the remainder of this section, we briefly outline how the UPPAAL model checker can be used to verify properties of a (simple) TDLM policy.

As an example, we take a security goal that is similar to (a simplified version of) the security goals for the smart meter: we wish to verify that certain data can only be read every 15 time units. The security policy enforced by our system is formulated as follows:

$$\{c : reader(x[15] >= 15)\}$$

Clearly, in this case it is trivial to verify manually that the policy satisfies the goal, but in a real system with even a moderate number of non-trivial policies, it quickly becomes infeasible. Instead we turn to the UPPAAL model checker to analyse the so-called *window of opportunity* for reading the labelled data, e.g., by an attacker or an insider. Figure 9 shows a partial screenshot of performing

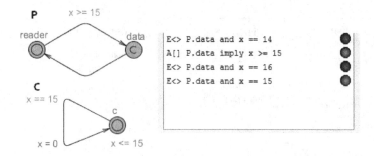

Fig. 9. UPPAAL window of opportunity analysis where upper limit is set to 15.

this window of opportunity analysis using UPPAAL. On the right hand side, the logical formulae verified by the model checker are shown, e.g., `A[] P.data imply x >= 15` that checks that for all possible system states when in the location *data* in the automaton P then the value of the clock x is larger than or equal to 15. This property is verified to be true which is the intended behavior of the system. For more details, we again refer to [16].

6   Conclusion

In this paper we have defined and formalised the *timed decentralised label model*, an extension of the decentralised label model with explicit handling of time through the use of timed automata. We have further shown how this formalism is well-suited for modelling and specifying the security policies for a smart meter system. Finally, we taken the first steps towards using the UPPAAL model checker to automatically verify and validate that the security policies in a system do indeed ensure the relevant security properties.

As future work we plan on investigating if the use of the modeling language Timed Input/Output Automata [9] and the Ecdar [10] tool to more concisely model the semantics of TDLM. As this tool uses a compositional verification method it would potentially allow for checking the policies of much larger TDLM models.

References

1. Alur, R., Dill, D.L.: A theory of timed automata. Theor. Comput. Sci. **126**(2), 183–235 (1994)
2. Anderson, R., Fuloria, S.: On the security economics of electricity metering. In: Proceedings of the 9th Annual Workshop on the Economics of Information Security (WEIS 2010), Cambridge, MA, USA, June 2010
3. Anderson, R., Fuloria, S.: Smart meter security: a survey. http://www.cl.cam.ac.uk/rja14/Papers/JSAC-draft.pdf (2011)

4. Behrmann, G., David, A., Larsen, K.G.: A tutorial on UPPAAL. In: Bernardo, M., Corradini, F. (eds.) SFM-RT 2004. LNCS, vol. 3185, pp. 200–236. Springer, Heidelberg (2004)
5. Bell, D.E., LaPadula, L.J.: Secure computer systems: Mathematical foundations. Tech. Rep. ESD-TR-73-278, ESD/AFSC, Hanscom AFB, Bedford, Mass, November 1973
6. Broberg, N., Sands, D.: Flow locks: Towards a core calculus for dynamic flow policies. In: Sestoft, P. (ed.) ESOP 2006. LNCS, vol. 3924, pp. 180–196. Springer, Heidelberg (2006)
7. Broberg, N., Sands, D.: Paralocks: role-based information flow control and beyond. In: Proceedings of the 37th ACM Symposium on Principles of Programming Languages (POPL 2010), Madrid, Spain, pp. 431–444, January 2010
8. Clark, D.D., Wilson, D.R.: A comparison of commercial and military computer security policies. In: Proc. of the IEEE Symposium on Security and Privacy (S&P 1987), pp. 184–194. IEEE (1987)
9. David, A., Larsen, K.G., Legay, A., Nyman, U., Wasowski, A.: Timed I/O automata: a complete specification theory for real-time systems. In: Johansson, K.H., Yi, W. (eds.) Proceedings of the 13th ACM International Conference on Hybrid Systems: Computation and Control, HSCC 2010, Stockholm, Sweden, April 12–15, pp. 91–100. ACM (2010)
10. David, A., Larsen, K.G., Legay, A., Nyman, U., Wąsowski, A.: ECDAR: An environment for compositional design and analysis of real time systems. In: Bouajjani, A., Chin, W.-N. (eds.) ATVA 2010. LNCS, vol. 6252, pp. 365–370. Springer, Heidelberg (2010)
11. Molina-Markham, A., Shenoy, P., Fu, K., Cecchet, E., Irwin, D.: Private memoirs of a smart meter. In: BuildSys 2010 (2010)
12. Myers, A.C.: Mostly-Static Decentralized Information Flow Control. Ph.D. thesis, Massachusetts Institute of Technology, January 1999
13. Myers, A.C., Liskov, B.: A decentralized model for information flow control. In: Proc. of the 16th ACM Symposium on Operating Systems Principles (SOSP 1997), pp. 129–142, October 1997
14. Myers, A.C., Liskov, B.: Complete, safe information flow with decentralized labels. In: Proc. of the IEEE Symposium on Security and Privacy (S&P 1998), pp. 186–197. IEEE, May 1998
15. Myers, A.C., Liskov, B.: Protecting privacy using the decentralized label model. ACM Transactions on Software Engineering and Methodology (TOSEM) **9**(4), 410–442 (2000)
16. Pedersen, M.L., Sørensen, M.H.: The Timed Decentralised Label Model. Master's thesis, Aalborg University (2015)
17. Sabelfeld, A., Sands, D.: Dimensions and principles of declassification. In: Proceedings of the 18th IEEE Workshop on Computer Security Foundations (CSFW 2005), pp. 255–269. IEEE (2005)

Privacy

Resilient Collaborative Privacy
for Location-Based Services

Hongyu Jin[✉] and Panos Papadimitratos

Networked Systems Security Group, KTH Royal Institute of Technology,
Stockholm, Sweden
{hongyuj,papadim}@kth.se
http://www.ee.kth.se/nss

Abstract. Location-based Services (LBSs) provide valuable services, with convenient features for users. However, the information disclosed through each request harms user privacy. This is a concern particularly with *honest-but-curious* LBS servers, which could, by collecting requests, track users and infer additional sensitive user data. This is the motivation of both *centralized* and *decentralized* location privacy protection schemes for LBSs: anonymizing and obfuscating LBS queries to not disclose exact information, while still getting useful responses. Decentralized schemes overcome the disadvantages of centralized schemes, eliminating anonymizers and enhancing users' control over sensitive information. However, an insecure decentralized system could pose even more serious security threats than privacy leakage. We address exactly this problem, by proposing security enhancements for mobile data sharing systems. We protect user privacy while preserving accountability of user activities, leveraging pseudonymous authentication with mainstream cryptography. Our design leverages architectures proposed for large scale mobile systems, while it incurs minimal changes to LBS servers as it can be deployed in parallel to the LBS servers. This further motivates the adoption of our design, in order to cater to the needs of privacy-sensitive users. We provide an analysis of security and privacy concerns and countermeasures, as well as a performance evaluation of basic protocol operations showing the practicality of our design.

Keywords: Location-based service · Security and privacy · Pseudonymous authentication

1 Introduction

The evolution and popularization of mobile Internet brings forth opportunities for service providers to cater to people's needs. Location-based Services (LBSs) in particular respond to user queries based on their locations, available at their location-aware mobile devices. However, the improved relevance and precision of responses comes at a cost: users' privacy can be harmed [8,26]; user location information can be used to reconstruct user trajectories and profile their

© Springer International Publishing Switzerland 2015
S. Buchegger and M. Dam (Eds.): NordSec 2015, LNCS 9417, pp. 47–63, 2015.
DOI: 10.1007/978-3-319-26502-5_4

activities or even infer their interests. In fact, the LBS itself, i.e., its server(s), is uniquely positioned to undermine users' privacy, collecting rich information over time, for all locations a user (client or mobile device/application) submits queries from. Moreover, it can have a financial motivation to do so, seeking to push advertisements to users. As a result, increased concerns have been voiced and numerous efforts to safeguard user privacy led to a number of proposals, both *centralized* and *decentralized*.

Centralized schemes [13,23,25] introduce a new entity, an *anonymizer*: it anonymizes a received client query (removing its identity attributes), obfuscates and/or blends the queries of multiple clients, and then sends them to the LBS server(s). The location is obfuscated to a corresponding region with the client and at least $k-1$ other clients included, to achieve k-anonymity: the user is indistinguishable among these k users. Clearly, these schemes are effective but this centralized approach seeks to solve the problem at hand based on the assumption that originally raised concerns for the LBS servers; they presume the anonymizer is trustworthy. But still, the anonymizer has all the rich information collected from client queries. If an LBS server can be curious and track or profile users, the question rises naturally: *Why couldn't an anonymizer also breach the user privacy the same way?*

This challenge motivated a number of works that proposed decentralized privacy schemes. Similar, in spirit, to decentralized approaches overcoming disadvantages of centralized approaches for privacy-related problems in many areas [12,17,24], LBSs user privacy protection can be achieved in a collaborative manner: without relying on an anonymizer. In particular, users can hide from the LBS server by obtaining LBS-provided information from their neighbors [29].

Nonetheless, opening up the system functionality is a double-edged sword: it reduces the user exposure to the curious provider (LBS or anonymizer) but it also exposes her to possibly faulty or misbehaving peers. In fact, risks in and abuses of, for example, peer-to-peer (P2P) systems [18,20,30] show that insecure decentralized schemes face serious problems. For example, users are threatened by exposure of their sensitive information to other peers or injected bogus data from malicious nodes. In [29], responses from the LBS server are signed, thus they are self-verifiable while passed to other peers. However, this does not comply with many existing LBS servers, which authenticate themselves and secure only pairwise communication over, e.g., a TLS channel, instead of signing the responses. In either case, peers could be uncooperative or offending.

This challenge exactly motivates our work, in the context of enhancing LBS user privacy. The decentralized or *collaborative* approach has clear advantages, enhancing the users' control over sensitive information: their exposure can be significantly reduced while they still obtain their sought quality of service (trading off mild delay for much better privacy). But this would be of no use if user peers could disrupt or even debilitate the collaborative querying part, by passing on bogus or irrelevant information, or excessively querying their peers. Even if LBS responses were signed, still, misbehaving peers can aggressively consume resources of benign peers and obstruct the peer query-response operation. Or, worse even, abuse peer queries to also harm users' privacy based on the peer-to-peer data exchange.[1]

This is what we address in this paper: we propose a security architecture for decentralized/collaborative privacy protection for LBSs. We are cognizant that already deployed LBS servers would be unwilling to change their operations, thus we propose new components that are orthogonal to the LBS servers and new functionality for the privacy-sensitive users. In fact, we conjecture that our scheme could even motivate LBS servers to adopt and offer the collaborative privacy-enhancing scheme to their interested users. While, in turn, the users would be further motivated to embrace it knowing that it protects them from unwanted risks (manipulation, overloading) and, at the same time, safeguards their privacy. Moreover, we impose constraints on pseudonym usage to further protect users from being inundated with bogus data.

In the rest of the paper, we first outline requirements and discuss related work (Sec. 2). Then, we present our proposed scheme (Sec. 3), we analyze the achieved security and privacy protection (Sec. 4), benchmark our protocol on mainstream mobile devices (clients) and provide a performance evaluation (Sec. 5), and conclude with our next steps (Sec. 6).

2   Problem Statement and Related Work

2.1   System and Adversary Model

System: Consider a general model, as illustrated in Fig. 1: Users' mobile clients, termed *nodes* in the rest of the paper, can be smartphones, tablet PCs, On-board Units (OBUs) in vehicles, etc. They are connected to the Internet through different channels (Wi-Fi and/or cellular network) and they are interested in different types of location-dependent information; e.g., specific Point of Interest (POI) information, traffic status, environmental conditions, etc. Nodes are able

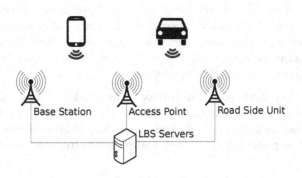

Fig. 1. System Model

---

[1] Although, of course, an adversary would need a massive number of peers to collect, each one locally, the same information an LBS would and is able to collect simply through its regular operations.

to request these information from LBS servers through the Internet. Nodes can in addition communicate with other nodes through ad-hoc connectivities, including Wi-Fi ad-hoc network, Wi-Fi Direct [5], LTE Direct [2] and Bluetooth. This allows them to exchange information with other nodes; thus sharing information with each other or aggregating data obtained from multiple peers. We assume this is an alternative way of obtaining location-dependent information while hiding from the LBS servers. This can be achieved by running an application on mobile devices; which obtains information from LBS servers through provided APIs [1,4], and shares the information with other nodes.

Adversaries: We assume that LBS servers are *honest-but-curious*: they follow the protocols, responding faithfully to their users' (nodes') queries. But they can trace the nodes (linking their queries), profile the nodes (recording their queries), and even deanonymize the nodes (inferring home and work sites). Such inferred sensitive data, based on the collected queries, could be commercially exploited. We maintain the same assumption for any third party, including the ones we introduce in our architecture (see Sec. 3).

Nodes can be honest, honest-but-curious or malicious. In the latter case, they can deviate from the collaborative protocol functionalities and policies, attacking the systems, notably their peer nodes: forging or tampering with responses, masquerading other nodes, excessively posting queries to their peers, seeking to exhaust their resources. The result could be degradation of the service users receive (i.e., being misled) or even a Denial of Service (DoS) on the collaborative exchange. These would not only affect quality of service but also force honest nodes to expose themselves to the LBS servers.

2.2   Security and Privacy Protection Requirements

We seek to thwart the aforementioned node misbehavior, while maintaining the benefit of "hiding" from the LBS servers and obtaining useful information.

Authentication and Integrity: Node messages, queries and responses, should allow their receiver to authenticate their sender and verify they were not modified or replayed from a previous exchange. We do not require strict identification of the sender (querier or responder) but at least validation that the sender is a legitimate participant of the P2P operation.

Non-repudiation and Accountability: The sender of any message (any action, in general) cannot deny having sent the message (taken the action). Any node can be tied to its actions, if need arises, and held accountable. Accordingly, it should be possible to have such nodes evicted from the system (the P2P operation).

Anonymity/Pseudonymity and Unlinkability: Nodes should not be identifiable, based on their P2P interactions, and have their messages linked to their identities. Anonymity should be conditional, allowing the system to identify a misbehaving node (and evict it). Ideally, we want to make it impossible for any observer to link any two messages (e.g., queries) to the same node. But, for practical operation and efficiency/lower cost reasons, we require that node actions (messages) can be linked at most over a protocol selectable period τ. Accordingly, any node can maintain one temporary identifier, a *pseudonym*, for that same period.

Confidentiality (optionally): The LBS-originating content should be accessible only by legitimately participating nodes, possibly registered with the LBS and the system/application that enables collaborative privacy protection.

2.3   Related Work

We discuss briefly decentralized approaches to enhance privacy for LBSs. As with centralized approaches, many decentralized schemes seek to provide k-anonymity: P2P spatial cloaking [11] and MobiHide [14] achieve k-anonymity by finding $k-1$ neighboring peers within a cloaked region. We do not dwell on how effectively this can be done (e.g., unlinkability under the assumption that nodes are not likely to move in the same direction). However, we note that the trust model among nodes (users) was not considered [11]; while MobiHide [14] relies on a central server who maintains a list of active nodes and supports them on joining the clusters, which is a privacy threat for users. Along the same lines, AMOEBA [28] protects user privacy by forming groups and delegating LBS queries to group leaders, proposed for vehicular communication systems; the predictable mobility helps in that case. The formation of groups, of course, imposes additional complexity and overhead. If the conditions allow such group operation and it is effective, it could be beneficial. But such group formation and provision of k-anonymity is orthogonal to our work here, and it could possibly co-exist with (and even be facilitated by) our scheme, by explicitly addressing trust assumptions and providing a security architecture.

Passing/sharing self-verifiable information among users helps to provide authentication and integrity [29]. Nodes cache information received from the LBS server and pass to its neighbors when requested, thus decreasing exposure to the LBS server. This is the approach we extend in this paper. It assumes that responses signed by the LBS server are self-verifiable (manipulation by a node will be detected). However, even with such signatures, assuming of course a change on the side of LBS (possibly considered unrealistic by some providers), a misbehaving node passing on tampered responses would remain "invisible" and continue attacking the system. This is exactly where this work comes in, protecting the system against node misbehavior. Moreover, it is interesting that this does not comply with many existing LBS servers: user-/node-server communication is authenticated (and kept confidential) through end-to-end security (a secure channel, e.g., TLS, with the LBS server), without signed responses.

The EU PRIME project [6] proposes the use of anonymous credentials in the context of LBS. This is related to our work, but a location intermediary is assumed between the LBS and the mobile operator. The use of non-traditional public key cryptographic protocols has also been considered in [9,10,22,27], with special care for sybil-free operations, in spite of the relatively higher overhead for those cryptographic primitives.

3 Our Scheme

3.1 Overview

We assume basic collaborative functionality for nodes, sharing location-dependent information [29]: before querying the LBS, a node queries its neighbors/peers, who respond if they can; if no appropriate response is obtained in this P2P manner, then the querier cannot but query the LBS. To secure such a system, as per the requirements in Sec. 2, we propose a security architecture and augment the basic P2P functionality, and the node-to-LBS communication. We assume nodes keep track of all communication in the vicinity, and react appropriately to P2P queries; listening if a query was already served by other nodes. This is straightforward to support in commodity wireless networks (e.g., Wi-Fi). Table 1 summarizes the used notation.

Table 1. Notation

$LTCA$	Long-Term Certification Authority
Lk/LK	Long-term Private/Public Key
LTC	Long-Term Certificate
PCA	Pseudonymous Certification Authority
Sk/SK	Short-term Private/Public Key
PC	Short-term (Pseudonymous) Certificate
$\{msg\}_\sigma$	Signed msg
$type_{poi}$	Type of POI
id	Node id or Query id
t/t_{now}	Timestamp/A fresh timestamp indicating current time
$T_{timeout}$	Timeout for peer response reception
SN	Serial Number
N	Number of needed responses to a peer query

Fig. 2 illustrates the proposed system architecture. We mandate that nodes are registered with an *identity and credential management facility* that equips them with *short-lived anonymized credentials*. To do so, we require the nodes be registered with an Long-Term Certification Authority (LTCA) that maintains their long-term identities and issues Long-Term Certificates (LTCs) for them. With the LTC, a node obtains a ticket from the LTCA and present the ticket to the Pseudonymous Certification Authority (PCA) to obtain *Pseudonymous Certificates (PCs)/pseudonyms*. The ticket is authenticated by the LTCA but

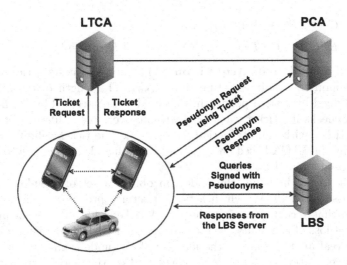

Fig. 2. System Architecture

anonymized: it does not reveal real identity of the node to the PCA. Therefore, neither the LTCA nor the PCA can link the real identity of the node to the issued pseudonyms (thus, the messages signed under the pseudonyms). The details of the operation are presented next (Sec. 3.2, 3.3).

We require that the pseudonyms be used to authenticate (with the corresponding cryptographic private key) P2P queries and responses. They can be optionally used to authenticate queries to the LBS (if its functionality allows that). The pseudonyms attest to the *legitimate participation* of the node in node-to-LBS or P2P communication. Furthermore, to prevent abuse of the node anonymity, our scheme provides *conditional anonymity* and allows *revocation of anonymity and eviction*. The node interactions with the facility entities are explained below. Moreover, we enforce ticket and pseudonym (lifetime) policies on the Certification Authorities (CAs) and nodes, so that user privacy is protected to the full extent and the nodes have *regulated access* to P2P part of the LBS. Finally, our extension of the P2P functionality allows for increasing resilience and user-control: the querying node can seek multiple responses and can regulate the maximum rate at which it responds to queries.

3.2 Protocols

Registration: All nodes register with an LTCA, which essentially acts as an identity provider. (1) A node generates a pair of long-term public/private keys, LK and Lk, and (2) submits a Certificate Signing Requests (CSR) (a self-signed LK and other relevant information) to the LTCA; (3) the node is issued with an LTC. The whole exchange is secured with a TLS channel or done offline.

$$C : Lk, LK \tag{1}$$

$$C \rightarrow LTCA : \{id_C, LK, others\}_{\sigma_{Lk}} \tag{2}$$

$$LTCA \rightarrow C : LTC_C = \{SN_{LTC}, id_C, LK, others\}_{\sigma_{LTCA}} \tag{3}$$

Ticket and Pseudonym Acquisition: (4) A node requests a ticket with a desired pseudonym validity starting time, t_{start}. The length of ticket validity period is defined by system policy, thus no need to be specified by the node. (5) The LTCA checks if a ticket was issued with an overlapping lifetime; if not, (6) it issues a ticket with validity period $[t'_{start}, t'_{end}]$. The ticket validity period is computed by the LTCA based on t_{start} and the policy defined in [19] to prevent ticket and pseudonym linkability.

With the ticket in hand, the node can obtain a set of pseudonyms (7-9) from any associated PCAs, which acts as a service provider itself. There can be multiple that recognize/accept the LTCA tickets; for the sake of presentation, without loss of generality, we refer to a single PCA. The anonymized ticket does not reveal anything about the identity of the node (and the user) to the PCA. This separation of duties concept is based on the work done in the context of vehicular communication systems [16,19]. Both ticket and pseudonym acquisitions are protected with TLS channels. The ticket request is protected by mutual authentication; while the pseudonym request is protected by uni-directional (PCA-only) authentication, since the node is authenticated with the presented ticket.

$$C \rightarrow LTCA : ticket\_req\{t_{start}\}_{\sigma_C} \tag{4}$$

$$LTCA : check(id_C, t_{start}) \tag{5}$$

$$LTCA \rightarrow C : ticket = \{SN_{ticket}, t'_{start}, t'_{end}\}_{\sigma_{LTCA}} \tag{6}$$

$$C : Sk, SK \tag{7}$$

$$C \rightarrow PCA : pseudonym\_req\{ticket, \{SK\}_{\sigma_{Sk}}\} \tag{8}$$

$$PCA \rightarrow C : PC = \{SN_{pc}, SK, t'_{start}, t'_{end}\}_{\sigma_{PCA}} \tag{9}$$

P2P Query: Algorithm 1 illustrates the querying thread of a node. As stated above, nodes cache locally responses received from the LBS server (and other peers). When POI information is needed, the local cache is checked first. If there is no match, it generates a signed query. To ensure unlinkability after a change of pseudonym, the node can randomly reset its IP and MAC address. The node waits for and possibly receives responses from its neighbors. It can specify in the query that N responses are required in total from its peers and assign a query id (id_q). It then verifies the responses and combine them to form a final response. Each receiver could overhear the responses to the same query while the query is queued, and serve the query only while less than N responses are overheard from the network (see Sec. 3.3 for detail). Moreover, a node could adapt to current CPU usage and battery amount remaining, the rate at which to serve peer queries for further reducing the overhead. We do not formulate what is a satisfactory response to a query, it can be specified in the preferences of the application or determined through UI (e.g., a button indicating the user wants to query the LBS server directly) after being presented the peer responses.

Algorithm 1. Querying thread (of a node)

1: Possesses a valid PC
2: $query = \{loc, type_{poi}\}$
3: $resp_{local} = search(query)$
4: **if** $resp_{local}$ is satisfactory **then**
5:     $resp_{final} = resp_{local}$
6: **else**
7:     $QUERY = \{id_q, t_{now}, query\}_{\sigma_{PC}}$
8:     $broadcast(\{QUERY, PC\})$
9:     Let $resp_{final} = \phi$, $n = 0$, $t = t_{now} + T_{timeout}$
10:     **while** $\{RESP_i, PC_i\} = receiveRespBefore(t)$ and $n < N$ **do**
11:         $RESP_i = \{id_q, t_{now}, resp\}_{\sigma_{PC_i}}$
12:         **if** $verify(PC_i, LTC_{PCA})$ and $verify(RESP_i, PC_i)$ **then**
13:             $resp_{final} = combine(resp_{final}, resp_i)$
14:             $n = n + 1$
15:         **end if**
16:     **end while**
17:     **if** $resp_{final}$ is not satisfactory **then**
18:         $resp_{final} = queryLBS(QUERY)$
19:     **end if**
20:     $cache(resp_{final})$
21: **end if**
22: **return** $resp_{final}$

LBS Query: Nodes query the LBS server only when they have to, e.g., when the information obtained from their neighbors is not satisfactory. The information obtained from the LBS server is the essential resource for supporting P2P function of our scheme. Nodes send the signed queries to the LBS server. Then, the responses from the LBS server are cached by the nodes.

P2P Query Processing: As shown in Algorithm 2, when a node receives a peer query, it first verifies the attached pseudonym and checks if the attached

Algorithm 2. Serving thread (of a node)

1: Possesses a valid PC
2: $\{QUERY_i, PC_i\} = receiveQuery()$
3: $QUERY_i = \{id_q, t_{now}, query\}_{\sigma_{PC_i}}$
4: **if** $verify(PC_i, LTC_{PCA})$ and $verify(QUERY_i, PC_i)$ **then**
5:     $query = \{loc, type_{poi}\}$
6:     $resp = search(query)$
7:     **if** $resp \neq \phi$ **then**
8:         $RESP = \{id_q, t_{now}, resp\}_{\sigma_{PC}}$
9:         $send(i, RESP)$
10:     **end if**
11: **end if**

pseudonym has been over-used (i.e., received queries signed under the same pseudonym exceeds the query rate allowed for one pseudonym). If not, it verifies the query and searches its cache. If successful in finding matching information, it signs and sends the response to the sender. This, of course, depends on whether or not N responses to the same query have been overheard from the network.

Reporting Misbehavior: We address post-misbehavior processing while the misbehavior detection is out of scope of this paper. However, we note that some types of misbehavior are straightforward to detect and confirm. For example, the honest LBS responses can help finding out which of the contradictory responses to a query is/are bogus information. When a misbehavior is detected by a node, (10) it sends to the Resolution Authority (RA), the messages related to the misbehavior with pseudonyms attached. In case (11) the messages are proved to be related to a misbehavior case, (12) it sends the pseudonym (or multiple pseudonyms) to the PCA, and (13) the PCA derives the SN_{ticket} of the ticket that had been used to issue the pseudonym. (14-15) With the help of the LTCA, the misbehaving node is exposed (and possibly evicted from the system).

$$C \rightarrow RA : \{\{msg\}_{\sigma_{PC_i}}, PC_i\}_{\sigma_{PC}} \tag{10}$$

$$RA : judge(msg) \tag{11}$$

$$RA \rightarrow PCA : PC_i \tag{12}$$

$$PCA \rightarrow RA : SN_{ticket} \tag{13}$$

$$RA \rightarrow LTCA : SN_{ticket} \tag{14}$$

$$LTCA \rightarrow RA : id_i \tag{15}$$

3.3   Optimizations for Query Processing

Processing a query requires searching the node cache and two signature verifications: one for the attached certificate (pseudonym) and one for the sender's signature. Similarly, the response validation requires two signature validations, and checking if the nonce and location matches that of the query. To reduce communication and processing overhead, we propose the following optimizations:

– **Optimization 1:** A node could sign multiple queries/responses under the same pseudonym, thus it may omit attaching it to some of those - thus reducing communication overhead. Accordingly, the receiving nodes need to validate the pseudonym of the said node only once throughout the pseudonym lifetime. Then, they cache validated pseudonyms and omit their verification for successive queries/responses signed under cached pseudonyms [10]. This way, the processing overhead is reduced, as only one signature needs to be validated for peer queries and responses. This is important, as the PCA key would in principle have high security level, thus relatively higher verification delay.
– **Optimization 2:** Each node could opportunistically cache responses to popular queries (both overheard and locally generated), assuming such information is likely to become useful later. The popularity can be determined by

occurrence frequency of type of POI in queries or responses, while it is proto-col selectable. In case an incentive scheme is used, caching popular responses would provide increased rewards.

- **Optimization 3:** Requesting multiple, N, responses allows cross-checking (Sec. 4), but could waste resources if responses are sent after the querier obtained all needed responses. Responders can back-off randomly and over-hear communications, counting responses to the specific query, based on its id_q; then, at the end of the back-off they respond only if less than N responses were overheard.

4   Security and Privacy Analysis

In this section, we explain how the security and privacy requirements are addressed and how malicious behavior is thwarted.

Authentication, Integrity, and Confidentiality: The communication of the nodes with the CAs and the LBS server is carried over TLS channels, thus providing end-to-end security. Signing P2P messages under pseudonyms pro-vides authentication and integrity. While confidentiality of P2P communication is optional, any two nodes can establish a shared session key and mutually authenticate each other leveraging their pseudonymous certificates, encrypting the response(s) with the session key. Thus, only users registered with the system have access to LBS-provided information.

Non-repudiation and Accountability: The use of public key cryptography and the digital signatures ensure non-repudiation. Any suspected misbehavior (messages deemed to be inconsistent, bogus, etc., by a node) can be linked to the signer's pseudonym. This can be reported to the security infrastructure and the LTCA and PCA can jointly identify the node and if necessary evict it - revoking valid pseudonyms and/or preventing it from obtaining new pseudonyms.

Unlinkability: Keeping ticket request records at the LTCA prevents nodes from excessively requesting pseudonyms with overlapping lifetimes - we enforce non-overlapping pseudonym lifetimes and similarly to [19] we enforce that all tickets and pseudonyms are issued at discrete times for all requests to the PCA. This precludes linkability of pseudonyms of the same node based on time of issuance and lifetime - the likelihood is inversely proportional to the number of all active pseudonyms in the system. Actions of a node are linkable only as long as the same private key (under the same pseudonym) is used, that is, only over the period τ. Setting this is a trade-off between unlinkability and efficiency. Changing node identifiers across the protocol stack (IP, MAC) precludes linkability across pseudonym changes.

Node Authentication and Exposure to the LBS Server: For subscriber-based LBSs, node authentication is necessary. Optionally, nodes can be authen-ticated to the LBS server with long-term credentials or pseudonyms based on the requirements of a specific LBS server. Use of long-term credentials would make the nodes identifiable and queries linkable. While pseudonymous authentication ensures nodes authentication without revealing their identities and breaching unlinkability, if done under different pseudonyms.

Non-verifiable Responses: If the LBS server signs responses, their integrity and timeliness can be readily verified. Otherwise, any malicious node could forge bogus responses, or any node create an arbitrary, valid yet unverifiable response based on its cache. We don't address this aspect here; we only suggest that queriers request redundant responses in order to cross-check them and infer valid information, e.g., extracting and using only information included in the majority of the responses from distinct peer nodes. Such a scheme warrants a separate investigation and it is part of future work. We note, however, that the authentication of the nodes and the constraints imposed by our scheme prevent an adversary from posing as multiple nodes and inundating the receiver with bogus responses.

Essentially, honest LBS responses can serve as ground truth for detecting injected bogus data. Nodes can examine suspicious responses (e.g., contradictory responses from different peers) by querying the LBS server, and consequently, downgrading and reporting deviant responders. Actually, a node dissatisfied by other responders trades off its exposure to the LBS server for precise and genuine information, while at same time, it contributes to the common objective: decrease and balance exposure of nodes to the LBS server.

Thwarting Clogging Attacks: An internal attacker could post a large amount of queries to fetch cached information from its neighbors and drain their resources. Limiting the number of received peer queries signed under a same pseudonym and enforcing non-overlapped pseudonym lifetimes address this problem. It ensures each node has only one valid pseudonym at any point; thus when the quota (with respect to one receiver) of currently valid pseudonym has been consumed completely, it will not have any more valid pseudonyms to generate queries. However, flooding with bogus pseudonyms or messages that attached with bogus signatures could consume a lot of client resources for verification, while they are not avoidable. This is the same even if LBS-obtained information are signed. Attackers can still pass forged data to their neighbors to consume resources of benign nodes. As a remedy for our system, keys with relatively low security levels could be used. Considering the ephemeral nature of information transmitted in the system and short lifetimes of credentials; even if the keys are cracked, the attacker will no longer be interested in expired credentials by that time. The decision on key choice will be made based on cryptographic benchmarks (see Sec. 5).

Exposure to the Security Infrastructure and Collusion with the LBS: Though authorities we introduce are designed in a manner that protects the nodes from being traced, they could be honest-but-curious. However, any of the honest-but-curious LTCAs or PCAs cannot trace a user's actions (based on an eavesdropped transcript) - we refer to the analysis in [19]. Moreover, if the the LBS server authenticated nodes with pseudonyms, its collusion with the LTCA would not reveal any information; collusion with the PCA would only reveal the batch of pseudonyms obtained with the one presented by the LBS server but not with past ones issued to the same node under a different ticket. Only the unlikely collusion of all three, the LBS server, the LTCA and the PCA, would expose the user.

5   Performance Evaluation

In this section, we demonstrate the practicality and applicability of our scheme. We show performance evaluation results for basic operations in our system with off-the-shelf components and popular platforms, i.e., RSA and ECDSA for public key cryptography and Android smartphone as user device. We find that a smartphone can easily handle high query rates from its neighbors, especially by using RSA keys with relatively low security levels.

Table 2. Processing delay of cryptographic operations

Key Type	Security Level (bits)	Generation (ms)	Sign (ms)	Verify (ms)	Signature Size (bytes)
RSA-1024	80	400.86	4.63	0.78	128
RSA-2048	112	2104.59	21.18	1.21	256
ECDSA-192	96	214.65	210.01	286.44	56
ECDSA-224	112	251.66	251.91	345.95	63

The most frequent and time consuming operations are signature generation and verification.[2] Encryption of P2P communication would incur also key establishment cost, thus some additional public key encryption, whose processing delay is on the same order of magnitude of signature verification delay. However, we do not explicitly consider it here, as it is optional. Table 2 shows processing delays for cryptographic operations on a *Sony Xperia Ultra Z* smartphone, which has a *Quad-core 2.2 GHz Krait 400* CPU. We choose RSA and ECDSA algorithms, commonly used for public key cryptography. Note that ECDSA is standard in other applications, notably Vehicular Ad-hoc Networks (VANETs) [7], due to its low key generation and signing delays and short signature sizes. However, the Spongy Castle library [3], the only library available for Android supporting ECDSA, is inefficient. We found that RSA key generation takes more time than ECDSA, but sign/verify operations take much less time than ECDSA. Actually, all the execution delays of ECDSA are abnormally high (compared to those in other libraries for other platforms). By checking the system logs of

---

[2] Compared to other domains [15,19], which need frequent pseudonym changes to ensure unlinkability of messages transmitted in high rate, a relatively longer pseudonym lifetime is acceptable in our scheme, as one can expect relatively lower message rates. Thus, the performance is less affected by key generation operations.

the smartphone, we found that for each cryptographic operation of ECDSA the application needs to free the heap 2 or 3 times. As a result, it increases significantly cryptographic latencies, due to the limited heap size of each application in Android and the high spatial overhead of ECDSA operations. Due to abnormalities of ECDSA operations in Android, RSA is preferred for our scheme.

Table 3. Processing overhead for different operations

Operation	*Processing Overhead*
Message verification with cached pseudonym	Message Verification
Message verification with non-cached pseudonym	Pseudonym Verification, Message Verification
Query generation	Message Signing
Response generation	Database Query, Message Signing

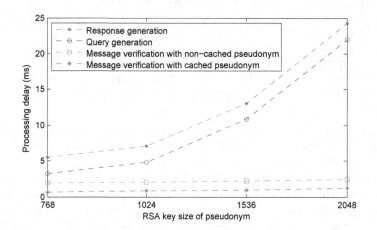

Fig. 3. Processing delay under pseudonyms with different RSA key sizes, assuming an RSA-2048 certificate of the PCA

Table 3 shows processing overhead for different operations and Fig. 3 shows processing delays on the smartphone. Consider, for example, mobile phone user density in Spanish cities [21]: Barcelona, the most densely populated in terms of mobile phone users in Spain, has around 3000 mobile phone users per km^2. Assuming Wi-Fi radio range of $100m$, there are around 100 peers within range. Assume all peers (e.g., in a landmark site or in the city center) need to query with a query rate per user equal to 1 $query/min$: this implies that a node would receive approximately 1.7 $queries/sec$. From Fig. 3, we can see that verifying a query, even with non-cached pseudonyms, would incur processing overhead for less than 3 *msec*, thus more than 300 *queries/sec* could be verified. Peer response generation delay is highly dependent on local cache implementation and size of the cache. It includes a searching process and a signing operation. In our experiment, we use SQLite database. We assume 50 pieces of POIs are stored in the cache and 5 pieces of them matches each query. From Fig. 3, we see it takes approximately 7 *msec* to generate a peer response with RSA-1024 key. This implies that a node could, if able and needing to, respond to 1.7 *queries/sec* (the query rate we calculated earlier).

Based on availability of relevant information in the cache, only a part of them could be served; moreover, the actual latency could be significantly lower thanks to optimizations we proposed in Sec. 3. More basically, a node can "decide," based on, e.g., current CPU usage and battery amount remaining, whether or not to serve peer queries. A protocol-selectable parameter, the maximum rate at which to respond, can further reduce the overhead.

Peer query and response sizes are application and implementation dependent. In our experiments, we assume 25 byte queries. By encoding public keys and signatures into Base64 format and encapsulating into JSON format; the total size of a peer query, with an RSA-1024 pseudonym (public key and signature from the PCA) attached, is 980 bytes. The size of a peer response depends on how many information pieces it contains; while the signature and attached pseudonym sizes are same as those for a query. With most smartphones supporting IEEE 802.11 b/g/n with throughput between 11 and 300 Mbps, the above mentioned query rate would not incur heavy communication overhead. Clearly, receiving queries would affect posting own queries, as responses are received over the same channel. But, as mentioned above, beyond optimizations, a node can always stop serving queries beyond a threshold, to ensure it can obtain own needed information.

6   Conclusion

We presented a decentralized secure and privacy protection scheme for LBSs. We leverage the concept of information sharing in P2P systems for POI information sharing, and further secure it in a privacy-preserving manner with pseudonym-based authentication. Through security and privacy analysis and performance evaluation, we show a system with high resiliency to different attacks and high practicality for the deployment. Our scheme can be extended in terms of optimizations we proposed. In our evaluation, we assume mobile nodes are evenly distributed. However, efficiency of our scheme in flash crowds needs to be evaluated with large scale simulation to show how peer queries for varying types of POI information can be handled by load balancing among the nodes in the crowds. Moreover, with simulation, we can quantify user privacy and determine optimal parameters for the optimizations we proposed. An incentive scheme and cross-checking mechanism can be integrated to promote user participation and improve attack resiliency.

References

1. Google maps api. https://developers.google.com/maps/
2. Lte direct. https://www.qualcomm.com/invention/technologies/lte/direct
3. The Spongy Castle Cryptography APIs. https://rtyley.github.io/spongycastle/
4. Uber api. https://developer.uber.com/
5. Wi-fi direct. https://rtyley.github.io/spongycastle/
6. PRIME Framework Version. 3 (2008). https://www.prime-project.eu/prime_products/reports/fmwk/
7. IEEE Standard for Wireless Access in Vehicular Environments Security Services for Applications and Management Messages. IEEE Std 1609.2-2013 (2013)
8. Barkhuus, L., Dey, A.K.: Location-based services for mobile telephony: a study of users' privacy concerns. In: INTERACT, Cape Town, South Africa, September 2003
9. Calandriello, G., Papadimitratos, P., Hubaux, J.-P., Lioy, A.: Efficient and robust pseudonymous authentication in vanet. In: ACM VANET, Montreal, Canada, September 2007
10. Calandriello, G., Papadimitratos, P., Hubaux, J.-P., Lioy, A.: On the performance of secure vehicular communication systems. In: IEEE TDSC (2011)
11. Chow, C.-Y., Mokbel, M.F., Liu, X.: A peer-to-peer spatial cloaking algorithm for anonymous location-based service. In: ACM GIS, New York, NY, November 2006
12. Cutillo, L.A., Molva, R., Strufe, T.: Privacy preserving social networking through decentralization. In: IEEE/IFIP WONS, Snowbird, Utah, February 2009
13. Gedik, B., Liu, L.: Protecting location privacy with personalized k-anonymity: Architecture and algorithms. IEEE Transactions on Mobile Computing, January 2008
14. Ghinita, G., Kalnis, P., Skiadopoulos, S.: Mobihide: a mobilea peer-to-peer system for anonymous location-based queries. In: SSTD, Boston, MA, July 2007
15. Gisdakis, S., Giannetsos, T., Papadimitratos, P.: Sppear: security & privacy-preserving architecture for participatory-sensing applications. In: ACM WiSec, Oxford, UK, July 2014
16. Gisdakis, S., Laganà, M., Giannetsos, T., Papadimitratos, P.: Serosa: Service oriented security architecture for vehicular communications. In: IEEE VNC, Boston, MA, December 2013
17. Han, L., Nath, B., Iftode, L., Muthukrishnan, S.: Social butterfly: Social caches for distributed social networks. In: PASSAT, Boston, MA, October 2011
18. Johnson, M., McGuire, D., Willey, N.: The evolution of the peer-to-peer file sharing industry and the security risks for users. In: HICSS, Waikoloa, Big Island, Hawaii, January 2008
19. Khodaei, M., Jin, H., Papadimitratos, P.: Towards deploying a scalable & robust vehicular identity and credential management infrastructure. In: IEEE VNC, Paderborn, Germany, December 2014
20. Kwok, S.H., Lang, K.R., Tam, K.Y.: Peer-to-peer technology business and service models: risks and opportunities. Electronic Markets (2002)
21. Louail, T., Lenormand, M., Cantu Ros, O.G., Picornell, M., Herranz, R., Frias-Martinez, E., Ramasco, J.J., Barthelemy, M.: From mobile phone data to the spatial structure of cities. Scientific Reports, June 2014
22. Martucci, L.A., Kohlweiss, M., Andersson, C., Panchenko, A.: Self-certified sybil-free pseudonyms. In: ACM WiSec, Alexandria, VA, April 2008

23. Mascetti, S., Bettini, C., Freni, D., Wang, X.S.: Spatial generalisation algorithms for lbs privacy preservation. Journal of Location Based Services (2007)
24. Mezzour, G., Perrig, A., Gligor, V., Papadimitratos, P.: Privacy-preserving relationship path discovery in social networks. In: Garay, J.A., Miyaji, A., Otsuka, A. (eds.) CANS 2009. LNCS, vol. 5888, pp. 189–208. Springer, Heidelberg (2009)
25. Mokbel, M.F., Chow, C.-Y., Aref, W.G.: The new casper: query processing for location services without compromising privacy. In: Proceedings of the 32nd International Conference on Very large Data Bases, Seoul, Korea, September 2006
26. Myles, G., Friday, A., Davies, N.: Preserving privacy in environments with location-based applications. IEEE Pervasive Computing (2003)
27. Papadimitratos, P., Calandriello, G., Lioy, A., Hubaux, J.-P.: Impact of vehicular communication security on transportation safety. In: IEEE INFOCOM MOVE, Phoenix, AZ, April 2008
28. Sampigethaya, K., Li, M., Huang, L., Poovendran, R.: Amoeba: Robust location privacy scheme for vanet. IEEE JSAC (2007)
29. Shokri, R., Theodorakopoulos, G., Papadimitratos, P., Kazemi, E., Hubaux, J.-P.: Hiding in the mobile crowd: Location privacy through collaboration. IEEE TDSC (2014)
30. Zhou, L., Zhang, L., McSherry, F., Immorlica, N., Costa, M., Chien, S.: A first look at peer-to-peer worms: threats and defenses. In: Proceedings of the 4th International Conference on Peer-to-Peer Systems, Konstanz, Germany, August 2005

Design of a Privacy-Preserving Document Submission and Grading System

Benjamin Greschbach[(✉)], Guillermo Rodríguez-Cano, Tomas Ericsson,
and Sonja Buchegger

KTH Royal Institute of Technology, Stockholm, Sweden
{bgre,gurc,te,buc}@kth.se

Abstract. Document submission and grading systems are commonly
used in educational institutions. They facilitate the hand-in of assignments
by students, the subsequent grading by the course teachers and the management of the submitted documents and corresponding grades. But they
might also undermine the privacy of students, especially when documents
and related data are stored long term with the risk of leaking to malicious
parties in the future. We propose a protocol for a privacy-preserving, anonymous document submission and grading system based on blind signatures.
Our solution guarantees the unlinkability of a document with the author-
ing student even after her grade has been reported, while the student can
prove that she received the grade assigned to the document she submitted.
We implemented a prototype of the proposed protocol to show its feasibility and evaluate its privacy and security properties.

1 Introduction

The pervasive collection of massive amounts of personal data is an increasing
threat to user privacy. Often, more information than necessary for the intended
purpose is collected and used for profiling or targeted advertisement. User choice
is often limited to either not using a given system or service, or to accepting the
loss of privacy that comes along with using the system. Designing systems that
collect or process personal user data should therefore have privacy in mind from
the beginning and employ best practices such as data minimization.

The focus of this work is the context of an educational institution, e. g., a university, where students take courses, work on assignments for these courses and
teachers grade these assignments. In this context, discriminatory grading may
be an issue, i. e., grading that is not solely based on the student's achievements
but also on the teacher's preconception about individual students or stereotypes
about certain groups of students. One approach to avoid this is to use blind
grading, where the student's identity is not known to the teacher while grading
the assignment. Only after the grade has been determined, the link between

---

S. Buchegger—This research has been funded by the Swedish Foundation for Strategic Research grant SSF FFL09-0086 and the Swedish Research Council grant VR
2009-3793.

S. Buchegger and M. Dam (Eds.): NordSec 2015, LNCS 9417, pp. 64–71, 2015.
DOI: 10.1007/978-3-319-26502-5_5

assignment and student identity is recovered, so that the grade can be assigned to the student. In some settings, one might even want to have what we refer to as *forward unlinkability*, i. e., the teacher not being able to link the student to the assignment even after the grades have been reported. For example if a course consists of two different assignments, the work done on the two assignments is linkable if students are likely to choose similar topics for both parts. In that case, without forward unlinkability, the teacher would know the student's identity during the grading of the second assignment. Another motivation for wanting forward unlinkability is the general aim of data minimization, which among other things protects against unintended leakages of personal data in the future. At the same time, the handling and grading of assignments has to guarantee that a student receives a certain grade if and only if she submitted work that was graded accordingly by the teacher. So while the student identity and the submitted document have to remain unlinkable, we want a *provable linkability* of the student's identity and the received grade.

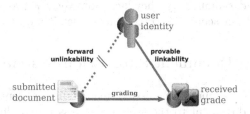

Fig. 1. Overview of system entities, their relations and desired properties.

Using the cryptographic technique of blind signatures [1], we propose a protocol for this use case: a privacy-preserving document submission and grading system that allows students to submit documents anonymously without compromising the correctness of the grade assignment process.

After presenting related work in Section 2, we formulate a system model and desired properties for the system in Section 3. In Section 4 we suggest a protocol design that meets these requirements, and evaluate the proposed protocol, discussing its privacy and security properties in Section 5. Furthermore, we show the practical feasibility of the proposed solution by having implemented a proof-of-concept prototype of the protocol, briefly described in the same section.

2   Related Work

Blind signatures schemes are widely used to enhance the privacy of protocols by providing unlinkability. Examples of their use include identity management in federated login systems, e. g., PseudoID [2], a project to protect the login data from the identity providers by means of blind digital signatures, or electronic payment systems, e. g., Taler [6], a digital currency approach close to Bitcoin with the additional benefit of governmental tax traceability without losing anonymity as blind signatures provide unlinkability to the transactions between customers and merchants but not between government and merchants. Secure voting schemes are another application area of blind signatures, e. g., CryptoBallot [7], a cryptographically secure online voting system where ballots cannot be traced back to the voter as they are blinded but their counting and the voter identities are publicly auditable. Even though these schemes have similarities with our problem, they would be unnecessarily complex to adapt for the use case of document submission and grading. Attribute-based anonymous credentials can be used for similar purposes, such as in an anonymous course evaluation system for universities [9]. The use-case of this project differs, however, from our problem statement, having a focus on smart-card based anonymous course attendance verification, introducing complexity not needed in our scenario. Whistleblower platforms, e. g., SecureDrop [5] or GlobaLeaks [8], allow a sender to submit documents anonymously to a receiver, such as a media organization. These systems employ anonymous and confidential communication and meta-data footprint minimization to increase the anonymity of the sender. While maximizing the sender anonymity, they lack, however, the provable linkability of feedback (grades in our scenario) to identifiers, that is required in our use case.

3   Anonymous Document Submission System

We aim to design a document submission and grading system, where each student can submit a document to the system before a public deadline. After the deadline passed, the teacher grades all submitted documents with either pass or fail. When all documents are graded, each student receives the grade that the teacher assigned to the document that was submitted by the student.

We assume that students can store credentials they receive in a secure way, do not pass them on to others and that they can communicate with the system in a mutually authenticated and confidential way (e. g., via a TLS secured web login), and at other times in an anonymous and confidential way (e. g., by using TLS over Tor[3]). We assume that they are careful to include no identifying information in the documents and that authorship attribution by stylometry is not feasible for the adversary. When discussing the security and reliability of the system from the teacher's perspective, we assume that the server cannot be compromised and that the teacher can handle secret keys in a secure way. Furthermore, protection against ghost writing is out of scope of this work, so we assume that students will not ask someone else to write their documents, which reflects a general limitation for home assignments that are allowed to be worked on outside a teacher-controlled environment. To achieve anonymity and correctness, we want the system to have the following two properties:

student–document forward unlinkability

A document cannot be linked to a student by anyone else than the student who submitted the document, and the unlinkability remains even after grades have been assigned to students.

student–grade provable linkability

If and only if a document was graded with a certain grade, the student who submitted the document can prove that she received this grade.

We want our system to both protect the student's privacy and to protect the teacher from dishonest students. Therefore we consider two different adversaries. The first adversary tries to break the student's anonymity and is capable of compromising any involved party except for the student herself. In particularly it can control the teacher, the server and any other student. Furthermore, we assume this adversary to be capable to passively intercept all network traffic and actively inject messages. The second adversary tries to break the correctness of the grade assignment and is used when discussing the security and reliability of the system from the teacher's perspective. This adversary is assumed to be able to compromise one student, to passively observe all network traffic and to actively inject messages.

4   Protocol Design

We implement the protocol that has the desired properties using a blind signature scheme as described in [1], that provides the functions $blind, unblind, sign$ and $verify$, with the property that blinding perfectly hides the data, but signatures on blinded data can still be verified after unblinding (informally: $unblind(sign(blind(x))) = sign(x)$). Section 4 shows the sequence of steps in our proposed protocol. First, the system server provides each registered student in the course with a unique, random, one-time identifier rID and stores the relation of student identifiers to rIDs for later use. Next, the student blinds the rID for both the pass verification key e_{pass} and the fail verification key e_{fail}, using two private, random blinding factors b_{pass} and b_{fail}, and sends the resulting $bID_{pass} = blind(rID, b_{pass}, e_{pass})$ and $bID_{fail} = blind(rID, b_{fail}, e_{fail})$ together with D, the document to submit, to the server over an anonymous, encrypted channel. At this point, the server does not learn who submitted the document because the blinding hides the rID, using the anonymous channel obfuscates the network address origin and the document D is assumed to not contain any identifying information about the student. After the deadline has passed, the teacher grades all submitted documents. If a document is graded as passed, the blinded identifier bID_{pass} that was submitted together with the document is signed with the private pass signing key d_{pass} of the teacher. If the grade is fail, bID_{fail} will be signed with the teacher's private fail signing key d_{fail}. When all documents are graded, the server publishes a list of all signed blinded

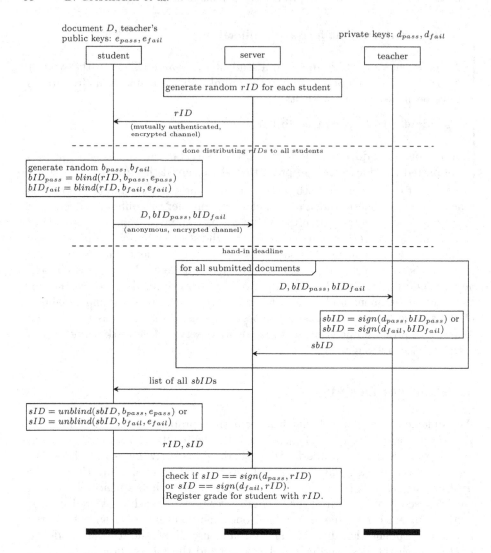

Fig. 2. Protocol realizing an anonymous document submission and grading system.

identifiers. The student fetches the list, picks the signed blinded identifier that belongs to her and unblinds it. The student will try both public verification keys e_{pass} and e_{fail} to check which grade she received. By this, the student obtains a signed identifier $sID = sign(rID)$ that proves that she received the grade corresponding to the signing-key. Finally, she sends sID to the server, the server checks the signature, looks up the student identifier that belongs to rID, and registers the corresponding grade for the student, not learning which document the student submitted.

5   Discussion and Evaluation

We have implemented a proof-of-concept prototype (see http://www.ter.se/dss/) which is a collection of C programs for the various operations performed by the student, server and teacher, realizing the described protocol. The prototype uses the free cryptographic library Libgcrypt [4]. In the following, we do an informal security and privacy evaluation, discussing why the previously defined properties hold and various attacks will not succeed. We do not cover implementation-based attacks though, such as cross-site-scripting attacks on a web-interface.

Student–document Forward Unlinkability. The student identity is directly linked to the random identifier rID. But when submitting the document D, the rID is perfectly hidden by the random blinding factors known only to the student. We assume that there is no identifying information contained in the document, so after submission the server cannot link student identifiers to documents. To achieve forward unlinkability, this has to hold even after the grades have been assigned to students. During grading, documents are linked to grades, which is a binary domain in our case. The grade information is attached to the blinded rID in form of a signature with one out of two keys, that can be transformed in a verifiable signature on the unblinded rID only by the student. The properties of the blind signature scheme provide the unlinkability between this unblinded signature and the blinded data that was submitted together with the document. At the same time, the signature is provided to the server together with the rID when the students claim their grades, so they provide an unambiguous mapping from every rID to a grade. As a consequence, we do not get perfect unlinkability of student identifiers and documents, but only *k-anonymity*, where k is the number of students who received the same grade. This is a general limitation of every system where the grading party is not trusted and the assignment of grades to student identifiers is verifiable. A worst-case example is a situation where only one student received the grade "fail", so the teacher can infer that the only document she graded with "fail" must belong to this student. Another limitation is the fact, that the anonymity for all students with a certain grade is reduced whenever one student with the same grade gives up their anonymity voluntarily or becomes compromised by the adversary.

Student–grade Provable Linkability. The provable linkability of student identifiers to grades has two directions: (a) soundness: if a student can prove that she received a certain grade, then she must have submitted a document that was graded accordingly, and (b) completeness: if a document submitted by a student was graded with a certain grade, then the student can prove that she received that grade. We show (a) by contrapositive, so we assume that the student did not submit a document that was graded with the grade that the student claims. Now we see that the student cannot prove that she received that grade: she cannot present a valid signature on the rID assigned to her, made with the private key corresponding to the grade, because the private signing key was used by the teacher only to sign other blinded rIDs that were submitted together with documents that were graded accordingly. For (b) we see directly that if a submitted document was graded with a certain grade, the teacher put a signature on the blinded rID submitted together with the document and publishes that later on. So the student can derive a valid signature on her rID by unblinding the published information and therefore can prove to anyone knowing the public verification key, that she received that grade.

Timing and Correlation Attacks. To avoid timing attacks, it is important that certain events in the protocol do not happen before others. For example, the hand-in of documents must not start before all students received their rIDs (denoted by the first dashed line in the message sequence chart in Section 4), otherwise the anonymity set for the submitting students is immediately reduced to those who already received their rID. For a similar reason it is important that the server publishes the result list with the signed, blinded rIDs after the hand-in deadline and as a complete list. The latter is important, because if students for example would request their individual entries without downloading the complete list, the server could correlate these requests for specific entries (that the server can link to documents) with requests for registering a grade (which contain the identifier rID), that might happen shortly after each other. End-to-end traffic correlation attacks are also relevant for the concrete implementation of the anonymous channel. Tor, for example, does not protect against an adversary that can observe both traffic going into the Tor network and traffic coming out of it [3], so the students should for example be advised not to use the university network when submitting their documents, because it is likely that the same party operates both the university network and the system server and therefore could observe both ends of the students' connections.

Impersonation and Replay Attacks. To avoid impersonation and replay attacks, it is important not to use a public or permanent student identifier such as the students' e-mail addresses. Otherwise, an attacker could impersonate a student, e. g., to damage her reputation by submitting a low-quality document in her name. Therefore, we use the unique, random, one-time identifier rID and distribute it over a mutually authenticated and encrypted channel to the student. This makes impersonation without the cooperation of the student impossible because the attacker does not know which rID was assigned to a student. It also prevents replay attacks, as the rID binds the messages both to the student and to the current course, because even if the same protocol is used for several courses, the same student will receive a new rID in each new protocol run.

Attacks on Combined Cryptographic Primitives. Attacks on the used cryptographic primitives, such as public key cryptography, hash functions and blind signatures, are out of scope of this work, so we assume them to be secure. However, we have to be careful to use these tools in a secure way, especially when combining them with each other. It is, for example, important to use two different blinding factors b_{pass} and b_{false} when blinding the rID. Otherwise, if for ease of implementation one would use only one common blinding factor b for both blindings, the server would be able to mount the following de-anonymization attack: The server generates specially prepared public keys $e_{pass} = \langle N, e \rangle$ and $e_{fail} = \langle N, e' \rangle$ with the property that both share the same modulus N and the public exponents have a difference of one: $e - e' = 1 \pmod{N}$. If the student blinds her rID for these keys using a common blinding factor b, she will submit the following two values to the server: $bID_{pass} = blind(rID, b, e_{pass}) = rID \cdot b^e \pmod{N}$, $bID_{fail} = blind(rID, b, e_{fail}) = rID \cdot b^{e'} \pmod{N}$. Now, the server can simply divide the two values to obtain the blinding factor b: $bID_{pass}/bID_{fail} = (b^e \cdot rID)/(b^{e'} \cdot rID) = b^{e-e'} = b \pmod{N}$. Having learned b, the server can unblind the bIDs and obtain rID, thus having de-anonymized the student.

6   Conclusions and Limitations

We have described a practical application for blind signatures schemes in the context of a document submission and grading system to improve the privacy of students without undermining the correctness of the grading process. We found that it is feasible to implement such a system, qualified only by the limitations derived from the scenario, e. g., that the provided k-anonymity depends on the number of other students who received the same grade, that students can choose not to reveal their grade, and that documents cannot be linked to students even where this might be desired for pedagogical reasons or penalty measures for plagiarism that go beyond grading the work with fail.

The basic protocol described here can be extended with more functionality such as having several teachers do the grading, using more fine grained grading scales (with the limitation that this decreases the anonymity sets), issuing submission acknowledgements or including individual feedback without breaking the anonymity properties.

References

1. Chaum, D.: Blind signatures for untraceable payments. In: Chaum, D., Rivest, R.L., Sherman, A.T. (eds.) Advances in Cryptology, pp. 199–203. Springer US (1982)
2. Dey, A., Weis, S.: PseudoID: Enhancing privacy in federated login. In: Hot Topics in Privacy Enhancing Technologies, pp. 95–107 (2010). http://www.pseudoid.net
3. Dingledine, R., Mathewson, N., Syverson, P.: Tor: The second-generation onion router. In: SSYM Proceedings, vol. 13. p. 21. USENIX Association, USA (2004)
4. Free Software Foundation (FSF): Libgcrypt (2007). http://www.gnu.org/software/libgcrypt/
5. Freedom of the Press Foundation (FPF): SecureDrop (2013). https://securedrop.org/
6. French Institute for Research in Computer Science and Automation (INRIA): Taler (2015). http://www.taler.net
7. Hayes, P.D.: CryptoBallot (2013). https://cryptoballot.com/
8. Hermes Center for Transparency and Digital Human Rights: GlobaLeaks (2011). https://www.globaleaks.org/
9. Stamatiou, Y., et al.: Course evaluation in higher education: the patras pilot of ABC4Trust. In: Rannenberg, K., Camenisch, J., Sabouri, A. (eds.) Attribute-based Credentials for Trust, pp. 197–239. Springer International Publishing (2015)

Towards Perfectly Secure and Deniable Communication Using an NFC-Based Key-Exchange Scheme

Daniel Bosk[1]([⊠]), Martin Kjellqvist[2], and Sonja Buchegger[1]

[1] School of Computer Science and Communication,
KTH Royal Institute of Technology, 100 44 Stockholm, Sweden
{dbosk,buc}@kth.se
[2] Department of Information and Communication Systems,
Mid Sweden University, 851 70 Sundsvall, Sweden
martin.kjellqvist@miun.se

Abstract. In this paper we first analyse the possibility for deniability under a strong adversary, who has an Internet-wide transcript of the communication. Secondly, we present a scheme which provides the desirable properties of previous messaging schemes, but with stronger deniability under the new adversary model. Our scheme requires physical meetings for exchanges of large amounts of random key-material via near-field communication and later uses this random data to key a one-time pad for text-messaging. We prove the correctness of the protocol and, finally, we evaluate the practical feasibility of the suggested scheme.

Keywords: Deniability · Deniable encryption · Authenticated encryption · Perfect secrecy · Off-the-record · Key-exchange · Near-field communication · Surveillance

1 Introduction

We have learned a lot about modern government surveillance from the Snowden revelations starting in 2013. For our current treatment, the most interesting ones are the tapping of fibre-optic cables [13], the storage of all intercepted encrypted data [9], the search [10] and visualization capabilities [11] for all intercepted data. It is not the details that are interesting, it is the fact that one actor can collect, store and search Internet-wide transcripts of communication. This paper focuses on the possibility of deniability in this setting.

Today, GNU Privacy Guard (GPG) [18], Off-the-Record (OTR) [3] and Text-Secure [16] are among the popular services used for private communication. GPG provides standard asymmetric and symmetric encryption, intended for use with email. In 2004, Borisov, Goldberg and Brewer [3] first described the OTR due to limitations of deniability in GPG. The design goal of the protocol is to achieve strong privacy properties for users' online communication, the same properties as expected from a face-to-face conversation. The main application at the time

© Springer International Publishing Switzerland 2015
S. Buchegger and M. Dam (Eds.): NordSec 2015, LNCS 9417, pp. 72–87, 2015.
DOI: 10.1007/978-3-319-26502-5_6

was Instant Messaging (IM). In 2010, OpenWhisperSystems adapted the OTR messaging protocol [8] for use in the smartphone text-messaging app TextSecure.

The construction used for deniability in OTR, and the derived protocols, is based on the principle "innocent until proven otherwise". While this holds true for most civil societies, it is not true everywhere. There are circumstances in which the principle "guilty until proven otherwise" is applied instead. For these circumstances, with an adversary that can record all network traffic, it is not possible to create any false witness (proof-of-innocence) due to the deterministic nature of the protocol. In Sect. 3 we show that this allows an adversary with transcripts of all network traffic to verify any statements about the conversation using the transcripts. To thwart this we need truly deniable encryption, as defined by Canetti et al. [4], which means that we need to introduce some randomness.

1.1   Our Contributions

We start from protocols like OTR, but we assume a stronger adversary (Sect. 2). This stronger adversary model breaks some assumptions in OTR-like protocols and removes the possibility for deniability. We still want to achieve the same basic properties, e.g. mutual authentication, but we also want to have stronger deniability. In Sect. 3 we show that an adversary who can record all communication in a network can use the deterministic properties of commonly used mechanisms to reject lies about any communication.

We then outline the security properties needed and formally describe them and some results about them (Sect. 4). We continue to present a scheme which is a combination of authenticated encryption and deniable encryption (Sect. 5). This protocol is stateful, and as such, is also secure against replay and out-of-order attacks. It is a general design, so any deniable encryption and message authentication schemes with the right properties can be plugged in.

To show that this scheme is practically feasible, we present an implementation (Sect. 6). We use Near-Field Communication (NFC) in smartphones to exchange large-enough amounts of random data when two users physically meet. Later, when the users are apart, this data is used to key a One-Time Pad (OTP) for use when communicating. To estimate the feasibility of this scheme we investigate

- the order of magnitude of random data needed to be able to cover everyday text-message conversation;
- if the NFC transmission rates and the random number generation in combination with the number of physical meetings can provide high enough exchange rates in practice; and
- how the continuous key-generation in this scheme affects battery life in the device.

We answer the first question by estimating the amount of private communication for some users (Sect. 6.1). We answer the second question by estimating the required number of physical meetings for the same users (Sect. 6.2). Since we have an estimate of the amount of exchanged randomness needed and the transmission rates for the NFC protocol, we can estimate how many physical meetings and how long transfers are needed to cover the needs. For the third question, we estimate the battery usage by performing key generation and exchanges using different Android-based phones while monitoring the battery consumption (Sect. 6.3).

2 The System and Adversary Models

In our system model, we assume that we have two communication channels: one private and one public. We can implement the private channel as an NFC channel and a public network-channel, e.g. the Internet. We can always use the public channel, but we can only use the private (NFC) channel more rarely, e.g. if we are in the same physical space.

We assume that a user can, at least once, use the private channel. They must do this before any secure communication over the public channel can be started. We assume that a device can generate cryptographically strong random data and that this key-material can be securely stored on the device.

For the adversary model, we assume a stronger adversary, Eve. Eve records all traffic in the public channel. This means that she records all traffic for the entire Internet. Thus Eve has a transcript of all communication that has taken place in the public channel and any future communication will also be entered into her transcript. But Eve cannot record any communication in the private channel. Also, Eve cannot access the devices used in the communication. Instead, she will force us to reveal the keys that produced the ciphertexts in her transcript. In summary, in related works, Eve has had the role of a prosecutor who must prove things to a judge. In our model, Eve has the role of being both prosecutor and judge, which is more the case in some surveillance states.

2.1 A Formal Definition of the Adversary

More formally, we summarize Eve's capabilities in the definition below. She has the transcript of all communication in the public channel and she forces Alice to reveal the keys used for the ciphertexts in the transcribed conversation with Bob. Eve's task is to decide whether Alice is trying to lie.

Definition 1 (Deniability under Surveillance-State Attack, DEN-SS).
Let A be an efficient adversary. Let $P = ((m_i, k_i))_{i=1}^{n}$ be pairs of messages and keys and let $T = (t_i = \mathsf{Enc}_{k_i}(m_i))_{(m_i, k_i) \in P}$ be transcript of ciphertexts corresponding to the entries in P. P and T are generated by some algorithm using the encryption scheme $S = (\mathsf{Keygen}, \mathsf{Enc}, \mathsf{Dec})$. Let ϕ be the challenge algorithm.

First let the adversary choose (the index of) a transcript

$$i \leftarrow A(r, T),$$

where $r \xleftarrow{\ \mathcal{C}\ } R$ is random coins sampled from a set R. We then create two challenges, c_0 and c_1:

$$c_0 \leftarrow k_i,$$
$$c_1 \leftarrow \phi(r', i, P),$$

where $r' \xleftarrow{\mathcal{C}} R$ is again some random coins. Next, we choose a bit $b \xleftarrow{\mathcal{C}} \{0,1\}$ uniformly randomly. Finally, the adversary outputs a bit

$$b' \leftarrow A(r, T, c_b).$$

We define the surveillance-state adversary's advantage as

$$\mathbf{Adv}_{\mathcal{S},\phi}^{DEN\text{-}SS}(A) = |\Pr[b = b'] - \Pr[b \neq b']|. \tag{1}$$

Eve's transcript T and Alice and Bob's plaintext transcript will be generated by a protocol. We we will present one in Sect. 6 for which Eve cannot win the above game. In the above, Alice uses the challenger algorithm ϕ to produce a key $k_i' \neq k_i$. The goal of our scheme is that the Eve cannot distinguish the two keys using the transcript T. Next we will outline the problems other protocols have against this adversary. We will use OTR as an example, but similar arguments can be made against similar protocols. Then we will return to our solution in Sect. 4 and onwards.

3   Why Alice and Bob Currently Must Forget Their Conversation

The security of today's popular services — GPG, OTR and TextSecure — rely on standard cryptographic mechanisms. These mechanisms provide strong security properties; in this section we outline why some of these properties are too strong for deniability in the setting where the adversary has a transcript of all communications.

GPG provides asymmetric and symmetric encryption intended to be used with email. Borisov, Goldberg and Brewer [3] have already presented arguments against GPG (and Pretty Good Privacy, PGP), but we will summarize them here. If Alice wants to send a message m to Bob, then she will encrypt it for Bob's public key k_B^{Pu}. She will then create a signature for the resultant ciphertext $c = \mathsf{Enc}_{k_B^{Pu}}(m)$ with her own private key k_A^{Pr}, i.e. $s = \mathsf{Sign}_{k_A^{Pr}}(H(c))$. Alice will then send the ciphertext block and the signature to Bob, and this transaction will be recorded in Eve's transcript. This scheme provides non-repudiation, i.e. Alice can not deny having sent the message m at a later time and Bob can also prove to a third party that Alice sent m. Further, Eve can also prove that Alice sent c, but she can only verify the plaintext m if Bob would reveal it to her.

In their paper, they suggested a scheme which does not have this property: the OTR messaging protocol. This protocol provides authentication for Alice and Bob, so that they can trust they are talking to the right person. But they can do no more than that, Bob can no longer prove to a third party what Alice has sent. They accomplish this by a continuous use of the Diffie-Hellman (DH) key-exchange and a Message-Authentication Code (MAC) based on symmetric keys.

We provide a simplified description here, mainly to give an understanding of the underlying ideas, see the original paper [3] for a detailed description. Alice chooses a secret exponent a and Bob chooses a secret exponent b. Alice signs g^a and sends

$$A \to B : g^a, \mathsf{Sign}_{k_A^{Pr}}(g^a)$$

to Bob. Bob conversely sends

$$B \to A : g^b, \mathsf{Sign}_{k_B^{Pr}}(g^b)$$

to Alice. By this time they can both compute the secret shared-key $k = g^{ab}$. Let H_E and H_M be two cryptographically secure hash functions, used for deriving encryption and MAC keys, respectively. When Alice wants to send the message m to Bob, she chooses a random a' and sends

$$A \to B : g^{a'}, c = \mathsf{Enc}_{H_E(k)}(i) \oplus m, \mathsf{MAC}_{H_M(k)}\left(g^{a'}, c\right),$$

where i is some counter, to Bob. Once she knows Bob has received the message she also sends the MAC key $H_M(k)$ to Bob. The next time Alice wants to send a message to Bob, she will use $k' = g^{a'b}$.

Now, Bob can no longer prove to a third party what Alice has said. This is due to the MAC being based on a secret key which Bob has access to. Also, since the encryption is done in counter mode [7], the ciphertext is malleable. This means that flipping a bit in the ciphertext, yields the same flip in the plaintext. Thus, anyone possessing the MAC key can modify the plaintext by flipping the bits in the ciphertext and then generate a new MAC.

3.1 Verifying Who Sent What

The arguments for forgeability using malleable encryption and publishing the MAC keys only hold if the adversary cannot trust the source of the transcript. This more powerful Eve (Def. 1) can ultimately trust the transcript since she collected it herself from the network. And *if* the courts trust Eve, if there are any courts, they also trust the transcript.

In this setting the forgeability property vanishes. Eve knows that no one has modified the ciphertext, she recorded in her transcript as it left Alice and arrived to Bob. She also recorded Alice publishing the MAC key used for the signature. This allows Eve to use the MAC for each ciphertext to verify them. She knows that Alice is the author of a message because she observes when Alice publishes the MAC key. Thus, Eve also knows that no one has used the malleability property, because if they did, that action would be recorded in Eve's transcript.

3.2 Verifying Encryption Keys

Furthermore, Eve also learns some information about the key from the ciphertext and MAC tag. Eve can use the MAC to discard false keys for the ciphertext.

Since Eve has $t = \mathsf{MAC}_{H_M(k)}(c)$ for a ciphertext c recorded in her transcript, she can reject a key $k' \neq k$ by verifying that $\mathsf{MAC}_{H_M(k')}(c) \neq t$. Hence, by having the MAC key depend on the encryption key, we automatically decrease the number of spurious keys and thus also reduce our possibility for deniability.

3.3   How Hard Is Deniability?

As suggested above, we have difficulty achieving deniability. This is illustrated by the following equations. Assume

$$\mathsf{Enc}_{H_E(k)}(m) = c = \mathsf{Enc}_{H_E(k')}(m')$$

and $k \neq k'$, then

$$\Pr\left[\mathsf{MAC}_{H_M(k)}(c) = \mathsf{MAC}_{H_M(k')}(c)\right] \approx \Pr\left[H_M(k) = H_M(k')\right].$$

I.e. our chance of lying about the key k, replacing it with a key k', is reduced to finding a collision for the hash function H_M. (There is also the negligible probability of $\mathsf{MAC}_x(c) = \mathsf{MAC}_{x'}(c)$ for $x \neq x'$ to consider.)

Furthermore, we find the key k' by finding the preimage of $H_E(k')$. And if the encryption system Enc is a trap-door permutation, then we will have to break that first, just to find $H_E(k')$ before we can attempt finding its preimage.

4   Required Security Properties

To be able to get deniability in our given scenario, Alice and Bob need to be able to modify the plaintext without modifying the ciphertext. They also need a MAC key independent of the encryption key. Then they can change the encryption key and the plaintext, but the ciphertext and MAC remains the same. In this section we will cover the needed security properties.

Canetti et al. gave the original formal definition of deniable encryption in their seminal paper [4]. We will give their definition of sender-deniable encryption for shared-key schemes here.

Definition 2 (Shared-key sender-deniable encryption). *A protocol π with sender S and receiver R, and with security parameter n, is a shared-key sender-deniable encryption protocol if:*

Correctness *The probability that R's output is different than S's output is negligible (as a function of n).*
Security *For any $m_1, m_2 \in M$ in the message-space M and a shared-key $k \in K$ chosen at random from the key-space K, then we have $\Pr[\mathsf{Enc}_k(m_1) = c] \approx \Pr[\mathsf{Enc}_{k'}(m_2) = c]$.*
Deniability *There exists an efficient "faking" algorithm ϕ having the following property with respect to any $m_1, m_2 \in M$. Let k, r_S, r_R be uniformly chosen shared-key and random inputs of S and R, respectively, let*

$c = \mathsf{Enc}_{k,r_S,r_R}(m_1)$ and let $(k', r'_S) = \phi(m_1, k, r_S, c, m_2)$. Then the random variables

$$(m_2, k', r'_S, c) \quad and \quad (m_2, k, r_S, \mathsf{Enc}_{k,r_S,r_R}(m_2))$$

are distinguishable with negligible probability in the security parameter n.

This means that given a ciphertext $c = \mathsf{Enc}_k(m)$ and a false plaintext m', there exists a polynomial-time algorithm ϕ such that $\phi(c, m') = k'$ yields a key k' and $m' = \mathsf{Dec}_{k'}(c)$. As we illustrated in Sect. 3.3, there exists no such polynomial-time algorithm ϕ for OTR or GPG. But one encryption system for which the algorithm ϕ is trivial is the OTP.

Definition 3 (One-Time Pad). Let $M = K = (\mathbb{Z}_2)^n$. Then let $m \in M$ be a message in the message-space M, let $k \in K$ be a uniformly chosen key in the key-space K. Then we define

$$\mathsf{Enc}_k(m) = m \oplus k \quad and \quad \mathsf{Dec}_k = \mathsf{Enc}_k.$$

Shannon [17] proved that this scheme is perfectly secret. But this requires that the key k is as long as the message m. The key must be uniformly chosen, i.e. never reused. This is why this scheme is usually considered impractical. However, we can easily see, and it is also pointed out in [4], that the OTP fulfils Def. 2. We can simply define $\phi(m_2, c) = m_2 \oplus c$ and this would yield k' such that

$$\mathsf{Dec}_{k'}(c) = c \oplus k' = c \oplus (m_2 \oplus c) = m_2.$$

When we use an encryption scheme for communication we also want authenticity. Bellare and Namprempre [2] treats authenticated encryption and how to create composed authenticated encryption schemes. We will use the encrypt-then-MAC (EtM) composition. This means that we will encrypt and then compute a MAC tag on the ciphertext. We use the same formal definition of EtM as in [2].

Definition 4 (Encrypt-then-MAC, EtM). Let $\mathcal{E} = (\mathsf{Keygen}^E, \mathsf{Enc}, \mathsf{Dec})$ be an encryption scheme and $\mathcal{A} = (\mathsf{Keygen}^A, \mathsf{Tag}, \mathsf{Verify})$ be a message authentication scheme. We can then construct the authenticated encryption scheme $\overline{\mathcal{E}} = (\overline{\mathsf{Keygen}}, \overline{\mathsf{Enc}}, \overline{\mathsf{Dec}})$ as follows:

function $\overline{\mathsf{Keygen}}$	function $\overline{\mathsf{Enc}}(K, m)$	function $\overline{\mathsf{Dec}}(K, C)$
$k \xleftarrow{\mathfrak{C}} \mathsf{Keygen}^E$	$k \parallel k^{\mathsf{MA}} \leftarrow K$	$k \parallel k^{\mathsf{MA}} \leftarrow K$
$k^{\mathsf{MA}} \xleftarrow{\mathfrak{C}} \mathsf{Keygen}^A$	$c \xleftarrow{\mathfrak{C}} \mathsf{Enc}_k(m)$	$c \parallel t \leftarrow C$
return $k \parallel k^{\mathsf{MA}}$	$t \leftarrow \mathsf{Tag}_{k^{\mathsf{MA}}}(c)$	**if** $\mathsf{Verify}_{k^{\mathsf{MA}}}(c)$ **then**
	return $c \parallel t$	$m \leftarrow \mathsf{Dec}_k(c)$
		return m
		return $\perp$

OTR, for instance, uses a variant of EtM composition. It is a variant since in OTR the MAC key is derived from a master key. The results of [2] are proved for independent keys. Remember, this is one problem with the OTR that we want to avoid: the construction where the MAC key is a witness for the correct key. Instead of deriving the encryption key and the MAC key by using two different key-derivation functions on the same master key, we have to use information-theoretically independent keys.

Bellare and Namprempre [2] proved some properties about EtM: If the encryption scheme $\mathcal{E}$ provides Indistinguishability under Chosen-Plaintext Attack (IND-CPA) and the message authentication scheme $\mathcal{A}$ provides Strong Unforgeability under Chosen-Message Attack (SUF-CMA), then the EtM scheme $\overline{\mathcal{E}}$ provides Integrity of Ciphertexts (INT-CTXT) and Indistinguishability under Chosen-Ciphertext Attack (IND-CCA). Consequently, we are interested in what happens if we use a deniable encryption scheme in EtM. Since this authenticates the ciphertext, and not the plaintext, it will not interfere with our deniability. Since the key for encryption and authentication are independent, we can lie about one but not the other. We summarize this in the following theorem.

Theorem 1. *If $\mathcal{D} = (\mathsf{Keygen}^D, \mathsf{Enc}, \mathsf{Dec}, \phi)$ is a shared-key sender-deniable encryption scheme and $\mathcal{A} = (\mathsf{Keygen}^A, \mathsf{Tag}, \mathsf{Verify})$ is a message authentication scheme, then the scheme $\overline{\mathcal{D}}$ formed from the composition of $\mathcal{D}$ and $\mathcal{A}$ as in Def. 4 is also a shared-key sender-deniable encryption scheme.*

Proof. Bellare and Namprempre [2] proved that the resulting scheme $\overline{\mathcal{D}}$ inherits the security properties from the original encryption scheme $\mathcal{D}$. So the security and correctness of Def. 2 remains.

Let $K = k \| k^{\mathsf{MA}} \xleftarrow{\mathfrak{c}} \overline{\mathsf{Keygen}}$. For any message M we have $C = c \| t = \overline{\mathsf{Enc}}_K(M)$ and $M = \overline{\mathsf{Dec}}_K(C)$. Use ϕ to derive a new k' as follows: $k' \leftarrow \phi(M, k, c, M')$, where M' is a new message such that $M \neq M'$. Now let $K' = k' \| k^{\mathsf{MA}}$. By the construction of $\overline{\mathsf{Dec}}$ (Def. 4) we will have $\overline{\mathsf{Dec}}_{K'}(C) = M'$. Thus the deniability property is retained as well. $\qquad\square$

Note that the independence of the encryption key and the MAC key is crucial in the above theorem. If they are not independent, as in OTR, then this will only work if there exists an algorithm that can generate a new MAC key with the property that the MAC algorithm generates the same tag t for the same ciphertext c but with this new different key.

We will call a scheme composed as in Thm. 1 a *deniable authenticated encryption* scheme.

5   Achieving Deniability Against the Surveillance State

Due to the deniability requirements outlined above, the randomness used for encryption cannot be extended by a Pseudo-Random Number Generator (PRNG): if we do, then we are in the same situation as when we were using a trap-door permutation — we cannot efficiently find a seed to the PRNG which yields a stream that decrypts the ciphertext to the desired plaintext. Instead we generate randomness continuously and then exchange as much as needed using the private channel. This way we can use the everyday chance-encounters for exchanging the generated randomness when we meet, and then use it to key a deniable authenticated encryption scheme when physically apart.

5.1   A Protocol

Alice and Bob want to communicate securely with the possibility of deniability. They agree on using a stateful deniable authenticated encryption scheme $\overline{\mathcal{D}} = (\overline{\mathsf{Keygen}}, \overline{\mathsf{Enc}}, \overline{\mathsf{Dec}}, \phi)$. The scheme $\overline{\mathcal{D}}$ provides Indistinguishability under Stateful Chosen-Ciphertext Attack (IND-SFCCA), Integrity of Stateful Ciphertexts (INT-SFCTXT) and shared-key sender-deniability.

Alice and Bob start by each generating a string of random bits. Alice generates the string $k_A \xleftarrow{\mathfrak{c}} \overline{\mathsf{Keygen}}$ of length $|k_A|$. When Alice and Bob meet, Alice sends k_A over the private channel. Thus Eve cannot see this traffic. Later Alice wants to send a message to Bob over the public channel. To send the message m, Alice computes $C = c \parallel t \xleftarrow{\mathfrak{c}} \overline{\mathsf{Enc}}_{k_A}(m)$ and sends it to Bob. We assume the scheme $\overline{\mathcal{D}}$ is stateful, so when Alice wants to send her next message to Bob she simply computes $C' \xleftarrow{\mathfrak{c}} \overline{\mathsf{Enc}}_{k_A}(m')$ and sends C' to Bob. (We can turn any scheme into a stateful scheme by e.g. adding a counter, cf. [1].)

The protocol is unidirectional. If Bob wants to send messages to Alice, he has to do the same set up: first generate $k_B \xleftarrow{\mathfrak{c}} \overline{\mathsf{Keygen}}$, then send the key to Alice over the private channel. After that he can encrypt messages to Alice using $\overline{\mathsf{Enc}}_{k_B}(\cdot)$. The reason we want the protocol unidirectional is to easily maintain the state of the encryption and decryption algorithms. The protocol, run once in each direction, is illustrated in Fig. 1.

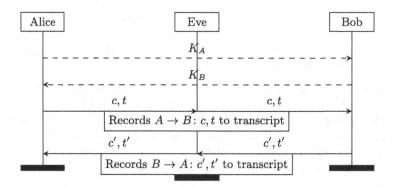

Fig. 1. A sequence diagram illustrating the protocol. K_A and K_B are long strings of bits sent over the private channel (dashed lines), Eve cannot record this. The messaging over the public channel is full lines: $c = \mathsf{Enc}_{k_{A,m}}(m)$ and $t = \mathsf{MAC}_{k_{A,m}^{\mathsf{MA}}}(c)$; $c' = \mathsf{Enc}_{k_{B,m'}}(m')$ and $t' = \mathsf{MAC}_{k_{B,m'}^{\mathsf{MA}}}(c')$. Eve records this data as it is sent over the public channel.

5.2   The Security of the Protocol

We will now show that the protocol just described yields negligible advantage to the surveillance-state adversary (Def. 1). However, to do this we need some more details to work with the formal definition of the adversary.

Let A be an algorithm representing Alice in the above protocol description. A is a randomized algorithm which generates a sequence of messages $M = (m_i)_{i=1}^n$ of n messages. A then generates a key $k_A \overset{\text{\textcent}}{\leftarrow} \overline{\text{Keygen}}$ by running the key generator of the scheme. Then A computes the sequence $T = (t_i \overset{\text{\textcent}}{\leftarrow} \overline{\text{Enc}}_{k_A}(m_i))_{i=1}^n$ by encrypting each message in the sequence M. The sequence T is the transcript of the surveillance-state adversary from Def. 1. While computing T, A also stores (possibly part of) the state of the decryption algorithm $\overline{\text{Dec}}_{k_A}(\cdot)$ in the following way: For each $t_i \overset{\text{\textcent}}{\leftarrow} \overline{\text{Enc}}_{k_A}(m_i)$ operation A will extract the state $K_i = k_i \parallel k_i^{\text{MA}}$ from $\overline{\text{Dec}}_{k_A}(\cdot)$ so that $\overline{\text{Dec}}'_{K_i}(t_i) = m_i$. We denote the sequence of states as $K = (K_i)_{i=1}^n$. And then we can form the sequence $P = M \times K$ in Def. 1 as the pairwise combination of M and K.

The first theorem shows that this scheme yields negligible advantage to the surveillance-state adversary. So our deniability properties holds.

Theorem 2 (Deniability against the surveillance state). *Given any adversary E_d against $\overline{\mathcal{D}}$, we can construct an adversary E'_d such that if E_d wins the DEN-SS game, then E'_d can distinguish between*

$$(m_2, k', r'_S, c) \text{ and } (m_2, k, r_S, \text{Enc}_{k, r_S, r_R}(m_2))$$

of $\mathcal{D}$ with non-negligible probability.

Proof. Assume that E_d has non-negligible advantage in the DEN-SS game of Def. 1. Then we can construct E'_d as follows. E'_d forms $T = (c)$ and runs $i \overset{\text{\textcent}}{\leftarrow} E_d(T)$. Then E'_d runs $b' \leftarrow E_d(T, k)$. If $b' = 1$, then E'_d knows that k was generated using the algorithm ϕ of $\mathcal{D}$. So E'_d can distinguish (m_2, k', r'_S, c) from $(m_2, k, r_S, \text{Enc}_{k, r_S, r_R}(m_2))$ with non-negligible probability.   □

The next theorem states that if the deniable encryption scheme $\mathcal{D}$ provides IND-SFCCA, then so will the scheme $\overline{\mathcal{D}}$.

Theorem 3 (Chosen-ciphertext security). *Given any adversary E_p against $\overline{\mathcal{D}}$, we can construct an adversary E'_p such that*

$$\mathbf{Adv}_{\overline{\mathcal{D}}}^{IND\text{-}SFCCA}(E_p) \leq \mathbf{Adv}_{\mathcal{D}}^{IND\text{-}SFCCA}(E'_p) \tag{2}$$

and E'_p makes the same number of queries as E_p does.

Proof (sketch). We use a similar construction as in [2,1], i.e. construct E'_p by letting E'_p generate and add the message authentication tags itself. Then E'_p will win IND-SFCCA$_{\mathcal{D}}$ when E_p wins IND-SFCCA$_{\overline{\mathcal{D}}}$.

6   Implementation and Evaluation

We want to make a practical implementation of the protocol described above. To do this we need an encryption scheme which is deniable (Def. 2) and provides IND-SFCCA. As pointed out above, OTP provides both. We will formulate this more rigorously below. We also need a message authentication scheme providing SUF-CMA. We will use this one to achieve INT-SFCTXT. But first we need to describe the stateful use of the OTP and MACs.

Definition 5 (Stateful OTP). *Let* Keygen *be an algorithm which generates a key k consisting of a string of $|k|$ uniformly random bits. Then we define the encryption and decryption functions for a message m and a ciphertext c, respectively, as follows:*

function Enc(k, m)	**function** Dec(k, c)
State s initialized to 0	State s initialized to 0
if $s + \lvert m\rvert > \lvert k\rvert$ **then**	**if** $s + \lvert m\rvert > \lvert k\rvert$ **then**
return $\perp$	**return** $\perp$
$k_m \leftarrow k[s, s + \lvert m\rvert]$	$k_c \leftarrow k[s, s + \lvert m\rvert]$
$s \leftarrow s + \lvert m\rvert$	$s \leftarrow s + \lvert m\rvert$
$c \leftarrow m \oplus k_m$	$m \leftarrow c \oplus k_m$
return c	**return** m

We call the scheme $\mathcal{E} = (\mathsf{Keygen}, \mathsf{Enc}, \mathsf{Dec})$ a stateful OTP encryption scheme.

The following theorem states that this scheme provides IND-SFCCA.

Theorem 4 (OTP implies IND-SFCCA). *If $\mathcal{E} = (\mathsf{Keygen}, \mathsf{Enc}, \mathsf{Dec})$ is the stateful OTP encryption scheme (Def. 5), then $\mathbf{Adv}_{\mathcal{E}}^{IND\text{-}SFCCA}(A)$ is negligible for any adversary A.*

Proof (sketch). By construction each encryption is perfectly secure. As such the adversary's advantage is no better than random guessing.

As mentioned above, we also need to have a stateful mechanism for message authentication. For this purpose, we now describe a stateful message authentication algorithm based solely on a MAC algorithm with SUF-CMA.

Definition 6 (Stateful MACs). *Let $\mathcal{A} = (\mathsf{Keygen}, \mathsf{Tag}, \mathsf{Verify})$ be a message authentication scheme yielding SUF-CMA and using random bit-strings of length $l_{\mathcal{A}}$ as keys. Let* Keygen *be an algorithm which generates a key k consisting of a string of $|k|$ uniformly random bits. Then we define the tag and verification functions for a ciphertext c and a tag t, respectively, as follows:*

function $\overline{\mathsf{Tag}}(k, c)$	**function** $\overline{\mathsf{Verify}}(k, c, t)$
State s initialized to 0	State s initialized to 0
if $s + l_{\mathcal{A}} > \lvert k\rvert$ **then**	**if** $s + l_{\mathcal{A}} > \lvert k\rvert$ **then**
return $\perp$	**return** $\perp$
$k_c \leftarrow k[s, s + l_{\mathcal{A}}]$	$k_c \leftarrow k[s, s + l_{\mathcal{A}}]$
$s \leftarrow s + l_{\mathcal{A}}$	**if** $\mathsf{Verify}_{k_c}(c, t) = 1$ **then**
$t \leftarrow \mathsf{Tag}_{k_c}(c)$	$s \leftarrow s + l_{\mathcal{A}}$
return t	**return** 1
	return 0

We call the scheme $\overline{\mathcal{A}} = (\overline{\mathsf{Keygen}}, \overline{\mathsf{Enc}}, \overline{\mathsf{Dec}})$ a stateful message authentication scheme.

Note that we only update the state if the verification is successful. We do not want to update the state in the case of an attack, that might bring the state of the verifying function out-of-sync with the state of the tagging function [1]. (Similarly for $\overline{\mathsf{Dec}}$ in Def. 4: to not bring Enc and Dec out-of-sync.)

We now show that the stateful message authentication mechanism provides INT-SFCTXT.

Theorem 5 (Stateful MACs implies INT-SFCTXT). *If the message authentication scheme* $\overline{\mathcal{A}} = (\overline{\mathsf{Keygen}}, \overline{\mathsf{Tag}}, \overline{\mathsf{Verify}})$ *is a stateful message authentication scheme, then* $\mathbf{Adv}_{\overline{\mathcal{A}}}^{INT\text{-}SFCTXT}(I)$ *is negligible for all adversaries I.*

Proof (sketch). By construction each tag will use a new key. As such the adversary's advantage is at best to randomly guess the next key.

The private channel for the protocol is implemented using the NFC protocol with smartphones. So Alice and Bob exchange the generated keys over the NFC protocol. From a user perspective, putting two phones together "charges the deniable encryption tool". This is probably a good metaphor to build on, since it builds on the mental model of a battery. Users are already familiar with this model, and thus, when running low on randomness, fewer messages should be exchanged until another physical meeting can be arranged to "charge" the tool again.

We have developed an app[1] for Android devices which implements the above ideas. It generates randomness continuously in the background to build up a pool of randomness. It can also exchange this randomness with another phone over NFC.

6.1   The Amount of Randomness Needed

Since we use the OTP, we need as much key material for encryption as we have plaintext. We need some additional key-material for the MACs, e.g. 128–256 bits per sent message. Thus we can estimate the total amount of randomness needed by estimating the exchange rate of plaintext. To do this we analyse the Enron email dataset[2].

We are interested in personal communication, i.e. we are not interested in newsletters and the like. To filter out the newsletter category of messages, we rely on emails found in the users "sent" directory, since these are emails sent by real users.

Since this dataset contains a mix of corporate and private emails, and is fairly small, it is hard to draw any general conclusions from it. So the Enron dataset is just one example. Another dataset, communication using other media,

---

[1] The source code is available at URL https://github.com/MKjellqvist/OTPNFCTransfer/.

[2] The source code for the data analysis described below is available at URL https://github.com/dbosk/mailstat/. The Enron dataset is available from URL https://www.cs.cmu.edu/~./enron/enron_mail_20150507.tgz.

e.g. text messages rather than email, would probably change the observed user behaviour and these numbers. But our main goal is to get an estimate of user communication to see whether our scheme is completely infeasible or not, and we argue that this dataset lets us reach that goal.

In the Enron dataset, we found that the average message was 1000 B excluding any headers and attachments. The standard deviation was 6000 B. The large standard deviation can probably be explained by the data being emailed: If a conversation requires a few rounds, then the previous messages accumulate in the body of the email as included history.

We also found that the average user communicates with 100 other users. The standard deviation was 200. If a user sends 5 messages per day (standard deviation: 15), then we need on average less than 137 KiB per day. This means that we need less than 50 MiB to store the key-material of one year — for all users.

We use Android's "SecureRandom" to generate our randomness. This is the only supported way to generate randomness on the Android platform, and it allows us to generate enough amounts of random data. Some research [5,14] suggest that "SecureRandom" under certain circumstances uses a low entropy seed. However, the documentation states that SecureRandom can be relied upon for cryptographic purposes. With these contradictory statements, the security of SecureRandom for use with the OTP must be investigated further.

6.2   The Number of Meetings and Transfer Time

From the above analysis, we know the average amount of data communicated between users per day. We also know that the NFC protocol can achieve a transmission rate of up to 424 kbit/s [15]. Considering this, we can see that even if a user sends *ten times* the average amounts, the time required for key-exchanges is still on an order of 10s of seconds per day. (Order of minutes weekly or half-hours yearly.) This number is divided among the contacts with whom the user communicates. More frequently communicating contacts will require a larger share of the time. The times provided does not include the set up of the NFC radio channel, only actual transmission is considered. The set up phase takes about 5 s on the tested devices.

6.3   The Battery Consumption

To estimate the effects on battery consumption we find a typical RF-active rating of 60 mA for the NFC chip [15]. The battery effects of this is negligible and on the order of 2 ‰ of the battery charge at the considered usages.

To estimate the effects on battery consumption we first build a baseline. For this we used the Android systems built-in power-consumption estimates. We used one phone as a reference and two others running the app implementing our scheme.

For the component generating the randomness, tests were performed where we generated the annual demand of key-material. This provided no indication of battery drain. The processor load was measured at 2 % and the input-output load was measured at 15 %.

6.4   Some Extensions

A problem that can occur is that Alice and Bob might run out of key-material before they can meet again. One way to handle this is for them to communicate less as they are closing in on the end of their random bit strings and use the last of the randomness to schedule a new meeting.

An alternative way they can handle this problem is to switch to another scheme, but with the knowledge that it is no longer deniable. In a similar fashion, Alice and Bob might not need deniability for all their communications. Thus they can switch to e.g. OTR or TextSecure when they do not need deniability against Eve, and then switch back when they want deniability. This strategy would use less randomness and they need to meet less often.

An extension to the protocol (Sect. 5.1): Alice can do as in OTR and publish the MAC key when she receives a reply from Bob. The effect we get through this is that the MAC key is recorded in Eve's transcript, and this might lower the trust in Eve's transcript.

7   Conclusions

We set out to design a scheme which provides users with deniability in a stronger adversary model. Provided that we can generate random data with high-enough entropy, then our protocol provides perfect secrecy, authenticated and deniable encryption. However, to achieve this scheme and these properties, we require physical meetings to exchange the randomness. If Alice and Bob run out of randomness they can fall back to e.g. OTR, but then they lose deniability against Eve. In either case, they are never worse off than using OTR or TextSecure.

We also showed that our scheme is usable. We found that a typical exchange of key material requires less than 10 s daily to complete. If you exchange the key-material on a weekly basis, then it is still less than a minute, while monthly and bimonthly require up to five minutes. Thus the transmission rates are not a usability concern. Also, the effects on battery life under the considered use is not a limiting factor in neither the generation of the key-material nor the transmission of the key-material.

The method for estimating the needed amount of data can be improved. This estimate depends on the type of communication, e.g. corporate emails differs from personal text-messaging. To get more accurate estimates, it might better to evaluate a dataset from other settings. To better estimate communication needs for private individuals, it might be better to use text-messages (SMSs). However, we intended to show that our scheme is feasible, and we argue that we have reached that goal.

The only issues found in the scheme are related to the "if" regarding high-enough entropy data. The security of SecureRandom for use with the OTP must be investigated further. In addition to [14,5], we also have the result of Dodis and Spencer [6] to consider.

As a final note, the design of the NFC API is hindering the flexibility of our and similar solutions. We are mostly concerned about the following points:

- There is no mechanism in which to stream data over NFC. This is desirable from a usability standpoint of the app, in particular with regards to interrupted transmissions. This might be solved by a more innovative implementation.
- The transmission must be done in the form of files, and currently these have to reside on a publicly readable file-system on the device. This is a concern for both the confidentiality and integrity of the key-material, as the transmitted files can be intercepted by a malicious app competing for the received files.

7.1   Future Work

There are several interesting directions to follow from this work. We start with the technical one. The security of the actual NFC transfer was out of the scope of this work. However, the security of the NFC protocol must be considered: in what proximity can Eve successfully record the NFC traffic? For instance, Koscher et al. [12] found that RFID tags could be read over 50 m away in a hallway. But more interestingly, can we make usable countermeasures?

Next, we can argue the need for deniability as compared to not being able to reveal any keys. An interesting first step in this direction would be to conduct a study with users: what is the users' perception of deniability, what is more convincing? This would also be interesting to contrast by looking into game theory to see what can be said about the behaviour of a probable liar: do we gain any credibility using this deniable scheme over simply not being able to disclose the keys? What are the differences if we have a rational adversary compared to an irrational one? Finally, there is the legal perspective, which could probably also benefit from exploring these questions.

Another direction, into usable security and privacy, would be to study suitable metaphors and mental models for this kind of system. We suspect that the mental model of "charging deniability" when we exchange randomness is good, i.e. that it does not lead to any contradictory behaviours which might put the user's security and privacy at risk. Our guess is that this is more intuitive than e.g. asymmetric encryption.

Acknowledgements. This work was funded by the Swedish Foundation for Strategic Research grant SSF FFL09-0086 and the Swedish Research Council grant VR 2009-3793. We would like to thank the anonymous reviewers for valuable feedback and especially Peeter Laud for very valuable shepherding.

References

1. Bellare, M., Kohno, T., Namprempre, C.: Breaking and provably repairing the SSH authenticated encryption scheme: A case study of the Encode-then-Encrypt-and-MAC paradigm. ACM Transactions on Information and System Security (TISSEC) **7**(2), 206–241 (2004)
2. Bellare, M., Namprempre, C.: Authenticated encryption: Relations among notions and analysis of the generic composition paradigm. Journal of Cryptology **21**(4), 469–491 (2008)
3. Borisov, N., Goldberg, I., Brewer, E.: Off-the-record communication, or, why not to use PGP. In: Proceedings of the 2004 ACM Workshop on Privacy in the Electronic Society, pp. 77–84 (2004)
4. Canetti, R., Dwork, C., Naor, M., Ostrovsky, R.: Deniable encryption. In: Kaliski Jr., B.S. (ed.) CRYPTO 1997. LNCS, vol. 1294, pp. 90–104. Springer, Heidelberg (1997)
5. Ding, Y., Peng, Z., Zhou, Y., Zhang, C.: Android low entropy demystified. In: 2014 IEEE International Conference on Communications (ICC), pp. 659–664 (2014)
6. Dodis, Y., Spencer, J.: On the (non)universality of the one-time pad. In: Proceedings of the 43rd Annual IEEE Symposium on Foundations of Computer Science, pp. 376–385 (2002)
7. Dworkin, M.: Recommendation for Block Cipher Modes of Operation: Methods and Techniques. Special Publication 800–38A, National Institute of Standards and Technology (2001)
8. Frosch, T., Mainka, C., Bader, C., Bergsma, F., Schwenk, J., Holz, T.: How Secure is TextSecure? Cryptology ePrint Archive (2014)
9. Greenberg, A.: Leaked NSA Doc Says It Can Collect And Keep Your Encrypted Data As Long As It Takes To Crack It. Forbes (2013)
10. Greenwald, G.: XKeyscore: NSA tool collects nearly everything a user does on the internet. The Guardian (2013)
11. Greenwald, G., MacAskill, E.: Boundless Informant: the NSA's secret tool to track global surveillance data. The Guardian (2013)
12. Koscher, K., Juels, A., Brajkovic, V., Kohno, T.: EPC RFID tag security weaknesses and defenses: passport cards, enhanced drivers licenses, and beyond. In: Proceedings of the 16th ACM Conference on Computer and Communications Security, CCS 2009, pp. 33–42. ACM, Chicago (2009)
13. MacAskill, E., Borger, J., Hopkins, N., Davies, N., Ball, J.: GCHQ taps fibre-opticcables for secret access to world's communications. The Guardian (2013)
14. Michaelis, K., Meyer, C., Schwenk, J.: Randomly Failed! the state of randomness in current java implementations. In: Dawson, E. (ed.) CT-RSA 2013. LNCS, vol. 7779, pp. 129–144. Springer, Heidelberg (2013)
15. Nxp, NFC controller PN544 for mobile phones and portable equipment. 9397 750 16890. NXP Semiconductors (2010). http://www.nxp.com/documents/leaflet/75016890.pdf
16. Open Whisper Systems, TextSecure Private Messenger. https://play.google.com/store/apps/details?id=org.thoughtcrime.securesms&hl=en (accessed on November 5, 2014)
17. Shannon, C.E.: Communication theory of secrecy systems. Bell System Technical Journal **28**(4), 656–715 (1949)
18. The GnuPG Project, The GNU Privacy Guard. https://www.gnupg.org/ (accessed on June 7, 2015)

Cryptography

Faster Binary Curve Software: A Case Study

Billy Bob Brumley[(⊠)]

Department of Pervasive Computing,
Tampere University of Technology, Tampere, Finland
billy.brumley@tut.fi

Abstract. For decades, elliptic curves over binary fields appear in numerous standards including those mandated by NIST, SECG, and ANSI X9.62. Many popular security protocols such as TLS explicitly support these named curves, along with implementations of those protocols such as OpenSSL and NSS. Over the past few years, research in improving the performance and/or security of these named curve implementations has pushed forward the state-of-the-art: e.g. projective lambda coordinates (Oliveira et al.) and commodity microprocessors featuring carryless multiplication instructions for native polynomial arithmetic (Intel, ARM, Qualcomm). This work aggregates some of these new techniques as well as classical ones to bring an existing library closer to the state-of-the art. Using OpenSSL as a case study to establish the practical impact of these techniques on real systems, results show significant performance improvements while at the same time adhering to the existing software architecture.

Keywords: Applied cryptography · Public key cryptography · Elliptic Curve Cryptography · OpenSSL

1 Introduction

Of the many types of public key cryptography available, elliptic curve cryptography (ECC) offers many attractive advantages – the main being the small size of private and public keys. Furthermore, since the introduction in the 1990s ECC has undergone extensive standardization – including NIST [20, D.1.3], SECG, and ANSI X9.62. Generally, these standardized curves come in two flavors:

- Elliptic curves over prime fields $\mathbb{F}_p$;
- Elliptic curves over binary fields $\mathbb{F}_{2^m}$.

For elliptic curves in software, elliptic curves over $\mathbb{F}_p$ are a more popular choice for performance reasons because the finite field arithmetic is easier to implement efficiently since most microprocessors feature native integer multiplication instructions as a building block for multi-precision arithmetic. Recognizing this

Supported in part by TEKES grant 3772/31/2014 Cyber Trust and COST Action IC1306.

S. Buchegger and M. Dam (Eds.): NordSec 2015, LNCS 9417, pp. 91–105, 2015.
DOI: 10.1007/978-3-319-26502-5_7

practical limitation, academic efforts for high speed ECC placed more research efforts on elliptic curves over $\mathbb{F}_p$.

For elliptic curves over $\mathbb{F}_{2^m}$, historically software needed to revert to primitive table lookup methods for finite field arithmetic since it was uncommon (to say the least) to feature a native polynomial multiplication instruction. However, this trend shifted roughly five years ago when chip makers such as Intel, ARM, and Qualcomm started introducing such instructions into the Instruction Set Architecture (ISA) for commodity microprocessors. This left a gap in research for high speed ECC software for elliptic curves over $\mathbb{F}_{2^m}$ – for example, there were really no major innovations in projective coordinate systems since López and Dahab in 1999 [17]. Oliveira et al. changed that recently in 2014 with λ-projective coordinates [21].

This gap in academic research also left a gap in practical elliptic curve software libraries. The best example of this is OpenSSL, which – since introducing ECC support in 2005 – has seen no new optimizations for elliptic curves over $\mathbb{F}_{2^m}$, despite heavy optimizations for elliptic curves over $\mathbb{F}_p$.

The goal of this paper is to fill that gap and measure the real world impact of these new optimizations for elliptic curves over $\mathbb{F}_{2^m}$. The resulting OpenSSL source code patches yield performance improvements that remarkably approach 6-fold in some cases. Section 2 gives background on binary elliptic curves and discusses various coordinate systems. Section 3 gives an overview of the ECC software architecture within OpenSSL. Section 4 discusses the optimizations implemented in this paper, and gives benchmarking results. Section 5 draws conclusions.

2   Binary Elliptic Curves

For a finite field $\mathbb{F}_{2^m}$, fix curve coefficients $a_2, a_6 \in \mathbb{F}_{2^m}$ and all of the (x, y) solutions to the equation

$$E : y^2 + xy = x^3 + a_2 x^2 + a_6$$

over $\mathbb{F}_{2^m}$ for $x, y \in \mathbb{F}_{2^m}$ along with the identity element (∞, point at infinity) form a finite Abelian group relevant to applied cryptography. The majority of standardized curves of this form further restrict the values that curve coefficients a_2 and a_6 can take for efficiency reasons. Generally, there are two major types.

Pseudo-Random Curves. These curves fix $a_2 = 1$ and $a_6 \in \mathbb{F}_{2^m}$ derived pseudo-randomly. Curves of this type include, but are not limited to: B-163, B-233, B-283, B-409, and B-571.

Koblitz Curves. These curves [15] fix $a_2 \in \mathbb{F}_2$ and $a_6 = 1$. Curves of this type include, but are not limited to: K-163, K-233, K-283, K-409, K-571, and sect239k1.

2.1   Scalar Multiplication

Take ℓ-bit scalar $k \in \mathbb{Z}$ where k_i denotes bit i of k and a point $P \in E$. Then the scalar multiplication result kP satisfies the following formula.

$$kP = \sum_{i=0}^{\ell-1} k_i 2^i P$$

This is the classical way to compute scalar multiplication, scanning the bits of k from MSB to LSB (or vice-versa): double-and-add, where the cost – defined w.r.t. elliptic curve operations – is $\ell - 1$ point doublings and the number of point additions is equal to the weight of k. That is, one point addition for each non-zero digit of k.

Scalar multiplication is the performance benchmark for ECC. Its speed determines the efficiency of cryptosystems like ECDSA and ECDH. Since performance is such a driving force in applied cryptography, there is no shortage of research on improving the efficiency of scalar multiplication. While the majority of these methods are beyond the scope of this paper, a few specific methods that OpenSSL employs will be discussed later (otherwise, see e.g. [11, 3.3] for a good survey).

2.2   Coordinate Systems

Since scalar multiplication breaks down into a sequence of elliptic curve point doublings and additions, the cost of these operations is critical for performance. One way to improve the efficiency of these operations is by considering different coordinate systems – the aim being to reduce the number of expensive finite field inversions. A discussion on relevant coordinate systems for elliptic curves over $\mathbb{F}_{2^m}$ follows.

Affine Coordinates. The textbook method to perform addition and doubling of points on elliptic curves over $\mathbb{F}_{2^m}$ – defining the group law – is using affine coordinates [8, 13.3.1.a]. Here the inverse of $P = (x_1, y_1)$ is $-P = (x_1, x_1 + y_1)$.

Addition. Let $P = (x_1, y_1)$, $Q = (x_2, y_2)$ such that $P \neq \pm Q$. Then $P + Q = (x_3, y_3)$ is given by

$$x_3 = \lambda^2 + \lambda + x_1 + x_2 + a_2$$
$$y_3 = \lambda(x_1 + x_3) + x_3 + y_1$$
$$\lambda = \frac{y_1 + y_2}{x_1 + x_2}$$

Doubling. Let $P = (x_1, y_1)$ then $2P = (x_3, y_3)$, where

$$x_3 = \lambda^2 + \lambda + a_2$$
$$y_3 = \lambda(x_1 + x_3) + x_3 + y_1$$
$$\lambda = x_1 + \frac{y_1}{x_1}$$

López-Dahab Coordinates. Elliptic curve operations using affine coordinates require finite field inversions (to compute λ), often an expensive operation. To eliminate these inversions, projective coordinates introduce an additional coordinate to represent points on a projective equation. While projective coordinates come in many different flavors, López and Dahab introduce a popular one for elliptic curves over $\mathbb{F}_{2^m}$ [17]. Consider the projective equation

$$Y^2 + XYZ = X^3 Z + a_2 X^2 Z^2 + a_6 Z^4.$$

The LD-projective point $(X_1 : Y_1 : Z_1)$ corresponds to the affine point $(X_1/Z_1, Y_1/Z_1^2)$ when $Z_1 \neq 0$ and the point at infinity otherwise. Here the inverse of $(X_1 : Y_1 : Z_1)$ is $(X_1 : X_1 Z_1 + Y_1 : Z_1)$.

Mixed Addition. A sum $P + Q$ is often more efficient to compute if one operand is in affine and the other in projective – mixed addition, colloquially. The reason this makes sense algorithmically is that for scalar multiplication, the accumulator point will undergo projective doublings and additions, but the second operand for additions remains static in affine coordinates. For LD coordinates, Al-Daoud give a slightly more efficient formula for mixed addition [1]. Let $P = (X_1 : Y_1 : Z_1)$, $Q = (x_2, y_2)$ such that $P \neq \pm Q$. Then $P + Q = (X_3 : Y_3 : Z_3)$ is given by

$$A = Y_1 + y_2 Z_1^2, B = X_1 + x_2 Z_1, C = B Z_1,$$
$$Z_3 = C^2, D = x_2 Z_3, X_3 = A^2 + C(A + B^2 + a_2 C),$$
$$Y_3 = (D + X_3)(AC + Z_3) + (y_2 + x_2) Z_3^2$$

Doubling. Let $P = (X_1 : Y_1 : Z_1)$ then $2P = (X_3 : Y_3 : Z_3)$, where

$$A = Z_1^2, B = a_6 A^2, C = X_1^2, Z_3 = AC, X_3 = C^2 + B,$$
$$Y_3 = (Y_1^2 + a_2 Z_3 + B) X_3 + Z_3 B$$

Lambda Coordinates. The λ-affine representation [14, Sec. 2] of a short affine point $P = (x, y)$ is (x, λ) where $\lambda = x + y/x$ – note that indeed, λ is the slope from the affine doubling formula. Historically, λ-affine coordinates saw little use due to being out-performed by LD coordinates in most cases. Recently, Oliveira et al. introduce a λ-projective system [21], the performance of which remarkably eclipses LD coordinates. Consider the projective equation

$$(L^2 + LZ + a_2 Z^2) X^2 = X^4 + a_6 Z^4.$$

The λ-projective point $(X_1 : L_1 : Z_1)$ corresponds to the λ-affine point $(X_1/Z_1, L_1/Z_1)$ when $Z_1 \neq 0$ and the point at infinity otherwise. Here the inverse of $(X_1 : L_1 : Z_1)$ is $(X_1 : L_1 + Z_1 : Z_1)$.

Mixed Addition. Let $P = (X_1 : L_1 : Z_1)$, $Q = (x_2, \lambda_2)$ such that $P \neq \pm Q$. In this case the formula for $P + Q = (X_3 : L_3 : Z_3)$ is given in [21], but from the implementation perspective the restriction $P \neq \pm Q$ is problematic – what is actually needed for implementation is an algorithmic solution, depicted in Fig. 2 (Appx. A). Indeed, this algorithm handles these corner cases to ensure correct computation for all inputs. The algorithm expects P and Q in λ-projective and λ-affine coordinates, respectively – i.e. P would be the accumulator in a scalar multiplication routine.

Doubling. Let $P = (X_1 : L_1 : Z_1)$ then Fig. 3 (Appx. A) depicts the algorithm to compute $2P = (X_3 : L_3 : Z_3)$. The input and output are both in λ-projective coordinates.

General Addition. From the ECC implementation perspective, sometimes the sum of two projective points is required – e.g. in the (online or offline) precomputation step for scalar multiplication. Since that will be the case later in this paper, Fig. 4 (Appx. A) depicts the algorithm to compute $P+Q = (X_3 : L_3 : Z_3)$ where $P = (X_1 : L_1 : Z_1)$ and $Q = (X_2 : L_2 : Z_2)$ – again, compensating for the cases when $Q = P$ or $Q = -P$.

Computational Costs. To conclude this section, the goal is to select the coordinate system that has the lowest computational cost w.r.t. finite field operations – inversions, multiplications, and squarings. The cost of inversions is usually very high (e.g. at least eight times that of a multiplication), so affine coordinates are not immediately useful in that respect. Table 1 summarizes the costs for the previously discussed coordinate systems, assuming $a_2 \in \mathbb{F}_2$. Based on these numbers, clearly λ-projective coordinates have an efficiency advantage.

Table 1. Computational costs of elliptic curve operations in various coordinate systems w.r.t. finite field inversions (I), multiplications (M), and squarings (S)

Coordinates	double	add	negate
affine	$1I + 2M + 1S$	$1I + 2M + 1S$	–
LD-projective (mixed)	$4M + 5S$	$8M + 5S$	$1M$
λ-projective (mixed)	$4M + 4S$	$8M + 2S$	–
λ-projective	$4M + 4S$	$11M + 2S$	–

3 ECC in OpenSSL

OpenSSL integrated support for elliptic curves in 2005. At a high level, the ECC portion of OpenSSL generically supports elliptic curves in short Weierstrass form over $\mathbb{F}_p$ and $\mathbb{F}_{2^m}$, only the latter being immediately relevant to this paper. What follows is a discussion on the ECC portion of OpenSSL, from the architecture level and later to the concrete methods used for binary curve arithmetic.

3.1   Generic Curve Support

When an application or the library instantiates a curve, an `EC_GROUP` structure holds the curve parameters (e.g. finite field, curve coefficients, curve order, generator point, etc.) and an `EC_METHOD` structure controls computations and operations on the particular curve. The latter structure is critical to this paper – a description follows.

The `EC_METHOD` structure (overview in Fig. 1) contains a set of function pointers to carry out elliptic curve operations (e.g. double, add) as well as various interface and conversion operations (e.g. extracting points to strings). The reason this structure exists is modularity – it allows elliptic curves to be treated mostly generically from the interface perspective, but abstracts away implementation aspects of a particular curve. The simplest example of this is the library supporting both curves over $\mathbb{F}_p$ and $\mathbb{F}_{2^m}$ – the group law for these types of curves is entirely different, but both can be supported with their own `EC_METHOD` by setting function pointers such as `add` and `dbl` to distinct functions for their corresponding curve types. Conceptually, one way to view this is analogous with object-oriented programming where the function pointers correspond to class methods.

What follows is a brief discussion of function pointers that are relevant to this work, to help understand implementation considerations in later sections. Method `point_set_affine_coordinates` sets the coordinates of the `EC_POINT` given the short affine coordinates `x` and `y`. The `get` method is the inverse, returning the short affine coordinates of the point. Methods `add` and `dbl` compute elliptic curve additions and doublings, respectively, while invert sets P to $-P$. Method `is_on_curve` checks if the point satisfies the curve equation; `make_affine` converts a single point from projective to affine coordinates, while `points_make_affine` does the same but for an arbitrary number of points. Scalar multiplication method `mul` computes

$$aG + \sum_{i=0}^{n} b_i P_i$$

hence a fully generic multi-scalar multiplication supporting an arbitrary number of scalars and corresponding points. Since G is fixed for each `EC_GROUP`, some scalar multiplication techniques precompute various multiples of points to speed up scalar multiplication; `precompute_mult` carries out such precomputation and `have_precompute_mult` checks if said precomputation is present. Finally, `field_mul`, `field_sqr`, and `field_div` compute finite field multiplications, squarings, and divisions for the particular field in `EC_GROUP` – finite field parameters often have a special form that allow e.g. fast modular reduction, so having dedicated function pointers offers the implementer a convenient way to integrate such optimizations.

```
struct ec_method_st {
...
    int (*point_set_affine_coordinates) (const EC_GROUP *, EC_POINT *,
                                         const BIGNUM *x, const BIGNUM *y,
                                         BN_CTX *);
    int (*point_get_affine_coordinates) (const EC_GROUP *, const EC_POINT *,
                                         BIGNUM *x, BIGNUM *y, BN_CTX *);
...
    int (*add) (const EC_GROUP *, EC_POINT *r, const EC_POINT *a,
                const EC_POINT *b, BN_CTX *);
    int (*dbl) (const EC_GROUP *, EC_POINT *r, const EC_POINT *a, BN_CTX *);
    int (*invert) (const EC_GROUP *, EC_POINT *, BN_CTX *);
...
    int (*is_on_curve) (const EC_GROUP *, const EC_POINT *, BN_CTX *);
...
    int (*make_affine) (const EC_GROUP *, EC_POINT *, BN_CTX *);
    int (*points_make_affine) (const EC_GROUP *, size_t num, EC_POINT *[],
                               BN_CTX *);
...
    int (*mul) (const EC_GROUP *group, EC_POINT *r, const BIGNUM *scalar,
                size_t num, const EC_POINT *points[], const BIGNUM *scalars[],
                BN_CTX *);
    int (*precompute_mult) (EC_GROUP *group, BN_CTX *);
    int (*have_precompute_mult) (const EC_GROUP *group);
    int (*field_mul) (const EC_GROUP *, BIGNUM *r, const BIGNUM *a,
                      const BIGNUM *b, BN_CTX *);
    int (*field_sqr) (const EC_GROUP *, BIGNUM *r, const BIGNUM *a, BN_CTX *);
    int (*field_div) (const EC_GROUP *, BIGNUM *r, const BIGNUM *a,
                      const BIGNUM *b, BN_CTX *);
...
} /* EC_METHOD */ ;
```

Fig. 1. OpenSSL's method structure for elliptic curves

3.2   Binary Curve Support

Since ECC integration in 2005, various EC_METHOD implementations started appearing in the OpenSSL code base for curves over $\mathbb{F}_p$ to optimize performance and/or security. For example, fast modular reduction routines for NIST curves P-192, P-224, P-256, P-384, and P-521; also fast and side-channel secure P-224 [13] and P-256 [10]. In contrast, for elliptic curves over $\mathbb{F}_{2^m}$ there remains only a single default EC_METHOD – an implementation of IEEE P1363 [12, A.10.2] that uses affine coordinates for elliptic curve point additions and doublings. To summarize, there is comparatively little to no optimization (such as projective coordinates) of binary curve operations in OpenSSL.

3.3   Finite Field Arithmetic

Software performance wise, elliptic curves over $\mathbb{F}_{2^m}$ historically lag behind those over $\mathbb{F}_p$ since most microprocessors feature integer word multiplication instructions, making the finite field multiplications more efficient in $\mathbb{F}_p$. Over the past few years, however, that trend is shifting as chips start to feature polynomial multiplication instructions – carryless multiplication, colloquially – suitable for $\mathbb{F}_{2^m}$ finite field multiplications. Some examples include:

- Intel's `pclmulqdq` instruction for 64-bit multiplication (2010);
- ARM's `vmull.p64` instruction on ARMv8 for 64-bit multiplication (2013);
- Qualcomm's `pmpyw` instruction [2, Sec. 4.1] on Hexagon DSP for 32-bit multiplication (2010).

OpenSSL integrated support for `pclmulqdq` in 2011. The implementation of polynomial multiplication is the Karatsuba method, and for chips featuring `pclmulqdq` the last level of recursion computes the product of two 128-bit polynomials – with three 64-bit multiplications, also using Karatsuba. In summary, OpenSSL has the potential for fast binary ECC since there is some acceleration of finite field operations, but currently lacks optimization of elliptic curve operations.

3.4   Scalar Multiplication

In OpenSSL, two scalar multiplication implementations are relevant for elliptic curves over $\mathbb{F}_{2^m}$.

Montgomery's Ladder. Building on their projective coordinate system result, López and Dahab combine their result with Montgomery's Ladder to yield an efficient scalar multiplication routine [17, Sec. 4.2]. OpenSSL has a fairly direct translation of their algorithm in function `ec_GF2m_montgomery_point_multiply`, taking remarkably six finite field multiplications and five squarings per scalar bit.

Interleaving. By default, if the `mul` scalar multiplication function pointer is not set OpenSSL uses Möller's interleaving with NAF splitting [18,19] in function `ec_wNAF_mul`. If precomputation exists, this implementation dramatically decreases the number of point doublings by precomputing small multiples of $2^i G$ (e.g. $i = 0, 8, 16, 24, \ldots$). If instead no precomputation is available, the NAF splitting goes away and the algorithm is then a fairly standard multi-scalar multiplication method with signed digits (NAF).

Code Path. As previously discussed, the sole `EC_METHOD` for elliptic curves over $\mathbb{F}_{2^m}$ uses short affine coordinates to implement the `add` and `dbl` function pointers – the scalar multiplication function pointer `mul` is different, however. The implementation is a short wrapper that looks at the number of scalar arguments:

- If the total number of scalars involved is more than two, or a single scalar multiple of the generator *with* precomputation, the wrapper calls `ec_wNAF_mul`.
- Otherwise, the wrapper iterates `ec_GF2m_montgomery_point_multiply`.

4   Improvements

This section discusses the implemented changes to the OpenSSL code base to achieve significantly better performance for scalar multiplication with elliptic curves over $\mathbb{F}_{2^m}$. This improved efficiency is then reflected in the timings for ECDH and ECDSA cryptosystems within OpenSSL.

4.1   Lambda Method

The goal of this new `EC_METHOD` is to provide λ-projective coordinate support but at the same time utilize the existing `ec_wNAF_mul` multi-scalar multiplication function. Some of the implementation considerations are as follows.

- For offline or online precomputation, `ec_wNAF_mul` calls function pointer `add` where both operands are potentially in projective form. So the new method implements `add` as a small wrapper that calls to either an implementation of Fig. 2 or Fig. 4 – i.e. the wrapper uses the more efficient formula when it can. Function pointer `dbl` is a direct translation of Fig. 3.
- After the precomputation stage, `ec_wNAF_mul` calls `points_make_affine` function pointer so as the scalar multiplication routine executes it can use more efficient mixed coordinate point additions. But in this case, the implementation converts from λ-projective to λ-affine.
- To handle negative scalar digits, `ec_wNAF_mul` tracks the sign of the accumulator point with a flag and inverts both the accumulator and flag as necessary. So in fact λ-projective coordinates are beneficial over LD coordinates in this regard, on average saving half a finite field multiplication per digit when implementing the `invert` function pointer.
- Function pointers `point_set_affine_coordinates` (and `get`) are critical to maintain interoperability – when a cryptosystem extracts the result of scalar multiplication, it needs to be in short affine coordinates. So for `set` this implementation converts from short affine to λ-affine, and `get` converts from λ-projective to short affine to maintain compatibility.

The resulting patch to the OpenSSL code base for this method is fairly independent and non-intrusive.

4.2   Finite Field Squaring

While OpenSSL has more efficient finite field multiplications with `pclmulqdq`, squarings are still done with legacy table lookups. This modification inserts the assembly instructions to perform squaring more efficiently using `pclmulqdq`, requiring one instruction per word since squaring is an $\mathbb{F}_2$-linear operation.

4.3   Side-Channel Countermeasures

Historically, OpenSSL is a popular target for side-channel attacks that target implementation and execution aspects that leak critical secret state through e.g. latency measurements. A brief discussion on side-channel considerations follows.

Timing Attacks. Previous timing attacks against OpenSSL's ECC implementation target traditional, insecure table lookups and irregular scalar encodings [7]. Although countermeasures and patches are publicly available [5], they have not been integrated into the OpenSSL codebase as of this writing.

Bug Attacks. Introduced by Biham et al. [3], bug attacks target intentional backdoors in implementations of cryptographic hardware that trigger with low enough probability to go undetected by random test vectors. They give applications to public key cryptography, using a hypothetical malicious integer word multiplication instruction as an example and show how to recover a private key with cleverly chosen inputs. In [6], the first practical bug attack targets instead a real world software defect in OpenSSL and uses it to recover private keys.

Originally proposed as a Differential Power Analysis (DPA) countermeasure, Coron's randomized projective coordinates [9, Sec. 5.3] is an extremely effective and efficient countermeasure against bug attacks. At a high level, the idea is to select a random representative from the set of projective points that map to the same affine point. While outlined for canonical projective coordinates, the exact steps to select this representative depend on the relationship between the projective and affine point.

For λ-projective coordinates, the λ-projective point $(X : L : Z)$ is in fact equivalent to $(\beta X : \beta L : \beta Z)$ for all $\beta \in \mathbb{F}_{2^m} \setminus \{0\}$. This is easy to see since the λ-affine point corresponding to $(X : L : Z)$ is $(X/Z, L/Z)$, so $(\beta X : \beta L : \beta Z) \mapsto ((\beta X)/(\beta Z), (\beta L)/(\beta Z)) = (X/Z, L/Z)$ for all $\beta \in \mathbb{F}_{2^m} \setminus \{0\}$ – i.e. yielding the same λ-affine point.

This randomization essentially makes the state of the scalar multiplication algorithm unpredictable, hence the iterative approach needed for bug attacks is no longer feasible. For this work, we implement this with a random β chosen at the start of the ec_wNAF_mul main loop, when the accumulator is initialized – i.e. randomize once per scalar multiplication.

4.4   Timings

The benchmarking environment in this section is an Intel Celeron 2955U 1.40GHz (ft. pclmulqdq) running 64-bit Ubuntu 14.04 with 2GB of memory. Timings are with OpenSSL's own benchmarking utility, openssl speed with options ecdh and ecdsa. The OpenSSL version is 1.1.0-dev, git branch OpenSSL-master tip[1].

ECDH Results. For ECDH, Tbl. 2 shows there is no significant change after the modifications. This is rather predictable since the code path for ECDH on stock OpenSSL executes the LD version of Montgomery's Ladder that is already fairly efficient. On the bright side, deprecating the stock code and introducing λ-projective coordinates does not hurt the average performance over all curves.

---

[1] Commit 5fced2395ddfb603a50fd1bd87411e603a59dc6f as of this writing.

Table 2. ECDH operations per second

curve	stock	modified	gain
nistk163	2107.7	2022.6	-4.0%
nistk233	1675.2	1670.2	-0.3%
nistk283	929.3	921.0	-0.9%
nistk409	589.5	563.8	-4.4%
nistk571	248.7	244.9	-1.5%
nistb163	2043.9	2011.4	-1.6%
nistb233	1600.9	1640.6	2.5%
nistb283	891.6	903.9	1.4%
nistb409	551.9	559.4	1.4%
nistb571	229.1	243.5	6.3%

ECDSA Results. The ECDSA numbers tell quite a different story, shown in Tbl. 3. The gains are fairly staggering – from roughly a 3 to 6 fold performance improvement for ECDSA signature generation, and roughly 1.6 to 1.8 for ECDSA signature verification.

Table 3. ECDSA operations per second

curve	stock (sign)	modified (sign)	gain (sign)	stock (verify)	modified (verify)	gain (verify)
nistk163	2304.1	6723.4	191.8%	1022.9	1617.6	58.1%
nistk233	1146.2	5147.5	349.1%	791.8	1313.5	65.9%
nistk283	770.6	3136.7	307.0%	442.6	744.2	68.1%
nistk409	341.0	1969.2	477.5%	280.2	456.4	62.9%
nistk571	158.2	896.0	466.4%	120.2	199.0	65.6%
nistb163	2300.3	6684.2	190.6%	983.1	1635.9	66.4%
nistb233	1174.2	5227.7	345.2%	765.0	1280.2	67.3%
nistb283	771.3	3142.4	307.4%	420.1	735.1	75.0%
nistb409	339.8	1952.7	474.7%	262.4	446.5	70.2%
nistb571	157.6	858.8	444.9%	111.1	197.7	77.9%

5 Conclusion

Leaning on recent academic results on more efficient elliptic curve operations for elliptic curves over $\mathbb{F}_{2^m}$, this work takes OpenSSL as a case study to bring the ECC portion of the library closer to state-of-the-art. This allows to measure the real world impact of these research results. For ECDH, the performance remains roughly the same but for ECDSA the performance approaches roughly an astounding 6-fold improvement. See Tbl. 4 in the appendix to get an idea of the comparative ECC performance for standardized curves over prime fields. Lastly, it is worth noting that these results can be used in tandem with curve-specific binary field arithmetic patches to compound the performance numbers – see e.g. [4].

The source code patches – available in OpenSSL's issue tracker (RT 4103) and on the `openssl-dev` mailing list[2] – are fairly non-intrusive, adhering to OpenSSL's existing software architecture and leveraging much of the code long present in the library, in particular the multi-scalar multiplication function. In conclusion, this work validates recent advances in efficient binary curve arithmetic and brings these research results to practice where they can have direct impact.

References

1. Al-Daoud, E., Mahmod, R., Rushdan, M., Kiliçman, A.: A new addition formula for elliptic curves over $GF(2^n)$. IEEE Trans. Computers **51**(8), 972–975 (2002). http://doi.ieeecomputersociety.org/10.1109/TC.2002.1024743
2. Avanzi, R., Brumley, B.B.: Faster 128-EEA3 and 128-EIA3 software. Cryptology ePrint Archive, Report 2013/428 (2013). https://eprint.iacr.org/2013/428
3. Biham, E., Carmeli, Y., Shamir, A.: Bug attacks. In: Wagner, D. (ed.) CRYPTO 2008. LNCS, vol. 5157, pp. 221–240. Springer, Heidelberg (2008)
4. Bluhm, M., Gueron, S.: Fast software implementation of binary elliptic curve cryptography. J. Cryptographic Engineering **5**(3), 215–226 (2015). http://dx.doi.org/10.1007/s13389-015-0094-1
5. Brumley, B.B.: Faster software for fast endomorphisms. In: Mangard, S., Poschmann, A.Y. (eds.) COSADE 2015. LNCS, vol. 9064, pp. 127–140. Springer, Heidelberg (2015)
6. Brumley, B.B., Barbosa, M., Page, D., Vercauteren, F.: Practical realisation and elimination of an ecc-related software bug attack. In: Dunkelman, O. (ed.) CT-RSA 2012. LNCS, vol. 7178, pp. 171–186. Springer, Heidelberg (2012)
7. Brumley, B.B., Hakala, R.M.: Cache-timing template attacks. In: Matsui, M. (ed.) ASIACRYPT 2009. LNCS, vol. 5912, pp. 667–684. Springer, Heidelberg (2009)
8. Cohen, H., Frey, G., Avanzi, R., Doche, C., Lange, T., Nguyen, K., Vercauteren, F. (eds.): Handbook of Elliptic and Hyperelliptic Curve Cryptography. Discrete Mathematics and its Applications(Boca Raton). Chapman & Hall/CRC, Boca Raton (2006)
9. Coron, J.: Resistance against differential power analysis for elliptic curve cryptosystems. In: Koç, Ç.K., Paar, C. (eds.) [16], pp. 292–302. http://dx.doi.org/10.1007/3-540-48059-5_25
10. Gueron, S., Krasnov, V.: Fast prime field elliptic-curve cryptography with 256-bit primes. J. Cryptographic Engineering **5**(2), 141–151 (2015). http://dx.doi.org/10.1007/s13389-014-0090-x
11. Hankerson, D., Menezes, A., Vanstone, S.: Guide to elliptic curve cryptography. Springer, New York (2004). Springer Professional Computing
12. IEEE: Standard specifications for public key cryptography. P1363 (1999)
13. Käsper, E.: Fast elliptic curve cryptography in OpenSSL. In: Danezis, G., Dietrich, S., Sako, K. (eds.) FC 2011 Workshops 2011. LNCS, vol. 7126, pp. 27–39. Springer, Heidelberg (2012)
14. Knudsen, E.W.: Elliptic scalar multiplication using point halving. In: Lam, K.-Y., Okamoto, E., Xing, C. (eds.) ASIACRYPT 1999. LNCS, vol. 1716, pp. 135–149. Springer, Heidelberg (1999)

---

[2] http://marc.info/?l=openssl-dev&m=144008703808363

15. Koblitz, N.: CM-curves with good cryptographic properties. In: Feigenbaum, J. (ed.) CRYPTO 1991. LNCS, vol. 576, pp. 279–287. springer, Heidelberg (1992)
16. Koç, Ç.K., Paar, C. (eds.): CHES1999. LNCS, vol. 1717. Springer, Heidelberg (1999)
17. López, J., Dahab, R.: Fast multiplication on elliptic curves over $GF(2^m)$ without precomputation. In: Koç, Ç.K., Paar, C. [16], pp. 316–327. http://dx.doi.org/10.1007/3-540-48059-5_27
18. Möller, B.: Algorithms for multi-exponentiation. In: Vaudenay, S., Youssef, A.M. (eds.) SAC 2001. LNCS, vol. 2259, p. 165. Springer, Heidelberg (2001)
19. Möller, B.: Improved techniques for fast exponentiation. In: Lee, P.J., Lim, C.H. (eds.) ICISC 2002. LNCS, vol. 2587, pp. 298–312. Springer, Heidelberg (2003)
20. NIST: Digital signature standard (DSS). FIPS 186-4, National Institute of Standards and Technology (2013). http://nvlpubs.nist.gov/nistpubs/FIPS/NIST.FIPS.186-4.pdf
21. Oliveira, T., López, J., Aranha, D.F., Rodríguez-Henríquez, F.: Two is the fastest prime: lambda coordinates for binary elliptic curves. J. Cryptographic Engineering 4(1), 3–17 (2014). http://dx.doi.org/10.1007/s13389-013-0069-z

A   Algorithms

Figures 2, 3, and 4 list the relevant formulae for λ-projective coordinate arithmetic in pseudo-code form, suitable for implementation. The algorithms assume $a_2 \in \{0, 1\}$.

B   Elliptic Curves Over Prime Fields

For reference, Tbl. 4 lists OpenSSL's stock performance for ECC operations for standardized curves over prime fields. The architecture and OpenSSL version are the same as for the previous performance numbers.

Table 4. Operations per second for standardized curves over prime fields

curve	ECDH	ECDSA sign	ECDSA verify
secp160r1	2309.6	7145.5	1933.9
nistp192	1987.5	6133.2	1575.3
nistp224	1414.7	4685.9	1173.2
nistp256	5817.6	9513.6	4013.5
nistp384	603.0	2141.6	504.0
nistp521	299.5	1035.6	239.8

Input: λ-projective $P = (X_1 : L_1 : Z_1)$, λ-affine $Q = (x_2, \lambda_2)$
Output: λ-projective $P + Q = (X_3 : L_3 : Z_3)$
if $Q = \infty$ **then return** P
if $P = \infty$ **then return** $(x_2 : \lambda_2 : 1)$
$t_1 \leftarrow \lambda_2 \cdot Z_1$
$t_2 \leftarrow t_1 + L_1$
$t_1 \leftarrow x_2 \cdot Z_1$
$t_0 \leftarrow t_1 + X_1$
if $t_0 = 0$ **then**
    if $t_2 = 0$ **then return** $2P$
    else return ∞
$t_1 \leftarrow t_1 \cdot t_2$
$t_3 \leftarrow X_1 \cdot t_2$
$t_0 \leftarrow t_0^2$
$X_3 \leftarrow t_1 \cdot t_3$
$t_3 \leftarrow Z_1 + L_1$
$t_2 \leftarrow t_0 \cdot t_2$
$t_0 \leftarrow t_0 + t_1$
$t_3 \leftarrow t_3 \cdot t_2$
$t_0 \leftarrow t_0^2$
$Z_3 \leftarrow Z_1 \cdot t_2$
$L_3 \leftarrow t_3 + t_0$
return $(X_3 : L_3 : Z_3)$

Fig. 2. Mixed addition of λ-projective and λ-affine points

Input: λ-projective $P = (X_1 : L_1 : Z_1)$
Output: λ-projective $2P = (X_3 : L_3 : Z_3)$
if $P = \infty$ **then return** ∞
$t_0 \leftarrow L_1^2$
$t_3 \leftarrow Z_1 \cdot L_1$
$t_1 \leftarrow Z_1^2$
$t_2 \leftarrow X_1 \cdot Z_1$
$t_0 \leftarrow t_3 + t_0$
if $a_2 = 1$ **then** $t_0 \leftarrow t_0 + t_1$
$X_3 \leftarrow t_0^2$
$Z_3 \leftarrow t_1 \cdot t_0$
$t_0 \leftarrow t_3 \cdot t_0$
$t_2 \leftarrow t_2^2$
$t_0 \leftarrow Z_3 + t_0$
$t_0 \leftarrow t_0 + X_3$
$L_3 \leftarrow t_0 + t_2$
return $(X_3 : L_3 : Z_3)$

Fig. 3. doubling a point in λ-projective coordinates

Input: λ-projective $P = (X_1 : L_1 : Z_1)$, λ-projective $Q = (X_2 : L_2 : Z_2)$
Output: λ-projective $P + Q = (X_3 : L_3 : Z_3)$
if $Q = \infty$ **then return** P
if $P = \infty$ **then return** Q
$t_3 \leftarrow X_1 \cdot Z_2$
$t_2 \leftarrow X_2 \cdot Z_1$
$t_0 \leftarrow L_2 \cdot Z_1$
$t_1 \leftarrow Z_2 \cdot L_1$
$t_0 \leftarrow t_0 + t_1$
$t_1 \leftarrow t_2 + t_3$
if $t_1 = 0$ **then**
    if $t_0 = 0$ **then return** $2P$
    else return ∞
$t_4 \leftarrow Z_1 + L_1$
$t_2 \leftarrow t_2 \cdot t_0$
$t_5 \leftarrow t_1^2$
$t_3 \leftarrow t_3 \cdot t_0$
$t_1 \leftarrow t_5 \cdot t_0$
$X_3 \leftarrow t_2 \cdot t_3$
$t_0 \leftarrow Z_2 \cdot t_1$
$t_1 \leftarrow t_5 + t_2$
$t_4 \leftarrow t_4 \cdot t_0$
$t_1 \leftarrow t_1^2$
$Z_3 \leftarrow Z_1 \cdot t_0$
$L_3 \leftarrow t_4 + t_1$
return $(X_3 : L_3 : Z_3)$

Fig. 4. Adding λ-projective points

WHIRLBOB, the Whirlpool Based Variant of STRIBOB
Lighter, Faster, and Constant Time

Markku–Juhani O. Saarinen[1](✉) and Billy Bob Brumley[2]

[1] Centre for Secure Information Technologies (CSIT) ECIT,
Queen's University Belfast, Belfast, UK
m.saarinen@qub.ac.uk

[2] Tampere University of Technology, Tampere, Finland
billy.brumley@tut.fi

Abstract. WHIRLBOB, also known as STRIBOBr2, is an AEAD (Authenticated Encryption with Associated Data) algorithm derived from STRIBOBr1 and the Whirlpool hash algorithm. WHIRL-BOB/STRIBOBr2 is a second round candidate in the CAESAR competition. As with STRIBOBr1, the reduced-size Sponge design has a strong provable security link with a standardized hash algorithm. The new design utilizes only the LPS or ρ component of Whirlpool in flexibly domain-separated BLNK Sponge mode. The number of rounds is increased from 10 to 12 as a countermeasure against Rebound Distinguishing attacks. The 8×8 - bit S-Box used by Whirlpool and WHIRL-BOB is constructed from 4×4 - bit "MiniBoxes". We report on fast constant-time Intel SSSE3 and ARM NEON SIMD WHIRLBOB implementations that keep full miniboxes in registers and access them via SIMD shuffles. This is an efficient countermeasure against AES-style cache timing side-channel attacks. Another main advantage of WHIRL-BOB over STRIBOBr1 (and most other AEADs) is its greatly reduced implementation footprint on lightweight platforms. On many lower-end microcontrollers the total software footprint of π+BLNK = WHIRLBOB AEAD is less than half a kilobyte. We also report an FPGA implementation that requires 4,946 logic units for a single round of WHIRLBOB, which compares favorably to 7,972 required for Keccak / Keyak on the same target platform. The relatively small S-Box gate count also enables efficient 64-bit bitsliced straight-line implementations. We finally present some discussion and analysis on the relationships between WHIRLBOB, Whirlpool, the Russian GOST Streebog hash, and the recent draft Russian Encryption Standard Kuznyechik.

Keywords: WHIRLBOB · STRIBOBr1 · Authenticated encryption · Sponge designs · Timing attacks · Whirlpool · Streebog · CAESAR competition

Much of this research was carried out during tenure of an ERCIM "Alain Bensoussan" Fellowship Programme at NTNU, Trondheim.

© Springer International Publishing Switzerland 2015
S. Buchegger and M. Dam (Eds.): NordSec 2015, LNCS 9417, pp. 106–122, 2015.
DOI: 10.1007/978-3-319-26502-5_8

1   Introduction

STRIBOBr2, or WHIRLBOB, is an Authenticated Encryption with Associated Data (AEAD) algorithm and a CAESAR ("Competition for Authenticated Encryption: Security, Applicability, and Robustness") [21] competition Second Round Candidate [58].

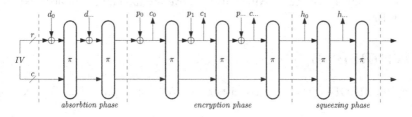

Fig. 1. A simplified view of a Sponge-based AEAD. Padded Secret Key, Nonce, and Associated Authenticated Data - all represented by d_u words - are first "absorbed" into the state. The π permutation is then also used to encrypt data p_i into ciphertext c_i (or vice versa) and finally to "squeeze" out a Message Authentication Code h_i.

AEAD algorithms and modes such as GCM [45] provide both confidentiality and integrity protection for messages in a single step, thus eliminating the need for a separate MAC algorithm such as HMAC [46]. This has clear advantages for performance and implementation footprint.

WHIRLBOB uses STRIBOBr1's BLNK Sponge AEAD mode and parameters without modification. Outside the CAESAR context, BLNK can be also used in a wider set of applications, even to build entire secure lightweight protocol suites [53]. A sponge mode requires only a single cryptographic component; an unkeyed cryptographic permutation π (See Figure 1). As with other provable Sponge modes, we assume that π is indistinguishable from a random permutation. This work focuses on π permutation design and implementation – for BLNK padding details and analysis we refer to [32,54,56,57].

The STRIBOBr1 CAESAR [56] candidate was derived from the Russian GOST hash standard Streebog [26]. In close examination Streebog appears to be modeled after the Whirlpool hash [4], with substantial modifications. However, STRIBOBr1 and WHIRLBOB only differ in the particular numerical selections for tables C, S, and L. These components, $L \circ P \circ S$ or the "LPS permutation" is derived directly from that of Whirlpool for WHIRLBOB. The program code of 64-bit reference implementations is essentially equivalent for both algorithms. Both STRIBOBr1 and WHIRLBOB have 12 rounds.

We show that the particular structure of the Whirlpool components allows WHIRLBOB to have much more efficient SIMD, constant-time, lightweight, and hardware implementations. One of our aims is to allow the same implementation core (such as a special instruction or coprocessor of a SoC [56]) to be also used for unkeyed hashing according to the Whirlpool standard. This is useful in applications that also require efficient standards-compliant certificate signature processing.

The corresponding standardized, Miyagushi-Preneel hash functions Streebog and Whirlpool require two (or more) times as much as state and processes data in bigger chunks when compared to STRIBOBr1 and WHIRLBOB. Our BLNK Sponge mode also supports randomized hashing and MACing without encryption. Our Sponge variants are slightly faster than the original hashes, yet have a provable security relation. All security parameters remain unmodified from STRIBOBr1.

2   WHIRLBOB

As with STRIBOBr1, the state consists of $b = 512$ bits, split in our BLNK mode as:

$r = 256$ - bit *rate* "block size", which directly interacts with output and input.
$c \approx 254$ - bit *capacity*, which is the secret state. Some bits are lost to padding.

These two halves are mixed together by a keyless, random-indistinguishable permutation π. According to theorems such as those given in [32,56] this is sufficient for $k = 192$ - bit secret key security level when less than 2^{64} bits are processed under same key and nonce pair. For the CAESAR variant the nonce length is fixed at $n = 128$ bits.

Despite having almost equivalent speed and size on generic 64-bit platforms, the size and performance characteristics of STRIBOBr1 and WHIRLBOB differ significantly on various implementation platforms such as FPGA, low-end microcontrollers, SIMD systems, and in bitslicing implementations.

WHIRLBOB's permutation π is indeed highly similar to AES. In case of STRIBOBr1, the "Russian 512-bit block AES" permutation had to be somewhat laboriously uncovered from the structure (see Section 5.3), but the particularities and history of Whirlpool make the connection immediately clear.

2.1   Structure of the π Permutation

The computation of π follows almost exactly the operation of the internal key schedule of Whirlpool 3.0 [4]. The only modification is that the number of rounds is increased from $R = 10$ to $R = 12$ for extra security margin against Rebound Distinguisher attacks [35,36]. [1]

To compute $\pi(x_0) = x_{12}$ we iterate the $\mathsf{LPS} = L \circ P \circ S$ composite mixing function with round constants C_r. For rounds $0 \leq r < 12$:

$$x_{r+1} = L(P(S(x_r))) \oplus C_r. \tag{1}$$

---

[1] These attacks would not be directly applicable with the BLNK mode anyway. This is because the attacker can never access more than r bits of the internal state.

If we use the AES-style notation of Whirlpool, S is equivalent to SubBytes, P corresponds to ShiftColumns, L to MixRows, followed by AddRoundKey.

We write the 512-bit state as a matrix $M[\,0\cdots7\,][\,0\cdots7\,]$ of 8×8 bytes, which can be serialized to a byte vector as $\text{vec}[\,8i+j\,] = M[\,i\,][\,j\,]$.

S: SubBytes: Each one of the 64 bytes in the state is substituted using the (singular) 8×8 - bit S-Box described in Section 2.2. For $0 \leq i, j < 8$

$$M'[\,i\,][\,j\,] \leftarrow S(M[\,i\,][\,j\,]). \tag{2}$$

P: ShiftColumns: A byte shuffle. For $0 \leq i, j < 8$

$$M'[\,(\,i+j\,) \bmod 8\,][\,j\,] \leftarrow M[\,i\,][\,j\,]. \tag{3}$$

L: MixRows: Each of the 8 row vectors

$$V_i = (\,M[\,i\,][\,0\,], M[\,i\,][\,1\,], \cdots M[\,i\,][\,7\,]\,) \tag{4}$$

is individually multiplied by a circulant, low-weight 8×8 MDS matrix in the finite field $\mathsf{GF}(2^8)$ characterized by primitive polynomial $p(x) = x^8 + x^4 + x^3 + x^2 + 1$.

$$V_i' = V_i \cdot \begin{pmatrix} 01 & 01 & 04 & 01 & 08 & 05 & 02 & 09 \\ 09 & 01 & 01 & 04 & 01 & 08 & 05 & 02 \\ 02 & 09 & 01 & 01 & 04 & 01 & 08 & 05 \\ 05 & 02 & 09 & 01 & 01 & 04 & 01 & 08 \\ 08 & 05 & 02 & 09 & 01 & 01 & 04 & 01 \\ 01 & 08 & 05 & 02 & 09 & 01 & 01 & 04 \\ 04 & 01 & 08 & 05 & 02 & 09 & 01 & 01 \\ 01 & 04 & 01 & 08 & 05 & 02 & 09 & 01 \end{pmatrix}. \tag{5}$$

C_r: AddRoundKey: The key schedule operation is effectively equivalent to the one used by Whirlpool's "internal block cipher" W. Blocks of eight bytes from the S-Box are used round keys C_r for the first row. For round $0 \leq r < 12, 0 \leq j < 8$:

$$M'[\,0\,][\,j\,] \leftarrow M[\,0\,][\,j\,] \oplus S(\,8r+j\,) \tag{6}$$

Rest of the rows are unaffected by C_r. For $1 \leq i < 8, 0 \leq j < 8$:

$$M'[\,i\,][\,j\,] \leftarrow M[\,i\,][\,j\,]. \tag{7}$$

We offer the listing of Appendix A as WHIRLBOB v1.0 π reference implementation. Whirlpool ISO Standard trace test vectors can be used to verify the correctness of this π implementation up to $r = 10$ [30]. One simply observes the keying "line" of these traces and ignores the encryption "line".

2.2   The S-Box

The Whirlpool and WHIRLBOB 8×8-bit S-Box design utilizes three 4×4 - bit "miniboxes" given in Table 1: E, E^{-1}, and R. Figure 2 shows how these are used to construct the 8×8 - bit S-Box.

Table 1. Three 4×4 miniboxes that are used to build the 8×8 S-Box in Whirlpool 3.0 and WHIRLBOB 1.0.

x	0 1 2 3 4 5 6 7 8 9 A B C D E F
$E(x)$	1 B 9 C D 6 F 3 E 8 7 4 A 2 5 0
$E^{-1}(x)$	F 0 D 7 B E 5 A 9 2 C 1 3 4 8 6
$R(x)$	7 C B D E 4 9 F 6 3 8 A 2 5 1 0

This computation can even be performed on the fly on 4-bit microcontrollers. FPGA implementations save a significant number of LUTs by explicitly utilizing the 4-bit structure rather than implementing a general 8×8 lookup table. These small S-Boxes can often fit into SIMD registers and accessed via constant-time shifts or shuffles, thus enabling implementations resistant to timing attacks.

2.3 BLNK Mode

The padding details and operation of BLNK Sponge mode for WHIRLBOB and STRIBOBr1 are equivalent. Please see [58] for details. The mode is based derived from the Blinker light-weight protocol [53], but limited to CAESAR use case.

3 Implementation

The entire byte-oriented implementation of π fits onto a single page; See Appendix A. Remarkably, in addition to π, only the S-Box `wbob_sbox[256]` (See Section 2.2) together with minimal BLNK logic are required for full AEAD implementation. On many microcontrollers WHIRLBOB's entire software footprint is in the 500B range. Slightly more is required for a shared secret handshake protocol and two-way secure BLINKER protocol [55].

This is a significant improvement over STRIBOBr1, which typically needs almost 2kB. STRIBOBr1 is also much slower and larger on low-end microcontrollers due to the "heavy" MDS matrix. The reference implementation is written for compactness and clarity; it is not optimal when it comes to speed or size. We refer to section 7.3 of [4] for techniques that greatly reduce the number of XORs required, resulting in increased processing speed. Additional tables will be required, however, and this will increase the overall implementation size.

3.1 Constant-Time SIMD Implementation

Due largely to Whirlpool's S-Box structure and generous parallelism, it is well suited for high speed, constant-time implementation on Single Instruction Multiple Data (SIMD) architectures. Here we focus on ARM's NEON as the reference architecture since the state layout fits the registers nicely, but also consider Intel's SSSE3 as another explicit example. The goal is to improve performance, while at the same time avoiding memory-resident table lookups that cause execution

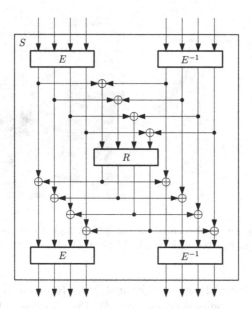

Fig. 2. The WHIRLBOB 8×8 - bit S-Box is constructed from three 4×4 - bit "miniboxes". In this diagram the most significant bits are on the left: E operates on the higher nibble.

time to depend on the data cache state and thus algorithm state (the crux of cache timing attacks).

Related work in this area includes simulated ISA extensions to a RISC architecture for parallel table lookups to speed up Whirlpool [28]. These extensions are then used to build essentially a hardware-assisted analogue of the traditional T tables software implementation – storing the state in rows and issuing a single instruction to perform 8 parallel lookups from the 8-bit S-Box input to the 64-bit linear layer output and XOR-summing the results, repeated for each row. AES [27] and Anubis [18] can also take advantage of SSSE3's variable byte shuffle instruction for fast and secure implementations.

NEON has 32×64 - bit SIMD registers and SSSE3 16×128 - bit. We store the state column-wise (one column per NEON register, two columns per SSSE3 register), i.e. byte position j of register i contains the state byte in column i and row j. The SubBytes step is not sensitive to this ordering, but both ShiftColumns and MixRows are. Since both of these architectures feature variable byte shuffle instructions (vtbl.u8 for NEON and pshufb for SSSE3), implementing SubBytes is a direct translation of Figure 2 to these instructions. This amounts to 40 NEON shuffles and half as many SSSE3 shuffles. For ShiftColumns, NEON uses vext for byte-wise register rotation and SSSE3 pshufb with constant rotation distances since each register holds two columns. For MixRows we use the row formula from the Whirlpool specification [4, Sec. 7.3] where the multiplications by x are a simple left shift (native on NEON,

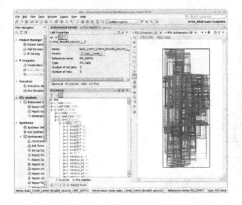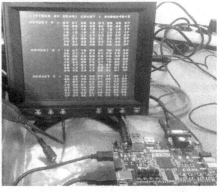

Fig. 3. WHIRLBOB was implemented on the FPGA logic fabric of Xilix Zynq 7010. The implementation integrates with the AXI bus of ARM Cortex A9 on the SoC chip.

integer addition on SSSE3) and conditional XOR (operand masked by signed right shift on NEON, comparison on SSSE3). The formula is fairly symmetric around even and odd byte positions – while NEON implements it as written with 24 multiplications, SSSE3 slightly rearranges a few registers to parallelize across the full 128-bit register width and use half as many multiplications.

3.2   Generic Constant-Time Bitsliced Implementation

The byte-oriented $8 \times 64 = 512$ - bit state can be rapidly split into eight 64-bit registers. The parallelism evident in Figure 2 helps to speed up bitsliced implementation. We see that for 2/3 of the time, the S-Box has effectively two independent 4-bit execution paths. Interleaving these may greatly reduce wait states due to the superscalar architecture employed by most modern CPUs.

Appendix B of the current 2003 Whirlpool specification [4] gives listings with 14-16 instructions/gates for each of the miniboxes (if ANDN instruction is allowed). Those were used in our reference bitsliced implementations.

3.3   Implementation Summary

We currently have six implementations of WHIRLBOB. They mainly differ in the implementation technique used for the π cryptographic permutation.

- **C 8-bit**: This is the minimal reference implementation which is optimized for clarity and low-resource platforms, corresponding to Appendix A.
- **C 64-bit**: Standard speed-optimized implementation for most platforms, utilizing large lookup tables. Apart from Whirlpool-derived tables, equivalent to the implementation of [56].
- **C Bitsliced**: Straight-line, fully bitsliced implementation without data-dependent branches or lookups. Resistant to timing attacks.

- **NEON Intrinsics**: Fast constant-time version that avoids table lookups by storing 4×4 - bit miniboxes in SIMD registers.
- **SSSE3 Intrinsics**: Similar but for 128-bit SIMD registers.
- **Verilog 12-cycle**: This is the hardware reference implementation. Source code is about 350 lines. Additional logic is required for AXI Bus integration.

Software Implementations. The first three implementations use only C99, and are hence easily portable. See Table 2 for implementation metrics. We also have various embedded implementations. Note that STRIBOBr2 is faster then the (out-of-box, Ubuntu 14.04 LTS) OpenSSL implementation of AES-192 on the same target.

Hardware Implementation. The hardware implementation has been proven on FPGA (Figure 3). The SÆHI proposal reports total post place-and-route utilization on Artix-7 of 4,946 logic units for a single round of WHIRLBOB, which compares favourably to 7,972 required for Keccak/Keyak [56]. Throughput is roughly 2 MB/s for each MHz.

Table 2. Comparing software implementations of WHIRLBOB π.

Target	Speed	Footprint		Source
	MB/sec	Code	Data	C lines
Single Core of 3.4GHz Core i7-4770				
8-bit C99 Reference	7.772	326	256	97
Bitsliced C99 Reference	49.02	4592	768	345
64-bit C99 Reference	139.2	1942	16512	128
SSSE3 (Constant-Time)	**162.3**	1290	1152	256
OpenSSL 1.0.1f AES-192 CBC	*145.6*			
BeagleBone Black 1.0GHz Cortex-A8				
8-bit C99 Reference	0.828	352	256	97
64-bit C99 Reference	3.343	6524	16512	128
Bitsliced C99 Reference	1.435	15704	768	345
NEON (Constant-Time)	9.208	1528	1072	320

4   Comparison with Other AEAD Schemes

At the time of writing the dominant AEAD scheme is the Galois / Counter Mode (GCM) for the AES block cipher [43,45], which is recommended for use with TLS, SSH and IPSec protocols by NSA as part of "Suite B" [19,29,48,59]. GCM message authentication is based on polynomial evaluation in the finite field $GF(2^{128})$. The required multiplication can be exceedingly slow on lightweight platforms. An LFSR-style implementation of a 128×128 - bit multiplication will require thousands of cycles on 8-bit targets.

It is often more efficient to use the CCM [44,63] double-mode of operation on lightweight platforms, since implementing a full extra AES operation can be

Table 3. Relative performance of some CAESAR candidates on a AMD64 reference system in SUPERCOP testing (smaller number indicates faster speed).

MORUS 1280 - 128 [64]	0.09
NORX 64-4-1 [3]	0.19
ASCON-128n [24]	0.89
WHIRLBOB Intel SSSE3 Constant-Time	**1.00**
WHIRLBOB and STRIBOBr1 64-bit Reference	1.26
Lake Keyak [12]	2.23
Ketje Sr. [6]	4.25
PRIMATES (HANUMAN, GIBBON, APE) [2]	50+

bench.cr.yp.to/web-impl/amd64-titan0-crypto_aead.html

faster than the finite field multiplication operation. CCM and GCM are currently the only two FIPS - standardized authenticated modes. The performance characteristics of AES-CCM AEAD can be expected to be very similar to WHIRLBOB due to their structural similarities and relative data bandwidth:

- WHIRLBOB: 12 rounds with 64 S-Boxes for 256 bits of data.
- AES-192-CCM: 2×12 rounds with 16 S-Boxes for 128 bits of data.

There are additional (patented) AES modes which will be faster on 8-bit platforms – such as AES-OTR [40] and AES-OCB [34], and dozens of others. Virtually all AEAD block cipher modes offer lower levels of integrity protection (2^{64} level even for 128-bit tags) and are not directly usable in wider Sponge applications such as non-randomized hashing.

Currently only unoptimized reference implementations are available for most CAESAR candidates [20], making fair performance comparisons difficult. Furthermore, no other CAESAR candidate is targeted at 192-bit security level (apart from AES modes) and little attention has been paid to 8-bit or hardware implementations.

We note that leading full-featured Sponge candidates, directly SHA3 / Keccak - based Ketje Keyak [12] and [6] have significantly slower reference implementation than STRIBOBr1 and WHIRLBOB (Table 3). WHIRLBOB falls very significantly from candidates such as NORX [3] and MORUS [64], which have been designed specifically with 64-bit targets in mind. Our proposal can claim a more conservative security margin when compared to these candidates, however.

5 Security Analysis and Design Notes

For analysis of the round function against classical Differential and Linear cryptanalysis we refer to Whirlpool literature [4]. Two additional rounds increase WHIRLBOB's resistance against best known attacks [35,36].

Most of the security arguments and proofs offered for STRIBOBr1 and BLNK in [56] also apply to the new proposal. These are based on indistinguishably arguments for the π permutation and a simple theorem (Thm. 1, Sec. 3.3. in [56]) that loosely ties the compression function in Miyagushi-Preneel mode [41,51] with the indistinguishably of π. A random-indistinguishable π and appropriate padding rules are sufficient to construct Sponge-based hashes [7], Tree Hashes [11], MACs [10], Authenticated Encryption (AE) algorithms [9], and pseudorandom extractors (SHAKEs, PRFs, and PRNGs) [8,47].

5.1   Side-Channel and Implementation Attacks

Due to the minibox structure, we may load the 4×4 - bit tables in registers and access them via constant-time shuffles on Intel SSSE3 and ARM NEON SIMD targets as noted in Section 3.1. WHIRLBOB is also relatively well suited for bitsliced implementation due to its particular S-Box and MDS design as noted in Section 2.2.

Being unconditional straight-line code without data-dependent table lookups, bitsliced and byte shuffling implementations are effective countermeasures against cache timing attacks, which can be mounted against cryptographic primitives with large tables such as AES [1,5,50,62].

A non-constant-time implementation of the S-Box on Whirlpool, Streebog, or STRIBOBr1 on 64-bit platforms typically requires lookup tables of up to $8 \times 256 \times 8 = 16384B$. Even though this size easily fits into the Level 2 cache of any 64-bit system, one may see that timing attacks are possible as L2 caches are not always shared even between different execution cores within a single CPU unit. This is due to the process switching operation of most 64-bit operating systems.

5.2   Historical Modifications to Whirlpool

Whirlpool has received a significant amount of analysis in the almost 15 years since its original publication. Whirlpool was the only hash function in the final NESSIE portfolio in addition to SHA-2 hashes [42]. Whirlpool has also been standardized by ISO as part of ISO/IEC 10118-3:2004 [30].

The amended MDS matrix used by current ('03) Whirlpool is also used by WHIRLBOB as a countermeasure to the structural observations given in [60]. Our design is based on Whirlpool 3.0.

Whirlpool was found to be vulnerable to a Rebound Distinguisher [35,36,39]. That 2^{188} attack applies to the 10-round variant; our 12-round version should offer a comfortable security margin, especially as our security target is 2^{192}. The way the round constants are derived from the S-Box allows this change to be made in a straightforward manner.

5.3   Notes on the Origins of Streebog, Kuznyechik, and STRIBOBr1

The 8-bit S-Box used by STRIBOBr1 was directly lifted from Streebog so that hardware and software components developed for Streebog could be shared or recycled when implementing STRIBOBr1. The same S-Box is also used by the recently proposed Russian Encryption Standard "Kuznyechik" [25,61].

The GOST R 34.11-2012 "Streebog" standard text [26] does not describe the linear step as a 8×8 matrix-vector multiplication with $\mathsf{GF}(2^8)$ elements like the STRIBOBr1 spec [56], but as a 64×64 binary matrix multiplication. One can see that $8 \times 8 \times 8 = 512$ bits are required to describe the former, but $64 \times 64 = 4096$ bits are required for the latter. The more effective description was discovered by Kazymorov and Kazymorova in [33] by exhaustively testing all 30 irreducible polynomial bases, revealing an AES-like MDS structure. The origin of the particular numerical values of that MDS matrix is still a mystery. They do not appear to offer similar avenues for size or performance optimization like those in Whirlpool 3.0 and STRIBOBr2 do.

Not much about the particular design criteria of the Streebog S-Box has been published. That S-Box was apparently selected at least 5 years ago as Streebog already appeared in RusCrypto '10 proceedings [38]. Very recent ongoing work has revealed it to also have an optimized representation [16], after all.

We can easily observe that the S-Box offers reasonable resistance against basic methods of cryptanalysis. Its differential bound [13] is $P = \frac{8}{256}$ and best linear approximation [37] holds with $P = \frac{28}{128}$. There does not seem to be any exploitable algebraic weaknesses. These are the exact same bounds as can be found for the Whirlpool and STRIBOBr2 S-Box, but fall short from the bounds of the AES S-Box.

By comparison, the Rijndael AES S-Box is constructed from finite field inversion x^{-1} operation in $\mathsf{GF}(2^8)$ (inspired by the Nyberg construction [49]) and an affine bit transform that serves as a countermeasure against, among other things, Interpolation Attacks [31] on the AES predecessor SHARK [52]. We refer to [23] for more information about the AES design process.

We had brief informal discussions with some members of the Streebog and Kuznyechik design team at the CTCrypt '14 workshop (05-06 June 2014, Moscow RU). Their recollection was that the aim was to choose a "randomized" S-Box that meets the basic differential, linear, and algebraic requirements. Randomization using various building blocks was simply iterated until a "good enough" permutation was found. This was seen as an effective countermeasure against yet-unknown attacks. At the time of Streebog S-Box selection (before 2010's) the emergence of allegedly effective AES Algebraic Attacks such as [22] was a major concern for much of the symmetric cryptographic community. Hence it was felt appropriate to avoid too much algebraic structure in either the S-Box or MDS matrix while also ensuring necessary resistance against known attacks such as DC and LC. Algebraic attack attempts of this type against AES have since largely fizzled out. We feel confident that the Whirlpool S-Box should be sufficient for our claimed security level, especially as it offers significantly better speeds in constant-time implementations when compared to an AES-Style S-Box.

One is left with the impression that Streebog is a "whitened" or randomized copy of the original Whirlpool design. Despite its partially unknown origins and relative shortcomings on some implementation targets, we consider STRIBOBr1 to be at least as secure as STRIBOBr2 if appropriately implemented. Indeed some of the more successful attacks on AES and Whirlpool have been based on their deep structural self-similarities and simplistic key schedules [14,15,17], so STRIBOBr1 may have some security advantages against "unknown" attacks.

6   Conclusions

We have introduced WHIRLBOB, an algorithm for Authenticated encryption with Associated Data. WHIRLBOB is a variant of the STRIBOBr1 first round CAESAR candidate but borrows its main components from the Whirlpool 3.0 hash. WHIRLBOB, also known as STRIBOBr2, is a CAESAR [21] second round candidate [58].

WHIRLBOB has extremely small implementation footprint on resource-limited software platforms – typically under half a kilobyte. Its particular S-Box and MDS design allows WHIRLBOB to have efficient constant-time bitsliced and SIMD byte shuffling implementations. This is an effective countermeasure against cache timing attacks, which are a concern against AES. The $b = 8 \times 64$ - bit state size is particularly suitable for bitslicing of a byte-oriented algorithm on 64-bit platforms and byte slicing for SIMD platforms.

WHIRLBOB has superb implementation characteristics on FPGA (ASIC), SIMD and lightweight embedded platforms. We recommend WHIRLBOB especially for those platforms. Furthermore WHIRLBOB offers provable security assurance through its security relationship with the well-analyzed Whirlpool hash.

We have also discussed the design choices for the STRIBOBr1 S-Box and other components used in the Streebog hash and Kuznyechik cipher, which are becoming standards for the Russian security market.

Acknowledgments. We thank Oleksandr Kazymyrov, Vasily Shishkin, Bart Preneel, and Paulo Barreto for their helpful comments.

Supported in part by TEKES grant 4681/31/2014 INKA EAKR Hardware Rooted Security. This article is based upon work from COST Action CRYPTACUS, supported by COST (European Cooperation in Science and Technology).

References

1. Acıiçmez, O., Schindler, W., Koç, Ç.K.: Cache based remote timing attack on the aes. In: Abe, M. (ed.) CT-RSA 2007. LNCS, vol. 4377, pp. 271–286. Springer, Heidelberg (2006)
2. Andreeva, E., Bilgin, B., Bogdanov, A., Luykx, A., Mennink, B., Mouha, N., Yasuda, K.: PRIMATEs v1 - Submission to the CAESAR Competition. CAE-SAR First Round Submission, March 2014. http://competitions.cr.yp.to/round1/primatesv1.pdf

3. Aumasson, J.-P., Jovanovic, P., Neves, S.: CAESAR submission: NORX v1. CAESAR First Round Submission, March 2014. http://competitions.cr.yp.to/round1/norxv1.pdf

4. Barreto, P.S.L.M., Rijmen, V.: The Whirlpool hashing function. NESSIE Algorithm Specification, 2000, revised May 2003. http://www.larc.usp.br/~pbarreto/WhirlpoolPage.html

5. Bernstein, D.J.: Cache-timing attacks on AES. Technical report, University of Chigaco, 2005. http://cr.yp.to/antiforgery/cachetiming-20050414.pdf

6. Bertoni, G., Daemen, J., Peeters, M., Van Assche, G., Van Keer, R.: CAESAR submission: Ketje v1. CAESAR First Round Submission, March 2014. http://competitions.cr.yp.to/round1/ketjev1.pdf

7. Bertoni, G., Daemen, J., Peeters, M., Van Assche, G.: Sponge functions. In: Ecrypt Hash Workshop 2007, May 2007. http://events.iaik.tugraz.at/HashWorkshop07/program.html

8. Bertoni, G., Daemen, J., Peeters, M., Van Assche, G.: Sponge-based pseudorandom number generators. In: Mangard, S., Standaert, F.-X. (eds.) CHES 2010. LNCS, vol. 6225, pp. 33–47. Springer, Heidelberg (2010)

9. Bertoni, G., Daemen, J., Peeters, M., Van Assche, G.: Duplexing the sponge: single-pass authenticated encryption and other applications. In: Miri, A., Vaudenay, S. (eds.) SAC 2011. LNCS, vol. 7118, pp. 320–337. Springer, Heidelberg (2012)

10. Bertoni, G., Daemen, J., Peeters, M., Van Assche, G.: The Keccak reference, version 3.0. NIST SHA3 Submission Document, January 2011. http://keccak.noekeon.org/Keccak-reference-3.0.pdf

11. Bertoni, G., Daemen, J., Peeters, M., Van Assche, G.: Sakura: a flexible coding for tree hashing. In: Boureanu, I., Owesarski, P., Vaudenay, S. (eds.) ACNS 2014. LNCS, vol. 8479, pp. 217–234. Springer, Heidelberg (2014)

12. Bertoni, G., Daemen, J., Peeters, M., Van Assche, G., Van Keer, R.: CAESAR submission: Keyak v1. CAESAR First Round Submission, March 2014. http://competitions.cr.yp.to/round1/keyakv1.pdf

13. Biham, E., Shamir, A.: Differential Cryptanalysis of the Data Encryption Standard. Springer (1993)

14. Biryukov, A., Khovratovich, D.: Related-key cryptanalysis of the full AES-192 and AES-256. In: Matsui, M. (ed.) ASIACRYPT 2009. LNCS, vol. 5912, pp. 1–18. Springer, Heidelberg (2009)

15. Biryukov, A., Khovratovich, D., Nikolić, I.: Distinguisher and related-key attack on the full AES-256. In: Halevi, S. (ed.) CRYPTO 2009. LNCS, vol. 5677, pp. 231–249. Springer, Heidelberg (2009)

16. Biryukov, A., Perrin, L., Udovenko, A.: The secret structure of the S-Box of Streebog, Kuznechik and StriBob. IACR ePrint 2015/812, August 2015. https://eprint.iacr.org/2015/812

17. Bogdanov, A., Khovratovich, D., Rechberger, C.: Biclique cryptanalysis of the full AES. In: Lee, D.H., Wang, X. (eds.) ASIACRYPT 2011. LNCS, vol. 7073, pp. 344–371. Springer, Heidelberg (2011)

18. Brumley, B.B.: Secure and fast implementations of two involution ciphers. In: Aura, T., Järvinen, K., Nyberg, K. (eds.) NordSec 2010. LNCS, vol. 7127, pp. 269–282. Springer, Heidelberg (2012)

19. Burgin, K., Peck, M.: Suite B Profile for Internet Protocol Security (IPsec). IETF RFC **6380**, October 2011

20. CAESAR. CAESAR: Competition for authenticated encryption: Security, applicability, and robustness, January 2014. http://competitions.cr.yp.to/caesar.html

21. CAESAR. CAESAR first and second round submissions, July 2015. http://competitions.cr.yp.to/caesar-submissions.html
22. Courtois, N.: How fast can be algebraic attacks on block ciphers? IACR ePrint 2006/168, May 2006. https://eprint.iacr.org/2006/168
23. Daemen, J., Rijmen, V.: The Design of Rijndael: AES - the Advanced Encryption Standard. Springer (2002)
24. Dobraunig, C., Eichlseder, M., Mendel, F., Schläffer, M.: Ascon v1 - Submission to the CAESAR Competition. CAESAR First Round Submission, March 2014. http://competitions.cr.yp.to/round1/asconv1.pdf
25. Dygin, D.M., Lavrikov, I.V., Marshalko, G.B., Rudskoy, V.I., Trifonov, D.I., Shishkin, V.A.: On a new Russian Encryption Standard. Mathematical Aspects of Cryptography **6**(2), 29–34 (2015). http://www.mathnet.ru/php/archive.phtml?wshow=paper&jrnid=mvk&paperid=142&option_lang=eng (Abstract In Russian)
26. GOST. Information technology. cryptographic protection of information, hash function. GOST R 34.11-2012 (2012). http://protect.gost.ru/v.aspx?control=7&id=180209 (In Russian)
27. Hamburg, M.: Accelerating AES with vector permute instructions. In: Clavier, C., Gaj, K. (eds.) CHES 2009. LNCS, vol. 5747, pp. 18–32. Springer, Heidelberg (2009)
28. Hilewitz, Y., Yin, Y.L., Lee, R.B.: Accelerating the whirlpool hash function using parallel table lookup and fast cyclical permutation. In: Nyberg, K. (ed.) FSE 2008. LNCS, vol. 5086, pp. 173–188. Springer, Heidelberg (2008)
29. Igoe, K.: Suite B Cryptographic Suites for Secure Shell (SSH). IETF RFC 6239, May 2011. https://tools.ietf.org/html/rfc6239
30. ISO/IEC. Information technology - security techniques - hash-functions - part 3: Dedicated hash-functions. ISO/IEC 10118–3:2004 (2004). https://www.iso.org/obp/ui/#iso:std:iso-iec:10118:-3:ed-3:v1:en
31. Jakobsen, T., Knudsen, L.R.: The interpolation attack on block ciphers. In: Biham, E. (ed.) FSE 1997. LNCS, vol. 1267, pp. 99–112. Springer, Heidelberg (1997)
32. Jovanovic, P., Luykx, A., Mennink, B.: Beyond $2^{c/2}$ security in sponge-based authenticated encryption modes. In: Sarkar, P., Iwata, T. (eds.) ASIACRYPT 2014. LNCS, vol. 8873, pp. 85–104. Springer, Heidelberg (2014)
33. Kazymyrov, O., Kazymyrova, V.: Algebraic aspects of the Russian hash standard GOST R 34.11-2012. In: CTCrypt 2013, June 23–24, 2013, Ekaterinburg, Russia, 2013. IACR ePrint 2013/556. https://eprint.iacr.org/2013/556
34. Krovetz, T., Rogaway, P.: OCB (v1). CAESAR First Round Submission, March 2014. http://competitions.cr.yp.to/round1/ocbv1.pdf
35. Lamberger, M., Mendel, F., Rechberger, C., Rijmen, V., Schläffer, M.: Rebound distinguishers: results on the full whirlpool compression function. In: Matsui, M. (ed.) ASIACRYPT 2009. LNCS, vol. 5912, pp. 126–143. Springer, Heidelberg (2009)
36. Lamberger, M., Mendel, F., Schläffer, M., Rechberger, C., Rijmen, V.: The rebound attack and subspace distinguishers: Application to Whirlpool. J. Cryptology **28**, 257–296 (2015)
37. Matsui, M.: Linear cryptanalysis method for DES cipher. In: Helleseth, T. (ed.) EUROCRYPT 1993. LNCS, vol. 765, pp. 386–397. Springer, Heidelberg (1994)
38. Matyuhin, D.V., Rudskoy, V.I., Shishkin, V.A.: Promising hashing algorithm. RusCrypto 2010. Workshop **02**, 2010 (2010). (In Russian)
39. Mendel, F., Rechberger, C., Schläffer, M., Thomsen, S.S.: The rebound attack: cryptanalysis of reduced Whirlpool and Grøstl. In: Dunkelman, O. (ed.) FSE 2009. LNCS, vol. 5665, pp. 260–276. Springer, Heidelberg (2009)
40. Minematsu, K.: AES-OTR v1. CAESAR First Round Submission, March 2014. http://competitions.cr.yp.to/round1/aesotrv1.pdf

41. Miyaguchi, S., Ohta, K., Iwata, M.: 128-bit hash function (n-hash). NTT Review **2**, 128–132 (1990)
42. NESSIE. Final report of European project number IST-1999-12324, named New European Schemes for Signatures, Integrity, and Encryption. NESSIE, April 2004. https://www.cosic.esat.kuleuven.be/nessie/Bookv015.pdf
43. NIST. Advanced Encryption Standard (AES). Federal Information Processing Standards Publication FIPS 197, November 2001. http://csrc.nist.gov/publications/fips/fips197/fips-197.pdf
44. NIST. Counter with Cipher Block Chaining - Message Authentication Code (CCM). NIST Special Publication 800–38C, May 2004
45. NIST. Recommendation for block cipher modes of operation: Galois/counter mode (GCM) and GMAC. NIST Special Publication 800–38D (2007). http://csrc.nist.gov/publications/nistpubs/800-38D/SP-800-38D.pdf
46. NIST. The Keyed-Hash Message Authentication Code (HMAC). Federal Information Processing Standards Publication FIPS 198–1, July 2008
47. NIST VCAT. NIST Cryptographic Standards and Guidelines Development Process: Report and Recommendations of the Visiting Committee on Advanced Technology of the National Institute of Standards and Technology, July 2014
48. NSA. Suite B Cryptography (2005). http://www.nsa.gov/ia/programs/suiteb_cryptography
49. Nyberg, K.: Differentially uniform mappings for cryptography. In: Helleseth, T. (ed.) EUROCRYPT 1993. LNCS, vol. 765, pp. 55–64. Springer, Heidelberg (1994)
50. Osvik, D.A., Shamir, A., Tromer, E.: Cache attacks and countermeasures: the case of AES. In: Pointcheval, D. (ed.) CT-RSA 2006. LNCS, vol. 3860, pp. 1–20. Springer, Heidelberg (2006)
51. Preneel, B.: Analysis and Design of Cryptographic Hash Functions. PhD thesis, K. U. Leuven (Belgium) (1993). http://homes.esat.kuleuven.be/~preneel/phd_preneel_feb1993.pdf
52. Rijmen, V., Daemen, J., Preneel, B., Bosselaers, A., De Win, E.: The cipher SHARK. In: Gollmann, D. (ed.) FSE 1996. LNCS, vol. 1039, pp. 99–111. Springer, Heidelberg (1996)
53. Saarinen, M.-J.O.: Beyond modes: building a secure record protocol from a cryptographic sponge permutation. In: Benaloh, J. (ed.) CT-RSA 2014. LNCS, vol. 8366, pp. 270–285. Springer, Heidelberg (2014)
54. Saarinen, M.-J.O.: Simple AEAD hardware interface (SÆHI) in a SoC: implementing an on-chip Keyak/WhirlBob coprocessor. In: TrustED 2014 Proceedings of the 4th International Workshop on Trustworthy Embedded Device, pp. 51–56. ACM (2014)
55. Saarinen, M.-J.O.: StriBob: Authenticated encryption from GOST R 34.11-2012 LPS permutation. In: Preproceedings of the CTCrypt 2014, 05–06 June 2014, Moscow, Russia, pp. 170–182, June 2014. https://eprint.iacr.org/2014/271
56. Saarinen, M.-J.O.: The STRIBOBr 1 authenticated encryption algorithm. CAESAR, 1st Round Candidate, March 2014. http://www.stribob.com
57. Saarinen, M.-J.O.: StriBob: authenticated encryption from GOST R 34.11-2012 LPS permutation. Mathematical Aspects of Cryptography **6**(2), 67–78 (2015). http://www.mathnet.ru/php/archive.phtml?wshow=paper&jrnid=mvk&paperid=146&option_lang=eng (Abstract In Russian)
58. Saarinen, M.-J.O., Brumley, B.B.: STRIBOBr 2: "WHIRLBOB", second round caesar algorithm tweak specification. CAESAR 2nd Round Candidate, August 2015. http://www.stribob.com

59. Salter, M., Housley, R.: Suite B Profile for Transport Layer Security (TLS). IETF RFC 6460, January 2012. https://tools.ietf.org/html/rfc6460

60. Shirai, T., Shibutani, K.: On the diffusion matrix employed in the Whirlpool hashing function. NESSIE Public Report (2003). http://www.cosic.esat.kuleuven.be/nessie/reports/phase2/whirlpool-20030311.pdf

61. Shishkin, V., Dygin, D., Lavrikov, I., Marshalko, G., Rudskoy, V., Trifonov, D.: Low-weight and hi-end: draft Russian encryption standard. In: Preproceedings CTCrypt 2014, June 05–06, 2014, Moscow, Russia. pp. 183–188, June 2014

62. Weiß, M., Heinz, B., Stumpf, F.: A cache timing attack on aes in virtualization environments. In: Keromytis, A.D. (ed.) FC 2012. LNCS, vol. 7397, pp. 314–328. Springer, Heidelberg (2012)

63. Whiting, D., Housley, R., Ferguson, N.: Counter with CBC-MAC (CCM). IETF RFC 3610, September 2003. https://tools.ietf.org/html/rfc3610

64. Wu, H., Huang, T.: The Authenticated Cipher MORUS (v1). CAESAR First Round Submission, March 2014. http://competitions.cr.yp.to/round1/morusv1.pdf

A   WHIRLBOB 1.0 π "8-bit" Reference Implementation

This ANSI C function implements the WHIRLBOB 512×512-bit π permutation.

```
void wbob_pi(uint8_t st[64])                    // WHIRLBOB Pi
{
  int r, i, j;
  uint8_t t[64], x, *pt;

  for (r = 0; r < 12; r++) {                    // 12 rounds
    for (i = 0; i < 64; i++) {
      t[(i & 7) + ((i + (i << 3)) & 070)] = // P
        wbob_sbox[st[i]];                       // S
    }

    // The round constants C come from the S-Box
    pt = (uint8_t *) &wbob_sbox[8 * r];
    for (i = 0; i < 8; i++)
      st[i] = pt[i];                            // C in first 8
    for (i = 8; i < 64; i++)
      st[i] = 0;                                // zero the rest

    // Apply the circular, low weight MDS matrix
    for (i = 0; i < 64; i += 8) {
      pt = &st[i];                              // start of row
      for (j = 0; j < 8; j++) {
        x = t[i + j];                           // Circular MDS
        pt[j & 7] ^= x;                         // 01
        pt[(j + 1) & 7] ^= x;                   // 01
        pt[(j + 3) & 7] ^= x;                   // 01
        pt[(j + 5) & 7] ^= x;
        pt[(j + 7) & 7] ^= x;

        // x <- 02
        x = (x << 1) ^ (x & 0x80 ? 0x1D : 0x00);
        pt[(j + 6) & 7] ^= x;                   // 02

        // x <- 04
        x = (x << 1) ^ (x & 0x80 ? 0x1D : 0x00);
        pt[(j + 2) & 7] ^= x;                   // 04
        pt[(j + 5) & 7] ^= x;                   // 01 + 04 = 05

        // x <- 08
        x = (x << 1) ^ (x & 0x80 ? 0x1D : 0x00);
        pt[(j + 4) & 7] ^= x;                   // 08
        pt[(j + 7) & 7] ^= x;                   // 01 + 08 = 09
      }
    }
  }
}
```

An Efficient Traceable Attribute-Based Authentication Scheme with One-Time Attribute Trees

Huihui Yang[(✉)] and Vladimir A. Oleshchuk

Department of Information and Communication Technology,
University of Agder, Kristiansand, Norway
{huihui.yang,vladimir.oleshchuk}@uia.no

Abstract. Attribute-based authentication (ABA) is a way to authenticate signers by means of attributes and it requests proof of possessing required attributes from the one to be authenticated. To achieve the property of traceability, required attributes should be combined with the signer's attribute private keys in order to generate a signature. In some schemes, signers' attribute keys are related to attribute trees, so changing attribute trees will cause the regeneration of all related attribute keys. In this paper, we propose an efficient traceable ABA scheme, where the generation of signers' attribute keys is independent from attribute trees. Thus the same set of attribute keys can be used with a different attribute tree for each signature generation and verification, which is called "one-time" attribute tree in this paper.

Keywords: Attribute-Based Authentication · ABA · Traceability · Attribute tree

1 Introduction

The approach how a signer is authenticated in attribute-based authentication (ABA) [8,14] schemes is different from traditional public key based authentication. Signers use attribute keys instead of private keys to generate signatures such that anonymous authentication can be achieved. Another goal of ABA schemes is to minimize information leakage. To illustrate ABA, let us assume Peter is an researcher in University A. His profile information includes his name, phone number, email address, office number, bank account number and so on. If Peter wants to borrow a book from the university library, it should be enough to prove that he is an employee in the university and there is no need to retrieve all his personal information from his profile. Another scenario is a teaching system. Students can mark and comment on teachers' lectures. Teachers can read these feedbacks but are not allowed to see who has done this. Students can also use the system to create study topics and discuss with each other. However, if someone abuses the system to distribute something illegal, the administrator should

© Springer International Publishing Switzerland 2015
S. Buchegger and M. Dam (Eds.): NordSec 2015, LNCS 9417, pp. 123–135, 2015.
DOI: 10.1007/978-3-319-26502-5_9

be able to trace the source of messages. Both scenarios can be solved within a traceable ABA scheme.

Except for anonymity and traceability, ABA can also have other properties, such as unforgeability, unlinkability and coalition resistance. Intuitively, unforgeability means that an adversary cannot impersonate a valid user to forge a signature and coalition resistance forbids users piling up their attributes to generate an signature together. Given enough signatures, if it is impossible to tell whether these signatures are generated by the same signer or not, the scheme provides unlinkability. Another optional property of ABA schemes is the dynamicity of attribute requirements. For example, in the above teaching system, a teacher assistant of a course can also be a student in other courses. When he accesses resources in these courses, the authentication requirements may differ from each other. If his attribute keys are bound to any of the requirements, he may not be able to be successfully authenticated to access resources of other courses.

To solve issues as described above, we propose an efficient traceable ABA scheme with a flexible attribute tree generation approach, to satisfy the need in a dynamic environment where attribute requirements change frequently. Meanwhile, this scheme can also be used in a comparatively static environment without any extra cost. This scheme is based on an untraceable ABA scheme proposed in [8], the purpose of which is to establish a shared session key at the end of the protocol. In our scheme, we have improved the scheme proposed in [8] in two main aspects. First of all, we add several parameters to achieve traceability. Secondly, we have applied the "shared key" to a keyed hash function to shorten the signature size and minimize computation complexity.

1.1 Related Work

There have already been many results on attribute-based schemes, such as attribute-based encryption (ABE) [11,16] and attribute-based signatures (ABS) [15]. The main goal of ABE is message encryption and decryption. Its security requirement is that an adversary cannot forge an valid ciphertext [11], while the "unforgeability" in ABA schemes is that an adversary cannot forge a valid signature. The privacy achieved in ABS schemes is based on the attribute set rather than signers' identities as in ABA schemes. Moreover, traceability is usually not discussed much in either ABE or ABS schemes in existing literatures. Therefore, we will narrow the survey scope from attribute-based schemes to results only related to cryptographic construction of ABA schemes.

In [14], Khader proposed a general framework how to build traceable ABA schemes based on group signatures [4]. All signers' attribute keys are generated based on signers' identifying information and an attribute tree, which causes an drawback that the cost of changing attributes requirements is very high, that is, all signers' attribute keys should be regenerated. The ABA scheme proposed in [8] is an ABA key exchange protocol, of which the main goal is to gain a shared secret key at the end of the protocol. Its security requirement is to prevent adversaries from learning any information about the secret key, which is slightly different from the main focus of this paper, i.e., authentication.

Two untraceable ABA schemes are proposed in [6,22], however, neither offers proof of unforgeability. The traceable ABA schemes proposed in [21] is based on a down-to-top attribute tree building approach, so that attribute trees are changeable. This scheme is efficient and flexible in dynamic environments, but its flexibility is achieved at the cost of a large central attribute tree and it increases the computation and storage costs.

The scheme of attribute-based credentials (ABCs) [17,18] is a special type of anonymous authentication and it is quite similar to our work. ABCs were proposed by the EU research project ABC4Trust [1,19]. This project focuses on privacy protection by anonymous authentication. Users obtain credentials for attributes they possess and they will use these credentials to generate tokens to prove their possession of these attributes. This project has generated lots of outputs, including publications [5] and codes for several testing examples. In [12], authors provide a detailed introduction of ABCs, consisting of descriptions of the architecture, cryptographic protocols underlying privacy-ABCs, mechanism comparisons of privacy-ABCs and implementation examples. However, the cryptographic protocol part has only covered possible underlying primitives without details how they are applied. Meanwhile, codes of implementation examples related to cryptographic protocols are not available as well and there is also not too much detailed information about the construction of credentials in the project publications.

2   The Proposed ABA Scheme

2.1   Attribute Trees

As described in [7,9,14], an attribute tree is a tree structure describing the logic relations among attributes. In an attribute tree, leaves represent attributes and interior nodes are threshold gates. We will use Fig. 1 as an example to explain the concept of attribute trees. Assume the related attribute set of attribute tree in Fig. 1 is $\{att_1, \cdots, att_5\}$, where leaf nodes indexed from 1 to 5 and interior nodes are index from 6 to 9. For an interior node x, let l_x and k_x be the numbers of x's children and the threshold respectively. If k_x is less than l_x, the interior node represents logical "OR". If k_x equals to l_x, the interior node represents logical "AND". For example, node 7 has two children and its threshold is one, so it represents logical "OR". The same is true for node 9. As for nodes 6 and 8, the number of their children and the threshold are two, so both represent logical "AND".

Suppose Γ is an attribute tree with rt as its root and Ψ as its attribute set. We use $ind(Node) \in \mathbb{Z}_p^*$ to represent the index of a random node denoted by $Node$. To construct Γ, we start from the root by selecting polynomials over $\mathbb{Z}_p^*$ of which all degrees equal to $k_{Node} - 1$ for all nodes, where $\mathbb{Z}_p^* = \{1, \cdots, p-1\}$ and p is a large prime. First of all, we select a random α from $\mathbb{Z}_p^*$ and assign $q_{rt}(0) = \alpha$, and then we randomly select a polynomial $q_{rt}(x)$ satisfying $q_{rt}(0) = \alpha$ for root rt. The value of the remaining nodes are computed by $q_{Node}(0) = q_{par(Node)}(ind(Node))$, where $par(Node)$ is the parent of node $Node$. Then a polynomial $q_{Node}(x)$ is

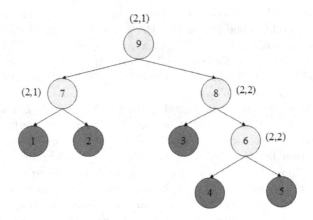

Fig. 1. Attribute tree: an example

chosen such that the equation $q_{Node}(0) = q_{par}(ind(Node))$ holds. For a leaf node, there is no related polynomial but only a constant value.

In the following, we use a specific example to demonstrate the generation of an attribute tree. The relations of all leaf nodes (green) in Fig. 1 can be represented as $(att_1 \vee att_2) \vee (att_3 \wedge (att_4 \wedge att_5))$. Assume $\alpha = 15$. We begin from the root, i.e., node 9 and the polynomials are set as following:

$$
\begin{array}{lll}
q_9(0) = 15 & q_9(x) = 15 & q_7(0) = q_9(7) = 15 \\
q_7(x) = 15 & q_8(0) = q_9(8) = 15 & q_8(x) = x + 15 \\
q_1(0) = 1_7(1) = 15 & q_2(0) = q_7(2) = 15 & q_3(0) = q_8(3) = 18 \\
q_6(0) = q_8(6) = 21 & q_6(x) = 2x + 21 & q_4(0) = q_6(4) = 29 \\
q_5(0) = q_6(5) = 31
\end{array}
$$

Since there is no polynomial rather than a constant value assigned to a leaf node, leaves 1 to 5 are assigned with 15, 15, 18, 29 and 31 respectively.

2.2 Two Approaches of Attribute Key Generation

Based on the above knowledge about attribute trees, we can use the example illustrated in Fig. 2 to explain the independence between attribute trees and attribute keys in our scheme. Both Alice and Bob want to be authenticated by the authenticator in the example. In Type 1, Alice's attribute keys are generated based on relation A and Bob's attribute keys are generated based on relation B. Both of them possess the required attribute set I otherwise they will never have the chance to be authenticated. However, since B's attribute keys are generated based on relation B rather than the required A, only Alice will be successfully authenticated.

In Type 2, A and B are attribute sets owned by Alice and Bob and their attribute keys are generated based on these sets. In this case, the authentication attribute requirements are represented by structure T. Assume $T(A) = 1$ and $T(B) = 0$, meaning that attribute set A satisfies structure T while B does not. Therefore, Alice will pass the authentication while Bob will fail. In our proposed scheme, we will apply the key generation approach described in Type 2.

2.3 The Construction of the Proposed Scheme

Our proposed scheme is based on pairings [3]. First of all, we define bilinear maps, DLP, q-SDH and DeLP as follows.

Definition 1. *[20] **(Bilinear Maps)** Let G, G_1 be cyclic (multiplicative) groups of prime order p, with $g \in G$ as the generator. Then $e : G \times G \to G_1$ is a bilinear map if it has the following properties:*
- *Bilinearity: for all $u, v \in G$ and $a, b \in \mathbb{Z}_p^*$, $e(u^a, v^b) = e(u, v)^{ab}$.*
- *Nondegeneracy: $e(g, g) \neq 1$.*

Definition 2. ***Discrete Logarithm Problem (DLP) in*** G *Let G be a cyclic group of prime order p with $g \in G$ as its generator. Given $h = g^k$, computing $k = \log_g h$ is considered as a discrete logarithm problem.*

Definition 3. *[21] **(q-Strong Diffie-Hellman Problem (q-SDH) in G)** Let G be a cyclic group of prime order p with $g \in G$ as its generator. Given input $(g, g^x, g^{x^2}, \cdots, g^{x^q}) \in G$, outputting a pair $(x_i, g^{1/(x+x_i)})$ where $x_i \in \mathbb{Z}_p^*$ is considered as a q-SDH problem.*

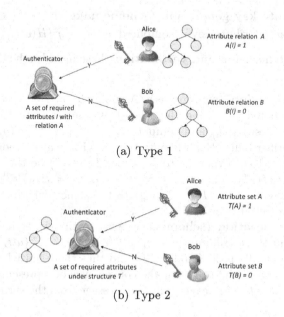

(a) Type 1

(b) Type 2

Fig. 2. Two types of ABA schemes

Definition 4. *[4, 14] (Decision Linear Diffie-Hellman Problem (DeLP) in G) Let G be a cyclic group of prime order p, with $u, v, h \in G$ as its generators. Given $u^a, v^b, h^c \in G$ $(a, b, c \in \mathbb{Z}_p^*)$ as the input, deciding whether $a + b = c$ or not is considered as a DeLP problem.*

System setup phase includes four algorithms as follows.

1) **System parameter generation (scheme.spg)** Assume k is the security parameter, G and G_1 are two multiplicative groups of prime order p with g and g_1 as their generators respectively. $e : G \times G \to G_1$ is a bilinear mapping. Assume DeLP and q-SDH is hard to solve in G. DLP is hard to solve in both G and G_1. $H_K : \{0, 1\}^* \to \mathbb{Z}_p^*$ is a keyed one way hash function. Select $h \in G$ and $\xi_1, \xi_2 \in \mathbb{Z}_p^*$. Set $u, v \in G$ such that $u^{\xi_1} = v^{\xi_2} = h$. Select $x_0 \in \mathbb{Z}_p^*$ as the top secret. The system public and private key sets are $S_{pk} =< G, G_1, g, g_1, h, u, v, w_0 = g^{x_0} >$ and $S_{sk} =< x_0, \xi_1, \xi_2 >$ respectively. The pair $tk =< \xi_1, \xi_2 >$ is used as the tracing key.

2) **Attribute key generation (scheme.akg)** Assume the system attribute set is $\Psi = \{att_1, \cdots, att_m\}$, where m is the size of Ψ. For att_j, randomly select a value $t_j \in \mathbb{Z}_p^*$ and compute $Apk_j = g^{t_j}$. The system public and private attribute key sets are $S_{Apk} =< g^{t_1}, \cdots, g^{t_m} >$ and $S_{Ask} =< t_1, \cdots, t_m >$ respectively.

3) **User key generation (scheme.ukg)** Suppose the system user set is $U =< U_1, \cdots, U_n >$ $(n = |U|)$. For each user U_i $(1 \le i \le n)$, randomly select $x_i \in \mathbb{Z}_p^*$ and compute $A_i = g^{1/(x_0 + x_i)}$. In a traceable ABA system, A_i should be registered in the opener's database.

4) **User attribute key generation (scheme.uakg)** For $att_{i_j} \in \Psi$ owned by U_i, U_i's private attribute key is computed as $T_{i_j} = g^{x_i} H(att_{i_j})^{t_{i_j}}$.

Signature generation and verification phase includes the following algorithms.

1) **Attribute selection (scheme.as)**: Assume the attribute set the verifier requires is denoted as Ψ' and the related attribute tree is Γ'. The verifier randomly chooses $\alpha \in \mathbb{Z}_p^*$ and compute $K_v = e(g, w_0)^\alpha = e(g, g)^{\alpha x_0}$. Based on Ψ', the verifier builds the attribute tree Γ' with r' as its root as described in Subsection 2.1 such that $q_{r'}(0) = \alpha$. Let $Leaf(\Gamma')$ be the leaf set of Γ'. For all $y \in Leaf(\Gamma')$, compute $C_y = g^{q_y(0)}$ and $C_y' = H(y)^{q_y(0)}$. The verifier sends $\{\Gamma', g^\alpha, \forall y \in Leaf(\Gamma') : C_y, C_y'\}$ to the signer, where $\forall y \in Leaf(\Gamma')$ represents every leaf node of Γ'.

2) **Signature generation (scheme.sg)**: Assume the signer has all required attributes and the attribute set is $\Psi_i \supset \Psi'$, where $\Psi_i = \{att_{i_1}, \cdots, att_{i_m}\}$. Since y is the attribute leaf node in Γ' and thus there must be an attribute $att_{i_j} \in \Psi_i$ corresponding to it. For the convenience of representation, we will use y instead of att_{i_j}. After receiving the message from the verifier, the signer calculates

$$DecryptNode(T_{i_j}, C_y, C_y', y) = \frac{e(T_{i_j}, C_y)}{e(Apk_j, C_y')} = e(g, g)^{x_i q_y(0)}.$$

If x is an interior node, then $DecryptNode$ proceeds as follows: for all x'
children z, $DecryptNode$ is called and the output is stored as F_z. Assume S_x
is the subset of all x's children z belonging to Ψ_i and define $\Delta_{S_x, index(z)} =$
$\prod_{l \in \{S_x - index(x)\}} \frac{l}{index(z) - l}$. Then

$$F_x = \prod_{z \in S_x} F_z^{q_z(0)\Delta_{S_x, index(z)}} = \prod_{z \in S_x} (e(g,g)^{x_i q_z(0)})^{\Delta_{S_x, index(z)}}$$

$$= \prod_{z \in S_x} (e(g,g)^{x_i q_{parent(z)}(index(z))})^{\Delta_{S_x, index(z)}} = e(g,g)^{x_i q_x(0)}.$$

The signer calls $DecryptNode$ for the root and gets the result $F_{r'} = e(g,g)^{\alpha x_i}$. Then it computes $K_s = e(A_i^{-1}, g^\alpha)/F_{r'} = e(g,g)^{x_0 \alpha}$ and uses K_s to in signature generation later. Then the signer randomly selects $\zeta, \alpha, \beta, r_\zeta, r_\alpha, r_\beta, r_x, r_{\delta_1}, r_{\delta_2} \in \mathbb{Z}_p^*$ and calculates

$$C_1 = u^\zeta, C_2 = v^\beta, C_3 = A_i h^{\zeta + \beta}, \delta_1 = x_i \zeta, \delta_2 = x_i \beta,$$
$$R_1 = u^{r_\zeta}, R_2 = v^{r_\beta}, R_4 = C_1^{r_x} u^{-r_{\delta_1}}, R_5 = C_2^{r_x} v^{-r_{\delta_2}},$$
$$R_3 = e(C_3, g)^{r_x} e(h, w_0)^{-r_\zeta - r_\beta} e(h, g)^{-r_{\delta_1} - r_{\delta_2}},$$
$$c = H_{K_s}(M, C_1, C_2, C_3, R_1, R_2, R_3, R_4, R_5) \in \mathbb{Z}_p^*$$
$$s_\zeta = r_\zeta + c\zeta, s_\beta = r_\beta + c\beta, s_\alpha = r_\alpha + c\alpha,$$
$$s_x = r_x + cx_i, s_{\delta_1} = r_{\delta_1} + c\delta_1, s_{\delta_2} = r_{\delta_2} + c\delta_2.$$

Finally, the signer sends the signature $\sigma =< M, C_1, C_2, C_3, c, s_\zeta, s_\beta, s_\alpha, s_{\delta_1}, s_{\delta_2} >$ to the verifier.

3) **Signature verification (scheme.sv)**: After receiving σ, the verifier computes

$$R_1' = u^{s_\zeta} C_1^{-c}, R_2' = v^{s_\beta} C_2^{-c}, R_4' = u^{-s_{\delta_1}} C_1^{s_x}, R_5' = v^{-s_{\delta_2}} C_2^{s_x},$$
$$R_3' = e(C_3, g)^{s_x} e(h, w_0)^{-s_\zeta - s_\beta} e(h, g)^{-s_{\delta_1} - s_{\delta_2}} \left(\frac{e(C_3, w_0)}{e(g, g)}\right)^c.$$

Finally, it checks whether $c = H_{K_v}(M, C_1, C_2, C_3, R_1', R_2', R_3', R_4', R_5')$ holds. If so, the verifier believes that the signer owns the required attributes and accepts the signature, otherwise rejects it. In the above algorithm, the verification of the signer's attributes is realized by the security of the keyed one way hash function.

Signature opening (scheme.so) The opener uses its tracing key $\{\varepsilon_1, \varepsilon_2\}$ to compute $A_i = C_3/(C_1^{\varepsilon_1} C_2^{\varepsilon_2})$.

From the above descriptions, we can see that attribute keys generated in this scheme are merely based on attribute sets without any limitations from relations among the attributes, which provides the probability of generating fresh attribute trees for each authentication. In addition, the use of a keyed hash function has voided computing and including a length of $|\Psi'|$ attribute related parameters in the signature [14].

3   Analysis of the Scheme

We analyze the correctness, security and efficiency in Subsections 3.1, 3.3 and 3.4 respectively in this section.

3.1   Correctness Analysis

Theorem 1. *(Correctness) The construction of the proposed traceable ABA scheme proposed in Subsection 2.3 is correct, which means:*

1) $K_v = K_s$.
2) $A_i = C_3/(C_1^{\varepsilon_1} C_2^{\varepsilon_2})$ holds.
3) $R_i = R'_i$, where $1 \le i \le 5$.

Proof. 1) From the algorithm description, we know that $K_v = e(g,g)^{x_0 \alpha}$. As long as the signer has the required attributes described in attribute tree Γ', it can compute K_s which also equals to $e(g,g)^{x_0 \alpha}$.
2) $C_3/(C_1^{\varepsilon_1} C_2^{\varepsilon_2}) = A_i h^{\varsigma+\beta}/((u^\varsigma)^{\varepsilon_1}(v^\beta)^{\varepsilon_2}) = A_i$.
3) R'_i $(1 \le i \le 5)$ are calculated as follows:

$$
\begin{aligned}
R'_1 &= u^{s_\varsigma} C_1^{-c} = u^{r_\varsigma + c\varsigma}(u^\varsigma)^{-c} = R_1 \\
R'_2 &= v^{s_\beta} C_2^{-c} = v^{r_\beta + c\beta}(v^\beta)^{-c} = R_2 \\
R'_3 &= e(C_3,g)^{s_x} e(h,w_0)^{-s_\alpha - s_\beta} e(h,g)^{-s_{\delta_1} - s_{\delta_2}} \left(\frac{e(C_3, w_0)}{e(g,g)} \right)^c \\
&= R_3 \left(e(C_3,g)^{x_i} e(h,w_0)^{-(\alpha+\beta)} e(h,g)^{-(\delta_1+\delta_2)} \frac{e(C_3, w_0)}{e(g,g)} \right)^c \\
&= R_3 \left(e(C_3 h^{-(\alpha+\beta)}, w_0 g^{x_i}) e(C_3, w_0)^{-1} \frac{e(C_3, w_0)}{e(g,g)} \right)^c \\
&= R_3 \left(e(A_i, w_0 g^{x_i})(g,g)^{-1} \right)^c = R_3 \\
R'_4 &= u^{-s_{\delta_1}} C_1^{s_x} = u^{-r_{\delta_1} - c\delta_1}(u^\varsigma)^{r_x + cx_i} \\
&= u^{-r_{\delta_1} - c\varsigma x_i}(u^\varsigma)^{r_x + cx_i} = C_1^{r_x} u^{-r_{\delta_1}} = R_4 \\
R'_5 &= v^{-s_{\delta_2}} C_2^{s_x} = v^{-r_{\delta_2} - c\delta_2}(v^\beta)^{r_x + cx_i} \\
&= v^{-r_{\delta_2} - c\beta x_i}(v^\beta)^{r_x + cx_i} = C_2^{r_x} v^{-r_{\delta_2}} = R_5
\end{aligned}
$$

3.2   Adversary Model

Before the security analysis, we first introduce the adversary model and its abilities based on the random oracle model [10,13] and we use **.Oracle** as suffix to represent the following oracles.

- **Syspara.Oracle**: An adversary can query this oracle about the tracing key tk generated by algorithm scheme.spg.
- **Userkey.Oracle**: An adversary can query this oracle about a user U_i's private key base bsk_i by sending the index i.

- **Attkey.Oracle**: An adversary can send an attribute $att_j \in \Psi$ ($1 \leq j \leq N_a$) to query the system private attribute key ask_j.
- **UserAttkey.Oracle**: An adversary can send the index i of U_i and $att_j \in \Psi$ to query attribute key $T_{i,j}$ and the oracle replies with $T_{i,j}$.
- **Signature.Oracle**: This oracle allows an adversary to obtain a user's signature. The adversary sends message M, the index i of user U_i and the required attribute set Ψ' to the signature oracle and will be replied with a valid signature δ based on $\{M, i, \Psi'\}$.
- **Opening.Oracle**: This oracle allows an adversary to obtain the signer's index i by sending $\{M, \delta, \Psi'\}$.

Assume A is an adversary with polynomial bounded computation abilities [2] and he has access to all public parameters. To formally define the security notions of anonymity and traceability, we first introduce games named as "Game.Anonymity" and "Game.Traceability".

Game.Anonymity includes the following steps:

- **System setup**: The system setup should be completed in this step.
- **Phase 1**: In this phase, the adversary A is allowed to query all oracles described above except for Syspara.Oracle.
- **Challenge**: A selects two indexes i_0 and i_1, a message M together with a selected attribute set Ψ', and then sends them to the system. The system replies with δ_b which is the signature generated based on $\{i_b, M, \Psi'\}$ ($b \in \{0,1\}$). One thing to notice that this challenge should not have been queried before.
- **Phase 2**: The adversary A performs the same as described in phase 1 but A is not allowed to query about the challenge described above.
- **Guess**: The adversary A output its guess $b' \in \{0,1\}$. If b equals to b', A wins the game. Otherwise, A fails.

Game.Traceability includes the following steps:

- **System setup**: The system setup should be completed in this step.
- **Phase 1**: In this phase, the adversary A is allowed to query all oracles described above.
- **Challenge**: The adversary decides to challenge now. It chooses the attribute requirement Ψ' and message M to be singed.
- **Phase 2** The adversary A repeats phase 1, but A cannot query about the challenge.
- **Output**: The adversary forges a valid signature δ and sends it to the opener. The opener opens the signature δ and gets the signer's index i'. If $U_{i'}$ is not registered in the system, the opener outputs 1 and A wins the game. Otherwise A fails.

Based on the above two games, now we can define the security notions of anonymity and traceability as Definitions 5 and 6.

Definition 5. (Anonymity) *Assume A is an adversary with polynomially bounded computational abilities. If the probability that A wins the game "Game.Anonymity" is negligible, the proposed scheme provides anonymity.*

Definition 6. (Traceability) *Assume A is an adversary with polynomially bounded computational abilities. If the probability that A wins the game "Game.Traceability" is negligible, the proposed scheme provides traceability.*

3.3   Security Analysis

Before proving security requirements that the proposed ABA scheme satisfies, we first describe some assumptions that will be used in the proof.

Definition 7. *[21]* **(Decision Linear Diffie-Hellman based Encryption (DLE) in G)** *In a DLE scheme, a user's public key is $u, v, h \in G$ and its private key is $\varepsilon_1, \varepsilon_2 \in \mathbb{Z}_p^*$, satisfying $u^{\varepsilon_1} = v^{\varepsilon_2} = h$. To encrypt message M, the user randomly chooses $\alpha, \beta \in \mathbb{Z}_p^*$ and computes the encryption message as a triple $< C_1, C_2, C_3 >$, where $C_1 = u^\alpha$, $C_2 = v^\beta$ and $C_3 = Mh^{\alpha+\beta}$. The decrypted message can be formed as $C_3/(C_1^{\varepsilon_1} C_2^{\varepsilon_2})$.*

Assumption 1. *[14, 21]* **(DeLP)** *Given the DeLP defined in Definition 4. for an algorithm A, if $|Pr[A(u^\alpha, v^\beta, h^{\alpha+\beta}) = (u^\alpha, v^\beta, h^c)] - 1/|G|| \leq \varepsilon$ holds, we say that A has a negligible advantage to solve DeLP in G and then we can assume DeLP is hard.*

Assumption 2. (IND-CPA Security) *[4] If DeLP holds, we say that DLE is semantically secure against a chosen-plaintext attack (CPA) or IND-CPA secure.*

Theorem 2. (Anonymity) *The proposed ABA scheme is fully anonymous if DLE is IND-CPA secure under the same attribute set. More specifically, given $A_{i(b)}$ with their corresponding signatures $\sigma_b = < M, C_1, C_2, C_{3(b)}, c, s_\zeta, s_\beta, s_\alpha, s_{\delta_1}, s_{\delta_2} > (b \in \{0,1\})$. Given a random toss $b \in \{0,1\}$, if an adversary A with polynomial computation ability has a non-negligible advantage to guess the correct b, we say that the proposed scheme is not fully anonymous. Otherwise, the scheme is fully anonymous.*

Proof. If adversary A can break the anonymity of the proposed scheme, A should have a non-negligible advantage to guess the correct b in the above statement. Given $A_{i(0)}$ and $A_{i(1)}$, one of which is the real signer's key, the adversary A has a non-negligible advantage to differentiate two signatures σ_0 and σ_1 which are related to $A_{i(0)}$ and $A_{i(1)}$ respectively. Therefore, A can distinguish the tuple $< C_1, C_2, C_{3(0)} >$ from the tuple $< C_1, C_2, C_{3(1)} >$ with non-negligible advantage. From the construction of the proposed scheme and Definition 7, we know that $< C_1, C_2, C_3 >$ can be considered as a DLE scheme with A_i as the message to be encrypted. According to Assumption 2, we know that $< C_1, C_2, C_3 >$ is IND-CPA secure. However, A can distinguish the tuple $< C_1, C_2, C_{3(0)} >$ from the tuple $< C_1, C_2, C_{3(1)} >$ with non-negligible advantage. It contradicts to Assumption 2. Therefore, the proposed scheme is fully anonymous.

Theorem 3. *(Traceability) As long as the keyed one way hash function H is collision resistant, the proposed ABA scheme is fully traceable if (1) given a valid signature $\sigma =< M, C_1, C_2, C_3, c, s_\zeta, s_\beta, s_\alpha, s_{\delta_1}, s_{\delta_2} >$, the opener can trace the identity of the signer and (2) an adversary A cannot forge a valid signature σ'.*

Proof. We first prove statement (1). According to the correctness analysis, we know (1) can be proven. Next we prove statement (2). It can be divided into two situations: a) the adversary uses $\{M, C_1, C_2, C_3, c, s_\zeta, s_\beta, s_\alpha, s_{\delta_1}, s_{\delta_2}\}$ to generate c to obtain the same signature σ; b) the adversary uses a different tuple $\{M', C_1', C_2', C_3', c', s_\zeta', s_\beta', s_\alpha', s_{\delta_1}', s_{\delta_2}'\}$ to generate a valid but different signature σ'. For situation a), the adversary needs the right K_v or K_s. Since DLP is hard to solve in G, the adversary cannot compute α from g^α, and therefore it cannot compute K_v via $e(g, g^{x_0})^\alpha$. The only way left is to compute as the signer does. However, from the algorithm described in Subsection 2.3, we can see that without the required attribute keys, it is impossible to recover K_s either. Therefore, it is impossible for A to generate the same signature σ. For situation b), without knowing the shared secret key K_v or K_s and given the security of the one way hash function, it is also out of the ability of the adversary A.

3.4 Efficiency Analysis

To our best knowledge, only the ABA schemes proposed in [14] and [21] are traceable, so we will only compare our schemes with them. The efficiency comparison focuses on computation complexity, storage and communication costs. For simplicity, we only assess the cost in one signature generation and verification. Since the scheme proposed [21] is based on a large central attribute tree, the storage cost in our scheme is obvious less considering the size of the attribute tree. The storage size in our paper is almost the same as in [14]. Suppose $|G|$ is the bit size of group, k is the bit size of numbers in $\mathbb{Z}_p^*$ and ρ is the computation cost of pairing. To simplify the comparison, we only count the computation of pairings and we will not include the size of message M or the size of attributes to be used in the signature. The comparison results are shown in Table 1, where [14].1 and [14].2 denote the schemes proposed in Chapters 5.4 and 5.5 in [14] respectively. It is worth noticing that the computation complexity to recover F_{root} is not included in the table because the cost should be the same given the same attribute requirements. From the results in Table 1, we can see that the computation complexity of our scheme is the same as [14].1 and [14].2, and the

Table 1. Computation and Communication Efficiency Comparison of ABA Schemes

Paper	Signature Size	Sign Complexity	Verify Complexity
[14].1	$5k + (|\Psi_i| + 5)|G|$	3ρ	5ρ
[14].2	$5k + 7|G|$	3ρ	5ρ
[21]	$8k + (|\Psi_i| + 4)|G|$	5ρ	9ρ
This paper	$6k + 3|G|$	3ρ	5ρ

signature size is much shorter than schemes proposed in [14].1 and [21] since it does not include parameters related to all required attributes.

4   Conclusions

In this paper, we proposed a traceable ABA scheme. In this scheme, the attribute tree generation is independent from attribute keys, such that the attribute tree can be freshly generated for each signature generation and verification without extra cost in signature size and computation complexity. This property makes our schemes very effective and practical in a dynamic system where the attribute requirements change frequently.

References

1. ABC4Trust. https://abc4trust.eu/
2. Bellare, M., Goldreich, O.: Proving computational ability. In: Goldreich, O. (ed.) Studies in Complexity and Cryptography. LNCS, vol. 6650, pp. 6–12. Springer, Heidelberg (2011)
3. Boneh, D.: Pairing-based cryptography: past, present, and future. In: Wang, X., Sako, K. (eds.) ASIACRYPT 2012. LNCS, vol. 7658, p. 1. Springer, Heidelberg (2012)
4. Boneh, D., Boyen, X., Shacham, H.: Short group signatures. In: Franklin, M. (ed.) CRYPTO 2004. LNCS, vol. 3152, pp. 41–55. Springer, Heidelberg (2004)
5. Camenisch, J., Dubovitskaya, M., Lehmann, A., Neven, G., Paquin, C., Preiss, F.-S.: Concepts and languages for privacy-preserving attribute-based authentication. In: Fischer-Hübner, S., de Leeuw, E., Mitchell, C. (eds.) IDMAN 2013. IFIP AICT, vol. 396, pp. 34–52. Springer, Heidelberg (2013)
6. Cao, D., Zhao, B., Wang, X., Su, J., Chen, Y.: Authenticating with attributes in online social networks. In: 2011 14th International Conference on Network-Based Information Systems (NBiS), pp. 607–611 (2011)
7. Emura, K., Miyaji, A., Omote, K.: A dynamic attribute-based group signature scheme and its application in an anonymous survey for the collection of attribute statistics. In: 2009 International Conference on Availability, Reliability and Security (ARES 2009), pp. 487–492, March 2009
8. Gorantla, M.C., Boyd, C., Nieto, J.M.G.: Attribute-based authenticated key exchange. In: Steinfeld, R., Hawkes, P. (eds.) ACISP 2010. LNCS, vol. 6168, pp. 300–317. Springer, Heidelberg (2010)
9. Goyal, V., Pandey, O., Sahai, A., Waters, B.: Attribute-based encryption for fine-grained access control of encrypted data. In: Proceedings of the 13th ACM Conference on Computer and Communications Security, CCS 2006, pp. 89–98. ACM, New York (2006)
10. Granboulan, L.: Short signatures in the random oracle model. In: Zheng, Y. (ed.) ASIACRYPT 2002. LNCS, vol. 2501, pp. 364–378. Springer, Heidelberg (2002)
11. Horváth, M.: Attribute-based encryption optimized for cloud computing. In: Italiano, G.F., Margaria-Steffen, T., Pokorný, J., Quisquater, J.-J., Wattenhofer, R. (eds.) SOFSEM 2015-Testing. LNCS, vol. 8939, pp. 566–577. Springer, Heidelberg (2015)

12. Rannenberg, K., Camenisch, J., Sabouri, A. (eds.): Attribute-based Credentials for Trust (2015)
13. Katz, J.: The random oracle model. In: Digital Signatures, pp. 135–142. Springer US (2010)
14. Dalia, Khader, D.: Attribute-based Authentication Scheme. Ph.D thesis, University of Bath (2009)
15. Maji, H.K., Prabhakaran, M., Rosulek, M.: Attribute-based signatures. In: Kiayias, A. (ed.) CT-RSA 2011. LNCS, vol. 6558, pp. 376–392. Springer, Heidelberg (2011)
16. Naruse, T., Mohri, M., Shiraishi, Y.: Attribute-based encryption with attribute revocation and grant function using proxy re-encryption and attribute key for updating. In: Park, J.J.J.H., Stojmenovic, I., Choi, M., Xhafa, F. (eds.) Future Information Technology. LNEE, vol. 276, pp. 119–125. Springer, Heidelberg (2014)
17. Sabouri, A., Bjones, R.: Privacy-ABCs to leverage identity management as a service. In: Preneel, B., Ikonomou, D. (eds.) APF 2014. LNCS, vol. 8450, pp. 143–153. Springer, Heidelberg (2014)
18. Sabouri, A., Krontiris, I., Rannenberg, K.: Trust relationships in privacy-ABCs' ecosystems. In: Eckert, C., Katsikas, S.K., Pernul, G. (eds.) TrustBus 2014. LNCS, vol. 8647, pp. 13–23. Springer, Heidelberg (2014)
19. Sabouri, A., Rannenberg, K.: ABC4Trust: protecting privacy in identity management by bringing privacy-ABCs into real-life. In: Camenisch, J., Fischer-Hübner, S., Hansen, M. (eds.) Privacy and Identity 2014. IFIP AICT, vol. 457, pp. 3–16. Springer, Heidelberg (2015)
20. Wan, Z., Liu, J.E., Deng, R.H.: HASBE: A hierarchical attribute-based solution for flexible and scalable access control in cloud computing. IEEE Transactions on Information Forensics and Security **7**(2), 743–754 (2012)
21. Yang, H., Oleshchuk, V.A.: A dynamic attribute-based authentication scheme. In: El Hajji, S., Nitaj, A., Carlet, C., Souidi, E.M. (eds.) Codes, Cryptology, and Information Security. LNCS, vol. 9084, pp. 106–118. Springer, Heidelberg (2015)
22. Zhu, S., Zhan, L., Qiang, H., Fu, D., Sun, W., Tang, Y.: A fuzzy attribute-based authentication scheme on the basis of lagrange polynomial interpolation. In: Zu, Q., Hu, B., Gu, N., Seng, S. (eds.) HCC 2014. LNCS, vol. 8944, pp. 685–692. Springer, Heidelberg (2015)

Trust and Fraud

FIDO Trust Requirements

Ijlal Loutfi[✉] and Audun Jøsang

University of Oslo, Oslo, Norway
ijlall@uio.no, josang@ifi.uio.no

Abstract. FIDO (Fast Identity Online) is a new online identity management architecture, developed and promoted by a large industry consortium. Its goal is to simplify and strengthen online user authentication by relying on local device user authentication. Another goal is to finally put passwords to rest. This solution requires strong trust between players and components in the architecture. These aspects have received little attention from the FIDO consortium. The aim of this paper is to analyze the trust requirements for FIDO, and assess the cost of establishing the required trust.

Keywords: FIDO · Trust · Identity · Passwords · Authentication · Federation

1 Introduction

Nowadays, consuming services online has become an exponentially growing trend within different industries. A robust online identity management solution to these services is a critical requirement for establishing trust between end users and service providers (SP). Within this context, Identity management is defined as the process of representing and recognizing entities as digital identities in computer networks. It includes many security constructs such as authentication, authorization and access control. Authentication, which is the focus of this paper, is an integral part of identity management, as it serves to verify claims about holding specific identities[12]. In todays online ecosystem, the average online end user holds multiple identities with multiple online SPs[10]. Password based authentication methods are by far the most prevalent deployed mechanism. However, their shortcomings are well documented and recognized. As a matter of fact, the rapid growth in the number of online services based on this model now results in the users being overloaded with identifiers and credentials that they need to manage. As a result, end users resort to adopting non secure password habits[20][9]. On the other hand, SPs also fail in protecting the users credentials they have stored on their servers. Early in 2013, the annual Data Breach Investigations Report published by Verizon, stated that approximately 90 percent of successful breaches in 2012 analyzed by Verizon started with a weak or default password, or a stolen and reused credential[13] [20]. For this reason, new identity management models are being proposed and implemented. Their goal is to

S. Buchegger and M. Dam (Eds.): NordSec 2015, LNCS 9417, pp. 139–155, 2015.
DOI: 10.1007/978-3-319-26502-5_10

either minimize the reliance on passwords, or eradicate passwords all together. Identity federation has marked the last decade as being the most prominent new authentication mechanism. However, Fast Identity Online (FIDO), which started in 2012 as an industry consortium, is currently gaining exponential momentum in the market with big identity management players, that can influence the reality of online authentication moving forward [4]. For instance, Microsoft is adopting FIDO2.0 protocols for its upcoming windows10 release [7], Google has already enabled FIDO authentication on its email services, and Samsung has equipped its Samsung galaxy S6 with FIDO compliant hardware [1][3]. FIDO, indeed, holds the promise to solve many of the problems inherent to password based authentication. However, it relies on a completely new architecture which introduces new trust requirements between different players and components. Identifying, understanding and quantifying these trust requirements are crucial in making us aware about what could go wrong while using FIDO, and if these are risks we are willing to incur.

2   Background and Related Work

FIDO came as a response to the shortcomings of the currently implemented identity management (IdM) models. It also build on many of their concepts. Hence, the first part of this section will focus on presenting the architectures of these models. The identity management architectures to be discussed are as follows:

1. Online isolated identity management.
2. Federated isolated identity management.
3. Local device identity management.
4. Fast Identity Online (FIDO).

2.1   Isolated Identity Management

In the simplest case where a set of users access a single SP, the traditional approach is to let users identify themselves through unique identifiers, and authenticate themselves using security credentials such as passwords. What we have here is an isolated IdM model because each identifier that a user possesses can only be used for one isolated service. This model, which is used for all types of access to online services and resources, as well as for digital rights management, is relatively simple for SPs [15]. In this architecture, online SPs act as both a credential provider and an identifier provider to their clients. They control the name space for a specific service domain, and allocate identifiers to users. A user gets separate unique identifiers from each service/identifier provider he transacts with. In addition, each user will have separate credentials, such as passwords associated with each of their identifiers. This is illustrated in Fig. 1.

This approach might provide simple IdM from the SP point of view, but is problematic for users, as the number of SPs that they transact with increases. Users are

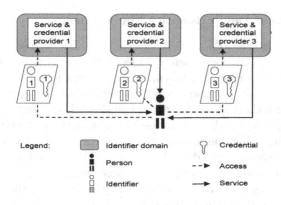

Fig. 1. Isolated Online Identity Management

faced with the daunting task of properly managing a large number of passwords. This has led to very inappropriate password behavior which compomises the security of end users (weak passwords, repeated passwords) [15] [11] [18].

Because of all the above, academia and industry alike have been working on alleviating the inherent problems of password based methods. One such approach evolved from the idea that we need to move away from a siloed isolated model, into a federated model. The latter would allow users to minimize the number of credentials they need to manage. Thanks to the ever more increasing adoption of social networks, federated IdM solutions have strongly impacted the commercial end user online IdM scene over the last decade, after having been confined to enterprise perimeters.

2.2   Federated Online Identity Management Solution

One of the purposes of identity federation is to address the type of inefficiencies described above. Identity federation can be defined in this context, as the set of agreements, standards and technologies that enable a group of SP to recognize user identifiers and entitlements from other SPs within the group. The basic idea is to link different identifiers, and thereby their associated identities, owned by the same user across multiple SPs. Then, allow the user to authentication himself with a single identifier to one of the service providers, and thereby be considered identified and authenticated by all the other SPs as well.The isolated identifier domains within a federated group becomes a single federated identifier domain [15]. This approach is illustrated in Fig. 2.

Identity federation comes in many variations but is typically based on the SAML1 standard which is implemented in applications such as Shibboleth,and FacebookConnect. However, Identity federation does not fundamentally solve the problem of identity overload. There will always be different federation domains, because not all SPs will merge their respective user identity domains into a single federated domain [16].

2.3   Local Owner Device Identity Management

While the two previous IdM models focused on online authentication, we will shift our focus now into local owner device authentication (referred to in the rest of the paper as user device authentication). Over the last decade, networked computing devices have become a common commodity. The global smartphone audience surpassed the 1,75 billion mark in 2014, while the number of computers is still increasing despite the saturation of many developed markets. Furthermore, we are witnessing the emergence of Internet of things where more and more devices are entering the digital world [16]. This trend has been facilitated by the decreasing costs of production of these devices. Numerous interesting aspects of computing have been challenged by this trend. In the context of this paper, the question that is most relevant to us is: How can end users identify themselves to their local devices?

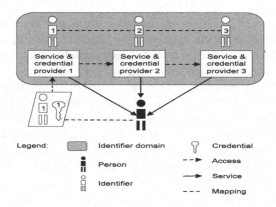

Fig. 2. Federated Online Identity Management

The answer to this question has long been simple: username,password pair. However, numerous alternate authentication mechanisms such as biometrics (fingerprint, iris) and TPMs are finding their place in user device authentication.

This is mainly due to two factors: the advancements made in the implementation of these new mechanisms. Also, its user acceptance is largely thanks to the fact that user device authentication happens locally, and does not require the disclosure of any sensitive information (e.g.: biometrics) to third party SPs. The market currently shows a growing trend in which users have accepted and embraced alternate authentication mechanisms for their local device authentication [6].

2.4   Fast Identity Online: FIDO

FIDO Philosophy: In July 2012, the FIDO alliance became a 501(c)6 non-prot organization. Its core idea relies on the following: leveraging local user device authentication for online user authentication. In a *Non FIDO scenario*, Bob would swipe his fingerprint into his mobile phone so as to authenticate himself to the device as his owner. He would then select the mobile application of the SP of his interest (e.g.: mybank), and use the corresponding online authentication mechanism (username and password) in order to start his transactions with his bank. In this scenario, Bob's local user (owner) device authentication, and his online authentication are two separate processes

On the other hand, in a *FIDO scenario*, Bob would have a different experience. In order to start his online transactions with his online bank, he would not be required to enter any username,password pair. Bob would only have to swipe his finger print, for example, into his smartphone, while being on the authentication page on the mobile application for his online bank. What is even more interesting in this new FIDO enabled scenario, is that from Bob's perspective, the authentication experience would be the same independently of the SP he is interacting with. If Bob wants to connect into his Facebook account, all he would have to do is open the Facebook mobile application and swipe his finger again into his smartphone. In this scenario, Bob's local user (owner) device authentication has become part of his online authentication, as illustrated in Fig. 3.(refer to section 2.4 for more details about the FIDO architecture).

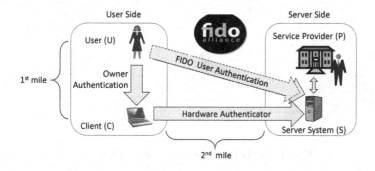

Fig. 3. FIDO Authentication: High Level Overview

First Mile Authentication: Figure 3 above introduces the concept of *hardware authentication* (hardware and authenticator will be used interchangeably). It is expected that users will acquire FIDO Authenticators in various ways: they purchase a new system that comes with an embedded FIDO Authenticator capability; they purchase a device with an embedded FIDO Authenticator, or they are given a FIDO Authenticator by their employer or some other institution such as their bank. After receiving a FIDO Authenticator, the user must go through an authenticator-specific enrollment process. For example, the user must register their fingerprint(s) with the authenticator. Once enrollment is complete, the

FIDO Authenticator is ready for registration with FIDO enabled online services and websites. Every time Bob wants to authenticate to an online SP, his *first mile* would be to authenticate himself to his FIDO device [5].

Second Mile Authentication: The first mile authentication required the interaction of Bob with his FIDO device/authenticator. However, the second mile authentication will be transparent to Bob, not requiring him to further interact with his device nor with the SP. After the completion of the first mile authentication (Bob authenticating to the his FIDO device), the authenticator can attest to its identity to online SPs, on behalf of Bob. This is achieved by relying on asymmetric public key cryptographic exchange.

FIDO User Authentication: Finally, after the completion of the second mile authentication, the SP will authenticate Bob to his service, if the key exchange was successful.Figure 4 below is a high level summary of the both the FIDO registration and authentication message flow.

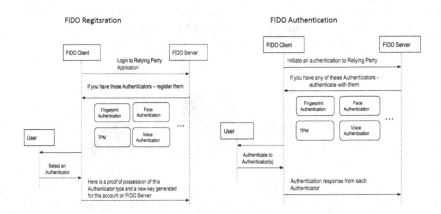

Fig. 4. FIDO Registration Message Flow

The Concept of FIDO Authenticator: At the heart of FIDO protocols, lies the concept of the authenticator. A FIDO Authenticator is a secure entity, connected to or housed within FIDO user devices, that can create key material associated to a SP. The key can then be used to participate in FIDO strong authentication protocols. For example, the FIDO Authenticator can provide a response to a cryptographic challenge using the key material. A FIDO authenticator can be implemented within the user space or completely separate from it. It is up to every SP to decide on the level of risk it wants to incur, and hence, the type of authenticators it allows its end users to use [5]. Some examples of authenticators are: a fingerprint sensor built into a mobile device, a PIN authenticator implemented inside a secure element, a USB token with built-in user presence verification, a voice or face verification technology built into a device.

FIDO authenticators' implementation are very varied. Each SP has the choice to accept users with using a specific type of authenticators (e.g.: only accept fingerprint readers that store the finger print and cryptographic keys in a secure element, and that are manufactured by hardware manufacturer xyz). Hence, in order to meet the goal of simplifying the integration of trusted authentication capabilities, a FIDO Authenticator will be able to attest to its particular type (e.g., biometric) and capabilities (e.g., supported crypto algorithms), as well as to its provenance. This provides SPs with a high degree of confidence that the user being authenticated is indeed the user that originally registered with the site [5].

So as to be able to perform the cryptographic operations defined in FIDO protocols, a FIDO authenticator needs to have some type of attestation mechanism. This is achieved through the key structure as illustrated in Figure 5:

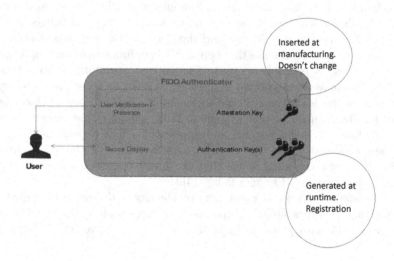

Fig. 5. FIDO Authenticator

The attestation key is used by an authenticator in order to attest to its type and provenance to the SP. FIDO Authenticators are created with attestation private keys used to create the signatures. FIDO SPs validate the signature using the corresponding authenticator's attestation public key certificate located in the authenticator metadata. The metadata holding attestation certificates is shared with FIDO Servers out of band [5].

Authentication keys: Every time a user wants to register with a new SP, the authenticator generates a new private/public key pair called authentication key pair. This key pair is unique for every combination of (end user, SP, authenticator). The authenticator stores the authentication private key. The corresponding authentication public key is communicated to the SP. After the successful completion of the registration process, the authenticator performs a challenge response exchange with the SP using the authentication keys, every time a new authentication in required.

FIDO Architecture: Figure 6 pulls all of the above FIDO concepts together, by showing a detailed architecture of both the client side and the server side of FIDO protocols.

2.5 Online Identity Management Trust Requirements

Now that we have introduced all the main IdM architectures, we will look at the extent to which their trust requirements have been studied and analyzed.

The Concept of Trust: Trust is typically interpreted as a subjective belief in the reliability, honesty and security of an entity on which we depend for our welfare. In online environments we depend on a wide specter of things, ranging from computer hardware, software and data, to people and organizations. A security solution always assumes that certain entities function according to specic policies. To trust is precisely to make this sort of assumptions, so a trusted entity is the same as an entity that is assumed to function according to policy. A consequence of this is that a trusted component of a system must work correctly in order for the security of that system to hold, meaning that when a trusted component fails, then the systems and applications that depend on it can no longer be considered secure. An often cited articulation of this principle is: a trusted system or component is one that can break your security policy (which happens when the trusted system fails) [14].[19].

The transfer of the social constructs of identity and trust into digital and computational concepts help in implementing large scale online markets and communities, and also plays an important role in the converging mobile and

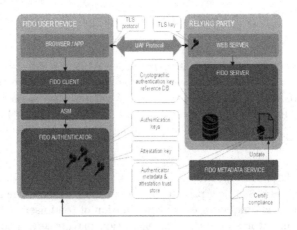

Fig. 6. FIDO Architecture

Internet environments. IdM (denoted IdM hereafter) is about recognizing and verifying the correctness of identities in online environments. Trust management becomes a component of IdM whenever different parties rely on each other for identity provision and authentication[14].

3   Trust Requirements Analysis

While the focus of this paper is on FIDO, we believe that an accurate understanding of its trust requirements cannot be achieved by analyzing them in isolation. They need to be compared and evaluated against the trust requirements of the other existing IdM solutions: isolated, federated. Hereby, we will be presenting in this section the trust requirements of all of the previously presently online IdM solutions, with a special focus on FIDO. Subsequently, we will discuss the implications of the varying trust requirements inherent to each solution.

3.1   Trust Requirements of Isolated Online Identity Management

In this architecture, the trust requirements between users and SPs are well understood in the form of specific security and privacy assumptions. In addition, the industry has had several decades of experience with this model, and users are familiar with it.

Trust complexity is greatly simplified when the same entity acts as identifier provider, credentials provider and SP. Under these conditions, the client and SP only need to trust each other for a small set of purposes [15]. Indeed, most of the trust requirements fall under one of the two categories:

Client Trust in Service Providers:

1. The service provider has the expected identity.
2. The service provider protects client privacy.
3. The service provider has implemented satisfactory user registration procedures and authentication mechanisms (from the clients perspective).

Service Provider Trust in Client:

1. The client handles their authentication credentials with adequate care.

3.2   Trust Requirements of Federated Online Identity Management

While identity federation is aimed at simplifying the user experience, it increases trust complexity both for the SPs and their clients. These trust requirements can be classified as follows [15]:

1. Trust between Federated Service.
   (a) Service access by assertions between SPs on behalf of users will only take place when legitimately requested by the client.
2. Trust in the Identity Mapping.
   (a) The mapping of identities between service providers is correct.
3. Client Trust in Service Providers.
   (a) The service provider adheres to the accepted policy for correlating personal data about the same client from other service providers.

3.3   Trust Requirements of FIDO

Given that FIDO is mainly an industry led initiative, and that its final protocols have only been released recently, we found no existing studies to its trust
requirements. As far as our knowledge goes, this study will be the first one to provide a basis for understanding FIDO trust issues that are seldom talked about.
They will help stakeholders who are joining FIDO better understand what can
go wrong with FIDO in real life. It will also help them understand the hidden
trust agreements they implicitly consent to, once they consent to using FIDO.
We arrived to these results by thoroughly studying FIDO protocols [5] and its
security reference[6] [2],then analyzing them against the claims put forward by
the FIDO consortium in its official release[5].

In order to provide a simple view for our FIDO trust requirements results,
we classified every single trust requirement under one of these categories:

1. Trust in FIDO consortium.
2. Trust in service providers.
3. Trust in hardware manufacturer.
4. Trust local device computing platform.
5. Trust in end users.
6. Trust in FIDO protocols.

3.4   Trust in FIDO Consortium

The FIDO consortium presents itself as an enabler for the promotion and education about FIDO open protocols. However, it is responsible for certifying the
hardware manufacturers. It also ensures that the right metadata and root certificates are being trusted. These tasks are detrimental to the overall trust of
FIDO as an IdM solution.

In this context, certification refers to the FIDO program that allows members and non-members to measure compliance and ensure interoperability among
products and services that support FIDO specifications. Companies completing
certification may display the FIDO Certified logo to demonstrate to consumers,
customers and partners that they have created a high-quality, interoperable
FIDO implementation that is known to work with other FIDO implementations. In the case of a FIDO authenticator that is certified, it will be characterized by a set of metadata information. This metadata is associated with an
AAID (Authenticator Attestation ID) and available from the FIDO Alliance.
FIDO Servers are expected to have access to up-to-date metadata to be able
to interact with a given authenticator. AAID is defined as a unique identifier
assigned to a model, class or batch of FIDO Authenticators that all share the
same characteristics, and which a SP can use to look up an Attestation Public
Key and Authenticator Metadata for the device. Finally, FIDO alliance needs to
explicitly trust a root certificate to which all authenticator attestation Certificates chain to, and that will be relied on by the SPs to assert to the validity of
the provided attestation certificates, and hence the metadata associated with it
[5] [6] [2]. The above process already introduces a number of trust requirements:

T1: *Trust that the FIDO consortium has identified the right set of metadata characteristics that are sufficient to identifying authenticators in ways that are meaningful to SPs to accept or reject them.*

T2: *Trust that the certification is still meaningful throughout the time it is valid.*

T3: *Trust that the FIDO consortium is able to detect and report authenticators breaching the metadata characteristics declared in their certification process, and update the metadata store accordingly.*

T4: *Trust in the validity of the FIDO PKI used (root certificate, attestation certificates).*

3.5   Trust in Service Providers

In the previous section, we have discussed how FIDO consortium is responsible for updating the content of the metadata. In this section, we will investigate how SPs make use of the attestation PKI as well as the authenticators metadata store. Indeed, SPs have the right to enforce policies about the type of authenticators they want their users to use while consuming their services. It achieves thit through the use of an authentication policy. The latter is defined as a JSON data structure that allows a SP to communicate to a FIDO Client the capabilities or specific authenticators that are allowed or disallowed for use in a given operation. The client then responds with an attestation certificate serving as a claim that it possesses an authenticator that is compliant with the policy. It is then the responsibility of the SP to ensure how genuine this claim is, by using information in his metadata store. The latter should always be in sync with the central FIDO metadata store that is supposed to hold the latest updates about all authenticators [5] [6] [2]. The above process introduces two new trust requirements:

T5: *Trust that the SP is able to correctly assess the risk level associated with the usage of his service by all his users.*

The above risk assessment directly influences the service provider's choice of the allowed authenticators, and hence how the authentication policy is defined. If the risk is estimated too high or too low, this will steer away consumers.

T6: *Trust that the SP establishes the appropriate network connection while updating the metadata store.*

3.6   Trust in Hardware Manufacturers

The architecture of FIDO has brought hardware manufacturers into prominence in the IdM trust requirements discussion. In all previous IdM models, hardware manufacturers did not incur any significant trust requirements nor liability. However, in the context of FIDO, hardware manufacturers have central responsibilities. For instance:

1. Manufacturing the hardware that is used as an authenticator for FIDO. The user owner local device authentication is the first step in the new FIDO authentication process.

2. Providing cryptographic evidence to the SP attesting to the type and provenance of the authenticator.

Furthermore, a main tenant of the FIDO privacy-by-design premise is hardware related. On one hand, as discussed in TR4, TR5, and TR6, FIDO protocols provide a mechanism for SPs to get information about the type of the and provenance of the authenticator being used. This is mainly achieved through the attestation certificate. However, this poses the risk of exposing the privacy of users, in the case that their authenticators can be identified individually by SPs. In order to resolve this issue, FIDO protocols proclaim the following requirement:

UAF authenticators can only be identified by their attestation certificates on a production batch-level or on manufacturer- and device model-level. They cannot be identified individually. The UAF specifications require implementers to ship UAF authenticators with the same attestation certificate and private key in batches of 100,000 or more in order to provide unlinkability [2].

All of these mechanisms introduce the following trust requirements:

T7: *Trust that hardware providers will not unintentionally break the unlinkibality property.*

Due to the recent privacy scandals in which governmental states have been involved, as well as the geopolitical changes the world is witnessing, the IT market tends to be compartmentalized. Indeed, there are a number of states that are wary of buying and using technology of its nonpolitical allies (Russia, china, Korea, USA). Especially at the beginning of FIDO adoption, this might lead the attestation certificate revealing more information than it ought to. This scenario can also happen in the case where specific hardware manufacturers are known to traditionally provide for certain industries (e.g.: military, banking). This risk becomes ever more relevant, with the recent news of the UK and US government entities joining the FIDO alliance[8].

T8: *Trust that hardware providers will not intentionally break the unlinkibality property.*

The FIDO consortium is not responsible for the ongoing testing process of all authenticator units produced by every hardware manufacturer. Furthermore, the metadata part of the metadata store and that are verified by APs during the attestation process, are only a subset of the authenticators characteristics. These facts give the opportunity to an evil hardware manufacturer to omit security relevant characteristics from the metadata characteristics disclosed during the certification process. This hardware manufacturer can then use this as a backdoor into manipulating some individual or entire authenticators, by making them susceptible for releasing private information for instance. As a more dangerous exploit, the hardware manufacturer can manipulate its authenticators into compromising the cryptographic material it stores. The latter scenario leads us into identifying another trust requirement [6].

T9: *Trust that hardware manufacturers will not keep a backdoor in the authenticator, and exploit it to release secret cryptographic information of its users.*

3.7   Local Device Computing Platform

The currently deployed online IdM solutions focus on defining more secure communication protocols between their end points (client, SP server, identity provider server). The question of whether the client computing platform (e.g.: computer, mobile phone) end users use to connect to SPs is compromised or not has been left out from their solutions. However, a number of the attacks that are directed against online IdM solutions do start from a compromised computing platform(a rooted computer, a keylogger, a compromised browser). This kind of threats is not very far fetched. According to PandaLabs estimates, 31.63 percent of the worlds PCs are infected with some sort of malware (Q2 2012) of 78.92 percent are Trojans [17]. This situation makes it so that even with the most carefully designed communication protocol between end points, and the most safely guarded server platform, the password of end users can still be compromised if they are authenticating to their SPs from a compromised device. Hence, one would deduce that any new online IdM solution aiming to improve the strength of its solution would not introduce the clients' computing platform as a component of its architecture. Unfortunately, this idea lies at the core of FIDO's architecture:

1. Besides the user agent (browser, app), FIDO has introduced the concept of the FIDO client. The latter communicates with both the FIDO authenticator and the user agent, and may be implemented in whole or in part within the boundaries of the user agent [6].
2. Furthermore, FIDO supports authenticators that are implemented as part of the computing platform, where secret cryptographic information are allowed be stored on the client's platform user space.

Indeed, while FIDO has introduced the client's computing platform as a main new component in its architecture, its solutions assumes that the client computing platform is not compromised by viruses or Trojans. Unfortunately, the reality could not be further from that as the studies show.

T10: *Trust that the user computing platform is not compromised by malicious software.*

3.8   End Users

The other side of trusting the local user computing platform to not be compromised is to have trust in the user not compromising it:

T11: *Trust the user will not expose his or her device to compromise in infected platforms.*

3.9   FIDO Protocols

FIDO is a very recent protocol. However, it has been interesting to see it gaining ground so rapidly with industry players that have a very large base of customer.

FIDO protocols have received little challenge from the security community. Most of the security reports and guarantees are coming directly from the FIDO consortium itself. In other words, FIDO protocols have not been put to the test of the market yet, decreasing hence the level of trust we can have in their strength. The trust In FIDO protocols can be expressed in two aspects.

T12:*Trust in the security of the protocol design.*

F13:*Trust in the security of the protocol implementation.*

Indeed, on the user computing platform, the FIDO architecture has introduced more layers of abstraction, that communicate with each other through FIDO specific API. As illustrated in figure 6, the layers of the abstraction from top to bottom are as follows: user agent (browser, app), FIDO client, ASM, FIDO authenticator. Except from ASM, all other components have already been introduced throughout the paper. ASM is a platform-specific software component offering an API to FIDO clients, enabling them to discover and communicate with one or more available authenticators.A single ASM may report on behalf of multiple authenticators. The interactions between all of these new layers are done through FIDO specific API which has so far received little challenge from the market.

4   Discussion

In order to arrive to an accurate assessment of FIDO trust requirements, it is important to evaluate them against the trust requirements of the currently deployed online IdM solutions (isolated, federated). In this discussion, we distinguish between three categories of FIDO trust requirements (hereafter referred to as TR): TRs that FIDO has inherited form the previous solutions, TRs it has eliminated, and finally TRs it has introduced.Table1 summarizes the trust requirements of all the previously discussed online IdM solutions. The TRs that are common to more than one solution are only cited once.

Eliminated Trust Requirements: One of the main **positive trust implications** of FIDO is the fact that it has freed service providers from a big liability they had to incur. This has been achieved by the FIDO architecture which doesnt rely on service providers storing end users secret information, e.g. passwords. With the increasing number of compromised service provider servers, this represents indeed a significant trust improvement for FIDO over both the isolated and federated online IdM solutions.

New Trust Requirements: FDO has introduced trust issues that were not present in the previous online IdM solutions, namely: authenticator hardware manufacturers and the FIDO consortium. As we can note from Table 1, a compromised authenticator can compromise both the secret key as well as the privacy of its user.In order to resolve and mitigate this trust issue, FIDO relies on its FIDO consortium, which will be responsible for controlling the ecosystem of hardware manufacturers (certification process and metadata store). We believe this is a

Table 1. Trust Requirements: FIDO Vs. Isolated IdM Vs. Federated IdM

Trust Requirements	FIDO	Isolated	Federated
The SP protects client privacy.		✓	✓
The SP has implemented satisfactory user registration procedures and authentication mechanisms.	✓	✓	✓
The client handles their authentication credentials with adequate care.	✓	✓	✓
Trust in the SP: ability to correctly assess the risk level associated with the usage of his service by all his users.	✓	✓	✓
Trust in the computing platform:it's not compromised by malicious software.	✓	✓	✓
Trust the user will not expose his device to compromise in infected platforms.	✓	✓	✓
Service access on behalf of users will only take place when legitimately requested by the client.	✓		✓
The SP adheres to the accepted policy for correlating personal data about the same client from other SPs.	✓		✓
Trust in FIDO consortium: it has identified the right set of meta-data.	✓		✓
The SP has the expected identity.	✓	✓	✓
Trust between Federated Service.			✓
Trust in the Identity Mapping.			✓
Trust in FIDO consortium: certificate is still meaningful throughout its lifetime.	✓		
Trust in FIDO consortium: its ability to detect and report authenticators breaching the metadata characteristics declared in their certification process, and update the meta-data store accordingly.	✓		
Trust in FIDO consortium: validity of the FIDO PKI used.	✓		
Trust in Hardware manufacturers: they will not unintentionally break the unlinkability property.	✓		
Trust in Hardware manufacturers: they not intentionally break the unlinkability property.	✓		
Trust in hardware manufacturers: they not keep a backdoor in the authenticators.	✓		

very weak solution for such a severe trust risk (please refer to section 2.3 for details about the trust requirements related to hardware manufacturers and the FIDO consortium).

Inherited Trust Requirements: Last but not the least, Table 1 shows that FIDO has just inherited several trust requirements from the previous online IdM solutions, as its architecture didnt resolve their underlying issue. The most severe of these Trust requirements are the ones related to trusting the computing platform. With 31.63 percent of the worlds PCs infected with some sort of malware (Q2 2012) of which most (78.92 percent) are Trojans [17], working under the assumption that the computing platform is not compromised is not reasonable.

This trust requirements is very relevant to FIDO because now the end user secret ket is not stored on the server side, but rather on his own authenticator, which has to be connected to his possible compromised computing platform.

The main claim of FIDO is that it is going to make authentication both more usable and stronger. While FIDO does indeed offer a better usability experience to its end users, by alleviating them from the burden of passwords, and unifying their authentication experience across all their (FIDO enabled) service providers, our trust requirement analysis shows that it falls short on the front of strengthening the authentication process. *The above discussions led us to conclude that instead of solving the trust requirements of the previous online IdM solutions, FIDO has just shifted them to other components in its architecture.* Indeed, FIDO has created a more complex ecosystem, with new components (authenticator hardware manufacturers and the FIDO consortium), to which previous trust requirements (mainly service provider ones) has been delegated. We believe this new FIDO trust requirements map, puts too much power and responsibility in the hands of entities that cannot be trusted, especially in a world where online digital attacks are increasingly becoming state affairs.

5   Conclusion

Adequate management of identities in open computer networks is crucial to providing security and improving efficiency. IdM requires an integrated and often complex infrastructure where all involved parties must be trusted for specific purposes depending on their role. The variety and complexity of the trust relationships required in the various IdM models can cause confusion for stakeholders. Satisfying the trust requirements also has a cost. Our study has tried to concisely analyze the trust requirements related to FIDO, and thereby allow these issues to be clarified. This study provides a basis for assessing the cost of satisfying the trust requirements, as well as for discussing and comparing IdM solutions [15]. We have concluded that instead of solving the real trust requirements of the previous online IdM solutions, FIDO has merely created a new complex ecosystem, with new components to which these trust requirements have been shifted. While we do recognize the great usability advantages this solution brings to end users, we think FIDO is not making online IdM necessarily stronger. it is crucial to not jump on the fast adoption bandwagon before being fully aware of its trust requirements. This study will help all stakeholders understand what can go wrong with such a solution. And if we have learned anything from the unfolding of many security scandals over the last years, it is that: If anything in computer security *can* go wrong, it *will* eventually go wrong. In which case, we need to be ready to accept or mitigate the consequences. As an academia community, we have a lot to offer to this big industry led initiative FIDO, especially in terms of reviewing its trust requirements of this.

References

1. FIDO Alliance. Chinas online giant alibaba endorses fido authentication (2014). www.fidoalliance.org/chinas-online-giant-alibaba-endorses-fido-authentication/
2. FIDO Alliance. Fido security reference (2014). www.fidoalliance.org/specifications
3. FIDO Alliance. Google launches security key, worlds first deployment of fido universal second factor authentication (2014). www.fidoalliance.org/category/news-events/news-more/
4. FIDO Alliance. Google, samsung, and 16 others receive post-password certification (2014). www.fidoalliance.org/google-samsung-and-16-others-receive-post-password-certification/
5. FIDO Alliance. Reference architecture (2014). www.fidoalliance.org/specifications
6. FIDO Alliance. Whitepaper: Privacy principles (2014). www.fidoalliance.org/specifications
7. FIDO Alliance. Windows hello waves off passwords (2014). www.fidoalliance.org/windows-hello-waves-off-passwords-2/
8. FIDO Alliance. Online identity atraction with governments (2015). www.fidoalliance.org/online-identity-group-gains-traction-with-government-involvement/
9. Cavusoglu, H., Mishra, B., Raghunathan, S.: The effect of internet security breach announcements on market value: Capital market reactions for breached firms and internet security developers. Int. J. Electron. Commerce 9(1), 70–104 (2004)
10. Florencio, D., Herley, C.: A large-scale study of web password habits. In: Proceedings of the 16th International Conference on the World Wide Web, pp. 657–666. Association for Computing Machinery Inc, May 2007
11. Herley, C.: More is not the answer. IEEE Security and Privacy magazine (2014)
12. ITU. Recommendation X.800, Security Architecture for Open Systems Interconnection for CCITT Applications. International Telecommunications Union, Geneva (1991)
13. Jennifer, W.: How to perform and interpret chi-square. SAS Global Forum (2012)
14. Jøsang, A.: Identity Management and Trusted Interaction in Internet and Mobile Computing. IET Information Security, (in press) (2013)
15. Jøsang, A., Fabre, J.: Trust requirements in identity management. In: ACSW Frontiers 2005, ACSW Workshops - the Australasian Workshop on Grid Computing and e-Research and the Third Australasian Information Security Workshop, pp. 99–108, Newcastle (2005)
16. Loutfi, I., Jøsang, A.: 1,2, Pause: lets start by meaningfully navigating the current online authentication solutions space. In: Jensen, C.D., Marsh, S., Dimitrakos, T., Murayama, Y. (eds.) IFIPTM 2015. IFIP AICT, vol. 454, pp. 165–176. Springer, Heidelberg (2015)
17. PandaLabs. PandaLabs Quarterly Report, Q2, June 2012
18. Prabhu, D., Adimoolam, M.: A novel dna based encrypted text compression. IJCA Special Issue on Network Security and Cryptography NSC(2), 36–41 (2011)
19. USDoD. Trusted Computer System Evaluation Criteria. US Department of Defence (1985)
20. Verizon. Control computer crime news (2013). www.verizonenterprise.com/resources

Using the RetSim Fraud Simulation Tool
to Set Thresholds for Triage of Retail Fraud

Edgar Alonso Lopez-Rojas[1]([✉]) and Stefan Axelsson[2]

[1] Blekinge Insitute of Technology, Karlskrona, Sweden
edgar.lopez@bth.se
[2] Gjovik University College, Gjøvik, Norway
stefan.axelsson@hig.no

Abstract. The investigation of fraud in business has been a staple for the digital forensics practitioner since the introduction of computers in business. Much of this fraud takes place in the retail industry. When trying to stop losses from insider retail fraud, triage, i.e. the quick identification of sufficiently suspicious behaviour to warrant further investigation, is crucial, given the amount of normal, or insignificant behaviour.

It has previously been demonstrated that simple statistical threshold classification is a very successful way to detect fraud [15]. However, in order to do triage successfully the thresholds have to be set correctly. Therefore, we present a method based on simulation to aid the user in accomplishing this, by simulating relevant fraud scenarios that are foreseeing as possible and expected, to calculate optimal threshold limits.

Our proposed method gives the advantage over arbitrary thresholds that it reduces the amount of labour needed on false positives and gives additional information, such as the total cost of a specific modelled fraud behaviour, to set up a proper triage process. With our method we argue that we contribute to the allocation of resources for further investigations by optimizing the thresholds for triage and estimating the possible total cost of fraud. Using this method we manage to keep the losses below a desired percentage of sales, which the manager considers acceptable for keeping the business properly running.

1 Introduction

The economic impact of fraud by staff can be substantial in several types of business. Thus the detection and management of fraud is an important topic. In the retail store the cost of fraud is of course ultimately transferred to the consumer, and finally impacts the overall economy. For example; in one recent case the major US home improvement chain *Home Depot* was the target of a fraudulent return scam where two inside members of staff netted several thousand dollars before being caught. They perpetrated the fraud by abusing their knowledge of the processes of the shipment and return of products [8]. Retail fraud was estimated to cost US retailers about 42 billion dollars in 2013 from which 43% was committed by dishonest staff [2]. Due to the seriousness of this type of fraud,

© Springer International Publishing Switzerland 2015
S. Buchegger and M. Dam (Eds.): NordSec 2015, LNCS 9417, pp. 156–171, 2015.
DOI: 10.1007/978-3-319-26502-5_11

both EU and US recently started to mandate the use of fraud detection as one part of the minimum security requirements for financial services [6,7].

The constant change of criminal behaviour and patterns, and the introduction of new fraud schemes makes this an important topic for researchers and practitioners alike. For a multitude of reasons (e.g., privacy related, legal, financial, or contractual) the state of practice in fraud research is to work with sensitive and hence secret data [12]. This difficulty hinders researchers to develop methods to detect, prioritize investigations (triage process), and finally share the results with other researchers without problem. We name this problem the *data secrecy problem*.

The *data secrecy problem* has previously been addressed by the use of synthetic data, generated by the RetSim simulator [14]. However, a simulator has other benefits aside from being able to share relevant data for research. One major advantage is that different scenarios can be tested. In these scenarios parameters such as the number of fraudulent staff, their propensity to perpetrate fraud, cost of merchandise etc. This enables the testing of e.g. new fraud detection schemes. These detection schemes can later be applied to real data, so we can prioritize and allocate resources for performing further investigation of fraud.

In this paper we address the problem of how to apply statistical threshold detection to perform triage by proposing a technique which uses synthetic data, generated by the RetSim simulator [14], to test different fraud scenarios so that thresholds can be set and the resulting performance studied. These methods can later be applied on real data.

In our study we target fraud caused by fraudulent refunds performed by sales staff. This is a common type of fraud and accounts for around 28% globally of the total fraud in a retail store, with this situation being more critical in North America [2]. This fraud scheme takes advantage of the lack of security controls inside the store and the difficulty to perform inventory control often in most of the retail business settings. Once the missing inventory is noticed by the inventory control officers, a digital forensic investigation can be performed over the available evidence to identify the people responsible, which in this particular case happens to be associated in most of the cases with the salesperson staff.

However, it is difficult to prioritise which of the staff members should be investigated, especially when we are dealing with a chain of stores with multiple branches and the corresponding number of staff. When investigating losses from theft and fraud in the retail setting, we are most often not interested in finding every last instance of fraud but rather of limiting our overall loss to an acceptable level, often put as a set percentage of overall turnover. Spending time and resources on the investigation of the pettiest of thefts of office supplies is counter productive, as the investigative resources are both scarce and expensive. It can also negatively affect the workplace atmosphere. Thus, being able to focus the investigative effort on the cases that can affect the bottom line is vital.

Thus there is an evident need to prioritize and allocate personal for performing such investigations of staff fraud in the retail sector. We do this by using a triage process model and categorising the fraud threat into critical, important and low impact. However, the financial and transaction data available is large and hence we need an effective way of performing triage, to focus efforts where they may make the most impact, and hence keeping the total loss to fraud at a set, acceptable, level.

2 Related Work

Simulations in the domain of retail stores have traditionally been focused on finding answers to logistics problems such as inventory management, supply management, staff scheduling and customer queue reductions [4,5,19]. We find no research focusing on simulations generating fraud data to be used for fraud detection in retail stores besides the RetSim simulator [14].

One of the reasons data is simulated instead of taken directly from the original source is the *data secrecy problem*. In our experience, the privacy of the customers has always been the main concern when disclosing any transactional data. This can be seen by the lack of any kind of public transactional data set that reflects financial statement of individual persons. Many anonymization techniques have been used to preserve the privacy of sensitive information present in data sets. But de-anonymizing data sets is not an insurmountable task, far from it [17]. This is one of the reasons why we have decided to use simulation techniques to keep specific properties of the original data set, such as statistical and social network properties, and at the same time providing an extra layer of insulation that pure anonymization does not provide.

However, using a simulator also has many other benefits, the main one being that the experimenter is in total control of the environment and can vary parameters to try different scenarios; increasing and decreasing the intensity and severity of fraud, for example.

There are tools such as IDSG (IDAS Data and Scenario Generator [11]) that were developed for the purpose of generating synthetic data based on the relationship between attributes and their statistical distributions. IDSG was created to support data mining systems during the testing phase, and it has been used to test fraud detection systems. The RetSim approach differs in that it is implementing an agent-based model which is based on agent micro behaviour rather, than a fixed statistical distribution of macro parameters.

Other methods to generate the necessary fraud data have been previously proposed [10,16,20]. The work by Yannikos et al. [20] lets the user specify the assumptions about the environment at hand; i.e., there is no need for access to real data. However, this will certainly affect the quality of the synthetic data. The work by Lundin et al. [16] makes use of a small sample of real data to generate synthetic data. This approach is similar to the one in RetSim. However, the direct use of real data to prime the generation of synthetic data is limited in that it makes it harder to generate realistic data with other characteristics than those of the original real data [20]. The work by Kargupta et al. [10] focused on privacy-preserving methods for data mining. However, that method also does

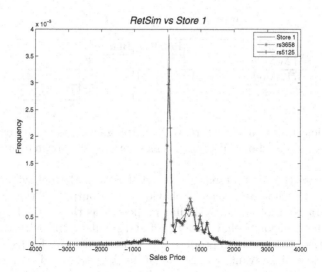

Fig. 1. Overlap of Two Runs of RetSim vs Real Data

not have the possibility of generating realistic data with other characteristics than those of the original data. RetSim, uses social simulation, which makes it possible to change the parameters of the agents in the model to create realistic synthetic data, potentially producing emergent behaviour in the logs which is hard to produce in other ways.

Previous research on fraud detection algorithms has showed that data mining and machine learning algorithms can identify novel methods of fraud by detecting those records that are different (anomalous) in comparison with benign records, e.g., the work by Phua et al. [18]. This problem in machine learning is known as *novelty detection*. Furthermore, supervised learning algorithms have been used on synthetic data sets to prove the performance of outlier detection [1,16]. More particularly in retail stores the use of pattern discovery to address retail fraud has been used by Gabbur et al. [9] with many limitations to train a classifier due to the lack of reliable fraud data. However none of these studies made use of synthetic data from retail stores. To our knowledge, there has been no investigation of what the limits of effectiveness of e.g. simple threshold based monitoring are over other complex techniques such as machine learning and pattern recognition.

3   RetSim: The Simulator for Retail Store Data and Fraud

Since we have access to several years worth of transaction data from one of the largest Scandinavian retail shoe store chains, we made use of *RetSim*[14], a *Ret*ail shoe store *Sim*ulation, built on the concept of Multi-Agents Based Simulation (MABS). *RetSim* is intended to be used in developing and testing

Table 1. Triage Threshold Limits

Data Set-Triage	Red 98%	Blue 95%	Green 90%
rs5125-No Fraud	0.136	0.133	0.128
rs3712-Moderate Fraud	0.191	0.182	0.147
rs3302-Aggressive Fraud	0.209	0.185	0.170

fraud scenarios at a retail shoe store, while keeping business sensitive and private personal information about customers consumption secret from competitors and others.

RetSim uses the relevant parameters that govern the behaviour in and of a retail store to simulate *normal* behaviour. The output of this process is a synthetic data set that contains similar properties as the original data set. We also model the malicious behaviour of staff and simulate this behaviour together with our normal behaviour to produce a rich data set useful for fraud research.

One of the main advantages of simulating data for fraud over real data is that it can quantify the loss due to the identification of malicious agents since the activities of these are known [12,13]. Due to this capability, one of the main results of previous research with RetSim is that in many cases a proper setting of a threshold detection control can be enough to keep the loss of a business to fraud, at a desired level, and at the same time avoiding the cost and complexity of more advance methods, such as data mining and machine learning.

Fraud in the retail setting is in many cases perpetrated by the staff so we have decided to focus on that. A common example of such fraud is *Refunds due to Fraudulent Returns*. In this paper we make use of the *RetSim* tool to study this specific fraud scenario that includes agents defrauding the store and performing known fraud behaviour patterns.

With the help of *RetSim*, we produced a simulation that results in data comparable to our real data set. The generated synthetic data set contains 36 salesmen and around 45,000 receipts and 81,500 articles sold. The simulation was seeded with a subset of about 11,000 articles from the real store (that we named *Store 1*). One of the challenges when simulating data is to evaluate how realistic the data is in comparison with the source. In Figure 1 there is evidence of the similarities from an overlapping plot of the generated distribution of sales by price of both: original data set (Store 1) and simulated data sets (*rs3658* and *rs5125*). In this paper we make use of *rs5125* as a reference data set for a *No Fraud* scenario. This evidence is part of previous work using this tool to generate a realistic data set for research [14].

Now that we have a proper data set simulated that resemble the original data, the next step is to inject malicious behaviour that can be used for research. In the chosen scenario of fraudulent returns we include cases where a salesman creates fraudulent refund slips, keeping the cash refund for him- or herself. In terms of the object model used in RetSim the refund scenario can be implemented by: Estimating the average number of refunds per sale and the corresponding standard deviation. Use these statistics for simulating refunds in the RetSim model. Fraudulent salesmen will perform normal refunds, as well as fraudulent one.

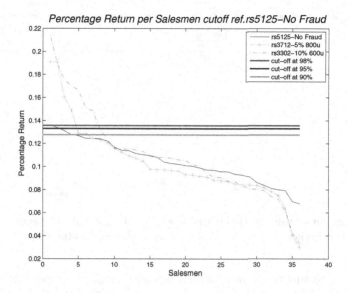

Fig. 2. Triage cut off using as reference no fraud behaviour

The volume of fraudulent refunds can be modelled using specific parameters that determine the *aggressiveness* of the fraudulent behaviour. The "red flag" for detection will in this case be a high number and value of refunds in average divided by the total sales for a salesman.

4 Triage Process in a Retail Store Scenario

When investigating the instance of fraud in a retail store, it is important to quickly eliminate all the normal background behaviour that is not indicative of fraudulent behaviour. This is of course (hopefully) the overwhelming majority of the transactions. So we need to perform some form of triage, where we quickly identify the abnormal behaviour and single that out for further investigation.

So inspired by the original triage,[1] we have chosen to divide the studied behaviour into three categories, bins, to classify suspicious activity of staff members: the first category requires *critical* or urgent investigation, Category one - red line in figures), the second category is *important* to detect significant loss to the business (Category 2 - blue line in figures), the last category is the category where investigation would probably not be fruitful and have *low impact* on business (Category 3 - green line in figures). The idea being an investigator ought to focus on the red category (Critical), maybe keeping an open mind regarding people in the blue category (Important), and disregard the green (Low Impact) as a cost of doing business if indeed any problematic behaviour should lurk in that category.

---

[1] From the French *trier* (v): to separate, sift, or select.

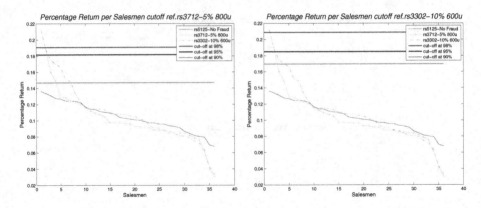

Fig. 3. Triage cut off using moderate fraud behaviour as reference

Fig. 4. Triage cut off using aggressive fraud behaviour as the reference

To illustrate this triage process in a fictitious retail store we use the return fraud scheme as an example, and we wish to set statistical thresholds to identify the limits of the categories. Staff that process many refunds in comparison to their sales are subject to investigation, therefore our definition of suspicious behaviour is: *An unusually high fraction of the total value of refunds to the total value of sales for the individual salesman in question, in comparison with the average value for the sales staff as a whole.* I.e. the fraud score for the individual salesman is:

$$FraudScore = \frac{ValueOfRefunds}{ValueOfSales}$$

However the task of finding the limits for each of the categories is not trivial. If we set the limits to high, much fraud will be unidentified. On the other hand if we set a lower limit we will experience many false positives. False positives are always a problem when doing any form of detection, and must be avoided [3].

To start formulating the problem we assume that all staff members have a similar probability of performing returns, and that returns of valuable articles are more interesting than lower priced articles from the criminal perspective. We chose, somewhat arbitrary, threshold cut-off limits of (90%, 95% and 98%) to cover at least 10% of the staff that are of particular interest due to suspicious fraud behaviour (higher amount of refunds). The calculated values for the thresholds limits are shown in table 1. We do this in order to show how a simulation tool can be used for setting these limits.

Figure 2 shows the values for both the normal behaviour, and two simulations with injected *return fraud*. This figure shows the total value of refunds divided by the total sales for each salesman as percentages, for the three simulations *rs5125, rs3712 and rs3302* explained below.

To model a normal sales scenario we used information about relevant parameters describing normal behaviour without any fraud and selected *rs5125* as the

No Fraud reference data set. As we said before in section 3, this data set was one of the two evaluated against the original data set to verify that we are using a realistic synthetic data set that resembles the original, and maintains interesting properties of sales without revealing specific details of particular customers.

In a normal situation the only information available is the normal behaviour of the refund process (no fraud). If we set up our threshold limits for triage using this data as a reference (as shown in figure 2), we notice that the limits are perhaps too close to each other due to the assumption, as perceived by studying the real data from the store, that each salesman has a similar probability of processing refunds.

The resulting triage processes using an arbitrary threshold for each of the simulations is not optimal for detecting fraud in most cases due to the possible high number of false positives needed to have sufficient effectiveness. For instance, if we set up the thresholds of triage using the data set that contains no fraud (First case Triage 1 in tables 2 and 3), we have many salesmen to investigate that are flagged as the top priority (red). This could lead to an overwhelming effort to investigate all the fraud without the necessary resources.

5   Tuning the Parameters of the Triage Set Up

In this section we propose a method to set up a triage process that fits the business expectations and limitations. To start, in section 4 we analysed the consequences of setting arbitrary thresholds due to lack of information of possible fraud. Our proposed method works for either detecting new fraud as it takes place or for the processing of historical data of refunds in order to perform a forensic digital investigation.

To begin, we make use of the RetSim simulator to generate a synthetic data set that contains information about an expected fraud behaviour scenario. In this study we started modelling two possible scenarios, one with moderate fraud behaviour and another one with aggressive fraud behaviour.

The first fraud simulation *(rs3712)* shows a conservative fraud behaviour agent where each of the fraudsters will attempt to commit fraud only if the sales

Table 2. Triage of moderate fraud data set with rs3712-5% 800u (Top Fraud Score)

ID Salesman	Fraction of Sales	Refunded	Total Sales	Total Stolen	Triage1	Triage2	Triage3
S836051140	0.191	-20234	106026	3874	Red	Blue	Blue
S1068592722	0.191	-12774	67000	0	Red	Blue	Blue
S1408212765	0.160	-10168	63409	0	Red	Green	
S1948780723	0.149	-42865.86	287783.1	7702.857	Red	Green	
S1568033761	0.129	-406122.8	3155567	119662	Green		
S1434682851	0.128	-53809.7	418757.1	0	Green		
S193026137	0.124	-14805	118980.4	0			
S24105143	0.123	-35499.56	288014	0			
S705613182	0.120	-99021	822423.2	16449			

value is worth more than 800 units in the fictitious currency, and the frequency with which he/she commits this fraud is 5% of all sales. The total amount pilfered by all fraudulent agents in a year is 161,630 units in this scenario, which is around 0.43% of total revenue (39,085,000 units).

The second fraud simulation *(rs3302)* represents an aggressive fraud agent behaviour where the threshold to commit fraud is 600 units and the frequency is 10% of sales. The total amount defrauded by all agents is 400,451 units per year, which is around 1.09% of total revenue (36,584,000 units).

The percentage of returns per salesman for the three generated synthetic data sets are plotted together in figures 2, 3 and 4 for comparison purposes. One of the many benefits of using a simulator is that we can flag all sales refunds that are fraudulent. In a real data set this is unknown unless someone has already vetted the entire data set, which is difficult both from a practical and theoretical standpoint. In table 2 and 3 we can partially see the information concerning the plots for those salesmen with higher percentage of refunds per the total sales, more specifically information about total value of sales, value of refunds and the total value stolen.

Now that we have all information required of the expected fraud scenarios, we can make use of these two simulations to set up the same arbitrary thresholds limits of (90%, 95% and 98%). The thresholds limits are shown in figures 3 and 4 and we will name them Triage 2 and 3.

After looking more in detail into the second case (Triage 2 in table 3), we see that inside the categories that are detected as red and blue, there are only 2 salesmen detected. Finally the last case (Triage 3 in table 3), does not flag any salesman in the blue category. But we notice that the amount of red flags for investigation is considerably lowered in comparison to Triage 1.

The evaluation of the fraud detection methods using different triage processes is presented in table 4 and 5. From these tables we see that when the fraud is more aggressive, the triage process has a higher precision and recall than in any of the other triage set ups. However if the goal is to minimize the false positives we should carefully chose a threshold limit that minimize this value.

Table 3. Triage of aggressive fraud data set with rs3302-10% 600u (Top Fraud Score)

ID Salesman	Fraction of Sales	Refunded	Total Sales	Total Stolen	Triage1	Triage2	Triage3
S836051140	0.214	-3597	16783	1199	Red	Red	Red
S1068592722	0.189	-11087	58619.38	0	Red	Blue	Red
S1568033761	0.175	-553671.7	3160122	267760.9	Red	Green	Green
S1948780723	0.170	-10965	64498.8	5343	Red	Green	Green
S1063661000	0.166	-41420.67	249302.5	0	Red	Green	
S705613182	0.151	-185363	1225409	68065	Red	Green	
S1884511064	0.148	-55632	374763	29095	Red	Green	
S944780329	0.132	-51983.12	392897.4	28989	Blue		
S1888626692	0.123	-66295.58	537627.2	0			

Table 4. Fraud Detection Results for Triage of moderate fraud using rs3712

Statistic	Triage 1	Triage 2	Triage 3
True Positives	3	2	1
False Positives	3	2	1
False Negatives	3	4	5
Detected	131239	11577	3874
Not Detected	30392	150054	157757
Precision	50%	50%	50%
Recall	50%	33%	17%

Table 5. Fraud Detection Results for Triage of aggressive fraud using rs3302

Statistic	Triage 1	Triage 2	Triage 3
True Positives	6	5	3
False Positives	2	2	1
False Negatives	0	1	3
Detected	399253	371463	274302
Not Detected	0	28989	126149
Precision	75%	71%	75%
Recall	100%	83%	50%

If we aim to investigate moderate fraud we should carefully set up triage thresholds somewhere in between the settings for Triage 1 and 2. Triage 3 is very inefficient in this scenario as seen in table 4. From our results in table 5 for the aggressive fraud, we can see that the higher recall is of course with a very low threshold as in Triage 1, but the effort to investigate 8 members of the staff is higher than using Triage 3, where we are still able to detect most of the fraud but lower the number of staff to investigate by half and still detect about 68% of the fraud committed with just one false positive.

Finally, after having all the information available, a fraud investigator can decide on the goal of the investigation and calculate the effort needed to investigate each of the categories and establish new thresholds according to business strategy to detect and prevent fraud, with the certainty that the chosen triage fraud detection strategy will cover a specific fraud behaviour, and therefore minimise the risk of a big loss.

For example if the goal is to detect as much as possible without considering cost, we can set up very flexible thresholds to achieve this goal. If on the other hand the goal is to catch only substantial amounts of losses we can filter out the staff that has not had enough total refund value from the flagged staff to not spend any resources investigating them. However, if the goal is to deter thieves from stealing, then we can think about prosecuting even minor fraud that become evident and hence easy to flag due to a higher proportion of refunds versus sales.

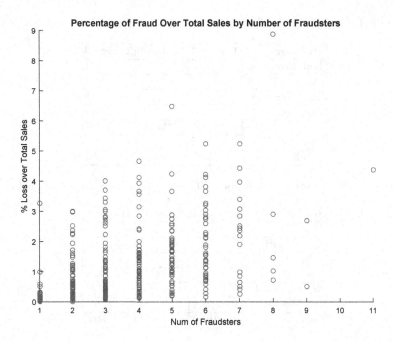

Fig. 5. Percentage of fraud divided by total sales grouped by number of fraudsters

6   Using the Triage Setup

Now we are ready to start using the threshold for triage. In the previous section we set the triage limits using 3 different ways (Table 1): using no fraud data (rs5125), moderate fraud behaviour (rs3712) and aggressive fraud behaviour (rs3302). In this section we make use of the RetSim simulator to simulate enough probable scenarios where the fraud can vary from none to aggressive fraud that rises up to nearly 9% of total sales as shown in fig. 5.

Using similar settings as the previous simulation we simulated scenarios for 48 different fraud behaviours each one 10 times randomly, which in total were 480 data sets. We did this by changing 3 different parameters of the fraud behaviour: the number of fraudsters, the minimum article value they are willing to defraud, and finally the frequency with which they steal and keeping the same parameters of sales for each store.

Each simulation is based on a store with 36 salesmen that according to different situations could work full time, part time or seasonally. The different circumstances vary the total amount of refunds considerably and the quantities sold by each salesman. This is the main reason for using *the fraction of total value of refunds divided by total value of sales per each staff* as a Fraud Score in our fraud detection model. We assumed that all the salesmen should perform at or below approximately the same value with this indicator. Any deviation is due to possible abnormal or fraudulent behaviour.

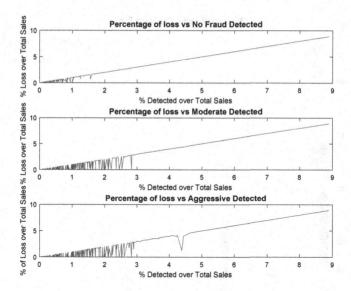

Fig. 6. Percentage of loss divided by Total Sales vs Detected

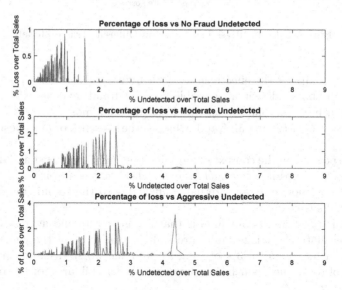

Fig. 7. Percentage of loss divided by Total Sales vs Undetected

With these scenarios the goal is to study how much fraud we can catch on average, and if we can keep the loss of the business below a certain level.

We will primarily focus on the red flags identified by the triage process since in most of the cases this would be the main focus of investigations, and also where most of the fraud investigation resources are placed.

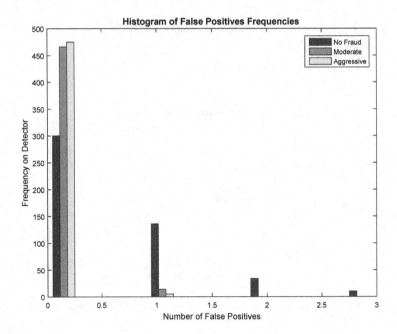

Fig. 8. False Positives Frequency on Different Triage Models

Figure 6 compares the effectiveness of the different methods. A perfect detection method should detect all possible cases of fraud, and as expected a low threshold such as the one for no fraud can detect almost all frauds. However there is a cost of detecting all fraud, which is the presence of false positives (see figure. 8).

A false positive in the context of a retail store might incur cost and difficulties to investigate all possible salesmen that matches the low suspicious criteria and perhaps if they notice it, an internal conflict due to the submission of staff to unwarranted suspicion.

One important fact about fig 6 is that the moderate and aggressive models used to calculate the triage limits are sufficient in most of the cases, to keep the loss to a maximum of 3% of total sales in the worst case, and most often below 2% of total sales, which are commonly accepted figures for fraud risk (see figure 7).

7   Discussion

The biggest threat to the validity of our research is concerning the synthetic data. Many would think that using a synthetic data set is not the same as using the original one. That is true to some extent. A synthetic data set is an abstraction of the original data set. The main goal in our case is to preserve the privacy of customers and business by keeping the original source secret but allowing third parties to interact with the essence of the data in order to provide access to the business through a simulation tool that aids to develop a layer of fraud protection.

Now moving to the retail store business, one of the biggest questions when inventory is missing is: where did it go? Missing inventory directly affects the revenue of many retail operations, especially in markets with lower margins. The causes can vary from customer theft, to staff fraud. In this paper we focus on the study of losses due to fraudulent refunds by the staff.

Gathering evidence of this fraud is a difficult task, specially when there is not a clear starting point. The triage process came about in wartime where medical first responders needed a way to prioritise how to allocate resources to wounded soldiers on the battle field. By analogy, using a similar triage process in the retail setting, when presented with evidence of loss due to fraud in the form of missing inventory, can be a useful way to allocate scarce investigative resources.

The goal of the investigation is an important variable when setting up the thresholds for triage. Often the investigation of small losses is costly for the business and we can reduce the number of investigations to those where the amount is substantial enough to affect the bottom line.

After the triage process is properly calibrated to fit the goals of the retailer, then a proper investigation can be carried out. There are many tools available for performing such an investigation, and discussing these go beyond the scope of this paper, but one could for example match the time stamps of refund receipts to video surveillance records of the cash register, to see if the receipts match the expected transaction.

The main concern of the retail fraud executives is to keep the business loss as low as possible. Reducing the cost of fraud is a constant process that requires business resources. Since the final cost of the fraud and the investment in fraud detection ends with the customer, managers have an important role to play in this process. They can either go for the detection of the minimum case of fraud with big investments, or accept that part of the business is to keep running at a certain low level of fraud which does not deeply affect the business end customer. The total percentage defrauded by all agents is in our aggressive simulation around 1.09% of total revenue. Most businesses would consider this an acceptable loss rate because it will not severely affect the final customer.

8   Conclusions

The RetSim simulator is a useful tool to implement a triage process based on a suspected fraud detection scenario. Without knowing the loss for a specific fraud scenario, retail loss prevention executives are basically left to set up arbitrary thresholds for the triage process. When using the RetSim simulator, they can model the expected cost of fraud by simulating and analysing a synthetic data set with already identified instances of fraud.

Developing a proper and effective triage process without knowing all the underlying details of the expected fraud is difficult. By using the RetSim simulator we can gather enough information for starting a digital forensic investigation since we can model and investigate how different parameters affect the situation.

For threshold detection to be effective, the reference data set that is used to calculate the cut off should contain enough fraud data. Otherwise the range of the categories for a triage process are in risk of being so slim that they can not detect any fraud or perhaps the fraud is outside of the region delineated by the thresholds.

The generation of synthetic fraud is necessary in many cases, to properly set up the triage categories. Our triage set up method substantially reduce the scope of investigation by using triage optimization based on simulated data generated from expected fraud scenarios. It is a management decision to properly set up the threshold according to the resources available for investigating more or fewer cases of suspicious staff returns, given the accepted overall loss to the business. It is off course a task for the managers to decide on the different thresholds to correspond with their business goals, which could be i.e. to maximise the fraud detection while avoiding the cost of invested resources for investigating many false positives, or keeping the total losses below 2% of turnover annually etc. In our examples above, we meet that level.

Further research on this topic will be focused on simulating new types of fraud and at the same time apply these results on the real business to measure the effectiveness of detecting simulated fraud versus real fraud *in vivo*. Another direction of research is to identify other domains where similar methods as those presented in this paper can be applied to circumvent the *data secrecy problem* such as when studying bank transactions, mobile payments and similar financial services.

Acknowledgments. This work is part of the research project "Scalable resource-efficient systems for big data analytics" funded by the Knowledge Foundation (grant: 20140032) in Sweden.

References

1. Abe, N., Zadrozny, B., Langford, J.: Outlier detection by active learning. In: Proceedings of the 12th ACM SIGKDD International Conference on Knowledge Discovery and Data Mining, KDD 2006, p. 504 (2006)
2. Arora, R., Khan, A., Deyle, E.: The global retail theft barometer 2014, pp. 1–81. Checkpoint Systems Inc., Thorofare. Acedido em, p. 60 (2014)
3. Axelsson, S.: The base-rate fallacy and the difficulty of intrusion detection. ACM Transactions on Information and System Security (TISSEC) **3**(3), 186–205 (2000)
4. Bovinet, J.: RETSIM: A Retail Simulation with a Small Business Perspective. West Pub. Co., Minneapolis/St. Paul (1993)
5. Chaczko, Z., Chiu, C.: A smart-shop system - multi-agent simulation system for monitoring retail activities. In: 20th European Modelling and Simulation Symposium, pp. 20–26 (2008)

6. Council, F.: Supplement to Authentication in an Internet Banking Environment, pp. 206–222 (2011). http://www.ffiec.gov/pdf/Auth-ITS-Final
7. E.C.B.: Recommendations for the Security of Internet Payments. Tech. Rep. January, European Central Bank (2013)
8. FBI: Ticket Switch Fraud Scheme at Home Depot (2013)
9. Gabbur, P., Pankanti, S., Fan, Q., Trinh, H.: A pattern discovery approach to retail fraud detection. In: Proceedings of the 17th ACM SIGKDD International Conference on Knowledge discovery and data mining, KDD 2011, p. 307 (2011)
10. Kargupta, H., Datta, S., Wang, Q.: On the privacy preserving properties of random data perturbation techniques. In: Third IEEE International Conference on Data Mining, pp. 99–106 (2003)
11. Lin, P., Samadi, B., Cipolone, A.: Development of a synthetic data set generator for building and testing information discovery systems. In: ITNG 2006, pp. 707–712. IEEE (2006)
12. Lopez-Rojas, E.A., Axelsson, S.: Money laundering detection using synthetic data. In: The 27th workshop of Swedish Artificial Intelligence Society (SAIS), pp. 33–40 (2012)
13. Lopez-Rojas, E.A., Axelsson, S.: Multi agent based simulation (MABS) of financial transactions for anti money laundering (AML). In: The 17th Nordic Conference on Secure IT Systems, pp. 25–32 (2012)
14. Lopez-Rojas, E.A., Axelsson, S., Gorton, D.: RetSim: A shoe store agent-based simulation for fraud detection. In: The 25th European Modeling and Simulation Symposium (2013). (Best Paper Award)
15. Lopez-Rojas, E.A., Gorton, D., Axelsson, S.: Using the RetSim Simulator for Fraud Detection Research. International Journal of Simulation and Process Modelling **10**(2) (2015)
16. Lundin, E., Kvarnström, H., Jonsson, E.: A synthetic fraud data generation methodology. In: Deng, R.H., Qing, S., Bao, F., Zhou, J. (eds.) ICICS 2002. LNCS, vol. 2513, pp. 265–277. Springer, Heidelberg (2002)
17. Narayanan, A., Shmatikov, V.: De-anonymizing social networks. In: 2009 30th IEEE Symposium on Security and Privacy, pp. 173–187, May 2009
18. Phua, C., Lee, V., Smith, K., Gayler, R.: A comprehensive survey of data mining-based fraud detection research (2010). Arxiv preprint arXiv: 1009.6119
19. Schwaiger, A., Stahmer, B.: SimMarket: multiagent-based customer simulation and decision support for category management. In: Schillo, M., Klusch, M., Müller, J., Tianfield, H. (eds.) MATES 2003. LNCS (LNAI), vol. 2831, pp. 74–84. Springer, Heidelberg (2003)
20. Yannikos, Y., Franke, F., Winter, C., Schneider, M.: 3LSPG: forensic tool evaluation by three layer stochastic process-based generation of data. In: Sako, H., Franke, K.Y., Saitoh, S. (eds.) IWCF 2010. LNCS, vol. 6540, pp. 200–211. Springer, Heidelberg (2011)

IncidentResponseSim:
An Agent-Based Simulation Tool
for Risk Management of Online Fraud

Dan Gorton[✉]

Center for Safety Research, Department of Transport Science,
KTH Royal Institute of Technology, Stockholm, Sweden
dan.gorton@abe.kth.se
http://www.kth.se

Abstract. IncidentResponseSim is a multi-agent-based simulation tool supporting risk management of online financial services, by performing a risk assessment of the quality of current countermeasures, in the light of the current and emerging threat environment. In this article, we present a set of simulations using incident response trees in combination with a quantitative model for estimating the direct economic consequences. The simulations generate expected fraud, and conditional fraud value at risk, given a specific fraud scenario. Additionally, we present how different trojan strategies result in different conditional fraud value at risk, given the underlying distribution of wealth in the online channel, and different levels of daily transaction limits. Furthermore, we show how these measures can be used together with return on security investment calculations to support decisions about future security investments.

Keywords: Risk management · Online fraud · Incident Response Tree (IRT) · Value at Risk (VaR) · Simulation · Return on Security Investment (ROSI)

1 Introduction

Banking is one part of our critical infrastructure [1], and as such, a threat against online banking may become a threat against the society.

Over the years, cyber criminals have become better organized and attacks against online banking services have grown more sophisticated [2]. A recent threat report from the European Network and Information Security Agency (ENISA) shows increasing trends for most of the attack vectors needed for online fraud [3].

To counteract this situation, authorities like the Federal Financial Institutions Examination Council (FFIEC) in the US and the European Central Bank (ECB) in Europe are stepping up their expected minimum security requirements for financial institutions, including requirements for risk management of online banking [2][4].

© Springer International Publishing Switzerland 2015
S. Buchegger and M. Dam (Eds.): NordSec 2015, LNCS 9417, pp. 172–187, 2015.
DOI: 10.1007/978-3-319-26502-5_12

For the financial institution, these requirements translate into a need to understand the incident response process protecting online services. However, existing tools like attack and protection trees [5][6][7][8][9], fail to capture chronological ordering of events [10].

In previous articles, we have presented the fundamentals of a derivation of event tree analysis for online fraud, which we call incident response tree (IRT) [11], and added a quantitative model inspired by current models for estimating credit risk [12].

In this article, we introduce IncidentResponseSim, an online bank simulation tool modeling the consequences of online fraud directed against online financial services.

The rest of this article is organized as follows. Section 2 presents the proposed model. In section 3, we simulate different scenarios using IncidentResponseSim. Section 4 presents an analysis of the consequences of different trojan strategies. In section 5, we present how the results from IncidentResponseSim can be used together with return on security investment (ROSI). Section 6 presents a discussion, and section 7 wraps up the article with conclusions.

2   Background

2.1   Online Banking

Wikipedia defines online banking as "... an electronic payment system that enables customers of a financial institution to conduct financial transactions on a website operated by the institution, such as a retail bank, virtual bank, credit union or building society" [13].

Financial institutions often provide multiple solutions for online banking, called "channels", with differing security and usability. Most often, a more secure channel provides more services, more information, and allows higher transaction amounts.

2.2   The Incident Response Process

The incident response process of online financial services is very important in that it protects customer and company assets. As noted, ENISA finds that the threat landscape is getting worse, making effective risk management of incident response a priority for financial institutions and governing bodies alike [3].

However, to investigate, develop, test, and improve different parts of the incident response process, detailed information about the current threat landscape and the effectiveness of current countermeasures is needed. Thus, information sharing is needed not only within the financial institution, but also in the form of information sharing among financial organizations. Additionally, it is very important to be able to model how emerging threat landscapes will affect current countermeasures. Information from, for example, simulations of potential future scenarios will make it possible to better plan for what might happen next.

For example, we can imagine a financial institution preparing for emerging threats which it has learned about from previous victims. The possible direct economic consequences are then estimated using simulation and further precautions are initiated, if deemed necessary. Other relevant situations to model include:

- Soon to be entered markets (with a different threat landscape)
- The introduction of a high usability (but less secure) online service
- Single point of failure (concerning for example prevention, detection, or response).

Furthermore, there is a lack of research in the domain of incident response. One reason for this is that information about fraud, and the effectiveness of current countermeasures is sensitive, something that is shared only sparsely within the financial institution, and preferably not at all with external parties.

Threats and Countermeasures. According to Julisch [14], there are three types of threats against online banking:

- Impersonation
- Deception
- Server-side attack.

Impersonation, which is the main focus of this article, corresponds to fraud where the fraudster impersonates the real user, using, for example, phishing, man-in-the-middle, man-in-the-browser, or social engineering, resulting in the user giving up his or her credentials. Deception corresponds to fraud where the fraudster tricks the user into register transactions on behalf of the fraudster, for example, using various fraud schemes like Nigeria Letters. Server-side attack corresponds to fraud where the fraudster hacks into the online banking environment and issues transactions from these servers directly. A recent example is the attacks by Carbanak (also known as Anunak) [15].

From an online financial service perspective, there are different ways to mitigate the effects of fraud; however, finding the right balance between different parts of countermeasures is not an easy task [16]. The likelihood of attacks can be mitigated by more effective preventive measures like multi-factor authentication, and more effective fraud detection and response. Additionally, the direct economic consequences of fraud can be lowered by temporarily closing down services like foreign payments, or lowering daily transaction limits.

To mitigate this situation, we developed a tool, based on event tree analysis which we called an incident response tree (IRT) [11].

Incident Response Trees. By using IRTs we are able to measure the effectiveness of different parts of countermeasures, for example, prevention, detection, and response.

Figure 1 shows an IRT for the initial event being a customer with a banking trojan which is actively targeting an online banking channel.

To measure the effectiveness of prevention, detection, and response, the incident response team needs to collect four different types of consequences, C_1 to C_4, to populate a basic IRT (most probably, some or all of these statistics are already collected separately by the fraud response team):

- C_1. The number of active attacks which were not detected by the bank. (This includes fraud detected by the customer after the fact, or by the financial institution during back testing against known money mules.)
- C_2. The number of active attacks which were detected by fraud detection, but not stopped by fraud response. (This includes fraud detected by batch fraud detection, where responsive countermeasures are not quick enough.)
- C_3. The number of active attacks which were detected by fraud detection, and stopped by fraud response.
- C_4. The number of active attacks which were identified and stopped by preventive measures, e.g., authentication and intrusion detection.

Using C_1 to C_4 frequencies, it is possible to create an IRT specific for the incident response process of the financial institution. Of course, with more detailed information documented during the incident response process, it should be possible to create more complex IRTs, for example, distinguishing between online and batch fraud detection, and automatic and manual response measures.

Furthermore, by using the frequencies, it is possible to calculate the conditional probabilities of prevention, detection, and response, given an active trojan attack. The generated statistics are then used as an indication of how effective the current countermeasures are against the specific threat, i.e., the higher the conditional probabilities for prevention, detection, and response, the less successful is the trojan.

However, to be able to estimate the direct economic consequences of an active trojan attack, the IRT tool needs to be complemented with an additional model.

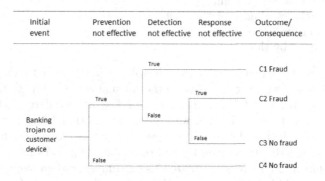

Fig. 1. Basic incident response tree [11].

Estimating the Direct Economic Consequences. When analyzing the possible direct economic consequences of fraud it is clear that the account balance of the victims and the transaction limit of the chosen online banking channel are important parameters; they both limit the size of the fraud. In [12], we notice that this situation is similar to current modeling of credit risk [17]. The model used is thus inspired by current models for credit risk, reusing some concepts from the advanced internal ratings-based approach for calculating credit risk [17].

By transferring these concepts to the domain of online financial fraud we end up with the following three concepts [12]:

- Exposure at Fraud (EAF_i) of customer i. Calculated as the minimum of the transaction limit (TL) and customer i:s account balance
- Probability of Fraud for a time period of one year (PF). Calculated from historical statistics or expert knowledge, as the number of fraud cases divided by the number of channel customers
- Loss Given Fraud (LGF_i) of customer i. Calculated for each customer, or based on historical statistics or expert knowledge, as the fraction of EAF stolen from defrauded customers.

In analogy with EL calculated for estimating the current credit risk [17], Expected Fraud (EF) is then calculated as:

$$EF = PF \cdot \sum_{i=1}^{N}(EAF_i \cdot LGF_i) \tag{1}$$

where N represents the number of channel customers, EAF_i represents the current exposure at fraud for each possible victim customer i, and PF and LGF_i represents values derived from historic events.

Thus, EF is conditioned on previous attacks targeting the financial institution, given:

- Number of defrauded customers
- Number of channel customers
- Account balance of each victim customer
- Transaction limit used for the specific channel
- Strategy used by the trojan.

However, with so many conditions, it will be hard for a fraud prevention manager to estimate how representative the calculated EF value is. One way to measure the accuracy of EF is to recalculate EF using a different set of victim customers, ceteris paribus. In [12], we present a conditional fraud value at risk (VaR) measure, which is defined as the level of loss that, for a specific scenario, will not be exceeded with a given level of confidence (e.g., 95%).

Conditional fraud VaR is calculated using simple random sampling over K different sets of victim customer accounts, where the number of customers in these sets is taken to be the expected annual number of defrauded customers I (which can be based on historical data known to the financial institution) [12].

Each sample will result in a sample-specific fraud loss (FL_k), calculated as:

$$FL_k = \sum_{i=1}^{I}(EAF_i \cdot LGF_i) \tag{2}$$

Additionally, K iterations of simple random sampling will generate a distribution of FL:s. EF is calculated as the mean of this distribution, and conditional fraud VaR is calculated by choosing the 95th percentile.

Furthermore, to be able to plan ahead for potential risks of an emerging threat environment, the fraud prevention manager will need to simulate future adverse scenarios, resulting in scenario-specific conditional fraud VaR.

To remedy this situation, we continue our research by creating a simulation tool for risk management of online fraud, which we call IncidentResponseSim. Additionally, we show how the results from these simulations can be used together with return on security investment calculations to support decisions about future investments.

3   Model

Our initial aim with IncidentResponseSim is to be able to simulate the effects of current and emerging threat landscapes directed against online financial services. The simulation environment is built on the concept of multi-agent-based simulation (MABS), which is a "class of computational models for simulating the actions and interactions of autonomous agents with a view to assessing their effects on the system as a whole" [18].

IncidentResponseSim is built using the Mason simulation environment [19]. This platform has previously been used in fraud detection research [20][21]. In contrast to earlier fraud detection research using the Mason simulation environment [20][21], IncidentResponseSim takes a broader perspective as it does not focus on any specific countermeasure technology, for example detection, but rather on the process of incident response as a whole, including the EF, and consequences of fraud using conditional fraud VaR.

The basic principle of IncidentResponseSim is the concept of fraudulent transactions. The banking trojan's objective is to attack the customers and transfer money out of the victim accounts. The concept of the channel plays a special role in the simulation. It serves as the scheduler for the next step of the simulation. Given the specific step of the simulation, the channel generates a supply of customers and malware.

In our simulation environment, the interaction between agents is always between malware and customer. The trojan randomly chooses a customer to attack. The agents do not perform any specific learning activities. Their behavior is given by probabilistic Markov models where the probabilities can be extracted from real incident response statistics, i.e., statistics calculated from an IRT.

Currently, there are three agents in IncidentResponseSim: (Online) Channel, Customer, and Trojan (Figure 2):

– Channel. This agent is responsible for scheduling customers and threats for the next step of the simulation.
– Customer. This agent is a fictional customer at the bank. The balance of the customer is drawn from a Beta distribution ($\alpha = 2, \beta = 7$) multiplied by 100,000. The assumption is that most customer balances are skewed towards lower amounts. Ideally, the bank estimates the actual distribution using the same underlying data that is required for reporting credit risk. Each customer can be in three different states: unaffected (non-victim), victim, and defrauded.
– Trojan. This agent is the only threat modeled in this first version of IncidentResponseSim. The Trojan can be in different states: active/non-active, and greedy/non-greedy (a greedy trojan is set to only attack wealthier customers with a current account balance above a set "greedy-limit").

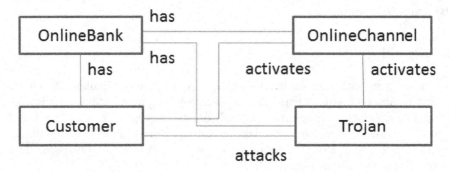

Fig. 2. Simplified model of IncidentResponseSim.

A normal step of the simulation starts out by identifying customers in the victim state. The customer is then "cured" with a probability P. In the initial version of IncidentResponseSim, this probability is set to 1.0, i.e., all previous victim customers are "cured" in the first part of every step.

In the second part of the step, the trojan agent is activated. The trojan randomly attacks a number of customers in the current online channel. Each victim customer is assigned a consequence, C_1 to C_4 (see Section 2.2), and all customers with a consequence of C_1 and C_2 are then defrauded according to the chosen trojan strategy; Max, Random, and Mean Transaction (Section 5).

3.1   Support for Different Types of Simulations

To be a valuable tool for a fraud prevention manager, IncidentResponseSim needs to support different types of simulations. We can imagine a fraud prevention manager that wants to estimate:

– The distribution of the number of victims, given scenario-specific IRT statistics

– The distribution of the direct economic consequences, given a scenario-specific number of victims and trojan strategy.

To accomplish this, IncidentReponseSim uses two main types of simulation; Simple Random Sampling of Defrauded Customers, and Simple Random Sampling of Direct Economic Consequences. Additionally, IncidentResponseSim supports a third simulation type, called Multi-step Simulation of Direct Economic Consequences, which first calculates the number of defrauded customers from IRT statistics, directly followed by a calculation of the direct economic consequences. They are all detailed below.

Simple Random Sampling of Defrauded Customers. During this simulation, the same step is performed N times by repeatedly calculating the number of defrauded customers, $C_1 + C_2$, given the conditional probabilities of prevention, detection, and response. Each customer is assigned as a victim with a probability of P_{IR}, according to the infection rate. Each victim customer is then further classified into the different consequences C_1 to C_4 according to the consequence-specific probabilities. The victim customer is first assigned to consequence C_4 with a probability P_P, according to the conditional probability of prevention. All victim customers that were not categorized into C_4, are then tested for C_1 with a probability $(1 - P_D)$, where P_D is the conditional probability of detection. Finally, the remaining customers are then categorized into C_3 with a probability P_R, the probability of effective response, and into C_2 with a probability $(1 - P_R)$. The number of defrauded customers per step is $y_n = C_1 + C_2$, resulting in a mean of:

$$\bar{y} = \frac{1}{N} \cdot \sum_{n=1}^{N} y_n \qquad (3)$$

In this article, we are conservative, aiming for an upper bound, and choose to set the number of defrauded customers as the 95 percentile of the distribution of y_n.

Simple Random Sampling of Direct Economic Consequences. In this first version of IncidentResponseSim, the simulation is started with a fixed number, M, of defrauded customers. During this simulation, the same step is performed K times by simple random sampling of M victim customers. Every victim is then defrauded according to the chosen trojan strategy (e.g., 90%), for example, $z_i = min(30000, x_i \cdot 0.9)$, where 30,000 represents the TL, and x_i represents the account balance of the customer. EF and conditional fraud VaR are then calculated according to the algorithm presented in Section 2.2.

Multi-step Simulation with Direct Economic Consequences. During this simulation, the behavior of the simulation is primed by relevant scenario statistics, for example, infection rate, and the conditional probabilities of prevention, detection, and response (given an actively targeting trojan). Additionally, the parameters can be changed from step to step to simulate a given fictive scenario. The actual logic is comparable to repeatedly performing one step of Simple Random Sampling of Defrauded Customers followed by one step of Simple Random Sampling of Direct Economic Consequences.

3.2 Data

Ideally, the data needed to support IncidentResponseSim is collected both internally from the fraud incident response process, and from external sources.

To be able to collect internal data, the financial institution probably needs to adjust its current incident response process in such a way that useful data is documented by the fraud response team, for example:

- The number of customers in the channel
- The frequencies of IRT consequences, C_1 to C_4
- Fraud-specific information:
  - The transaction limit of the channel
  - The account balance
  - The amount stolen
- The distribution of wealth in the channel (in line with existing credit risk calculations).

The financial institution also needs external data concerning the current and emerging threat landscape, as well as information about the quality of different types of countermeasures. The former is typically available from different types of security organizations, and the latter is data either acquired by information sharing, for example, between financial institutions, or by direct experience.

4 Simulating Relevant Scenarios Using IncidentResponseSim

In this section, we first present a baseline scenario describing our estimated current conditions, followed by scenarios where we evaluate how the current countermeasures handle different kinds of potential future stress, including:

- Newly entered markets (with different threat landscapes)
- Single point of failure (of different parts of the countermeasures)
- Emerging threat landscapes.

When simulation results are unacceptable, countermeasures, transaction limits, etc. can be adjusted to yield acceptable results (this should be tested using further simulation).

By performing "what-if" analysis using simulations like these, the fraud prevention manager can estimate, for example, scenario-specific conditional fraud VaR, which can be used together with models like return on security investment (ROSI) to support decisions about future security investments.

4.1   Baseline Scenario

Our fictional online channel has 100,000 customers. The maximum account balance of the online channel is set to 100,000 SEK, with a daily transaction limit of 30,000 SEK. According to our estimated (fictional) statistics, the trojan infection rate is 0.01, and the conditional probabilities of prevention, detection, and response is set to 0.8, 0.9, and 0.9 respectively. As this is our baseline scenario, the infection factor is set to 1.0. All simple random sampling simulations are set to 999 iterations. If further accuracy is needed, the number of iterations needs to be set to a higher value. All simulations use the random number seed 822075070.

The data used in the simulations are summarized below:

- Number of Customers = 100,000
- Max Balance = 100,000 SEK
- Transaction Limit = 30,000 SEK
- Number of Iterations = 999
- Infection Rate, $P_{IR} = 0.01$
- Infection Factor = 1.0
- Conditional Probability of Prevention, $P_P = 0.8$
- Conditional Probability of Detection, $P_D = 0.9$
- Conditional Probability of Response, $P_R = 0.9$
- Trojan Strategy = Max (i.e., the minimum of TL and account balance).

Throughout all simulations, we will be on the conservative side aiming for the 95 percentile results. The "Simple Random Sampling of Defrauded Customers" simulation generates a mean value of 38.10, a standard deviation of 6.07, and a 95% percentile of 48 (for $C_1 + C_2$).

We then insert the calculated number of defrauded customers at the 95 percentile, i.e., 48, into the "Simple Random Sampling of Direct Economic Consequences" simulation.

During the 999 iterations, EF was 941,426 SEK, with an FL standard deviation of 62,548 SEK. In 95% of all iterations, the stolen amount did not exceed 1,042,431 SEK, which is our conditional fraud VaR.

4.2   Newly Entered Markets

In this simulation, we can imagine a fraud prevention manager trying to model what might happen when the financial institution enters a new market using an online service which is very similar to one where they have access to baseline statistics. The main difference is the new threat landscape. We assume that the financial institution has a 2.75 times higher probability of native customers being infected with malware on the new market, using public malware infection statistics as a proxy [23]. In IncidentResponseSim we change the following information (compared to the baseline scenario):

- Infection Factor = 2.75

The "Simple Random Sampling of Defrauded Customers" simulation generates a mean value of 104.58, a standard deviation of 10.19, and a 95% percentile of 121 (for $C_1 + C_2$).

During the 999 iterations, EF was 2,379,053 SEK, with an FL standard deviation of 97,137 SEK. In 95% of all iterations, the stolen amount did not exceed 2,545,100 SEK, which is our conditional fraud VaR.

4.3   Single Point of Failure

In this simulation, we can imagine a fraud prevention manager trying to analyze what might happen when one of the main components of the countermeasures fails open, i.e., when the prevention system fails open, the detection system fails open, or the response system fails open. Information about the probable consequences of single points of failure will be helpful when estimating the fault tolerance of the incident response process.

Firstly, we set Probability of Prevention to 0. Simple Random Sampling of Number of Defrauded Customers results in 213 defrauded customers at 95 percentile.

Secondly, we set Probability of Detection to 0. Simple Random Sampling of Number of Defrauded Customers now results in 225 defrauded customers at 95 percentile.

Thirdly, we set Probability of Response to 0, which results in 225 defrauded customers at 95 percentile.

We then calculate the direct economic consequences given that 225 customers are defrauded (i.e., we chose to use the highest number). This results in an EF of 4,422,002 SEK, and an FL standard deviation of 135,992 SEK. In 95% of all iterations, the stolen amount did not exceed 4,636,140 SEK, which is our conditional fraud VaR.

4.4   Emerging Threat Landscapes

In this simulation, we model what might happen when the fraud prevention team proactively identifies an emerging threat that is highly contagious, and also very effective at overcoming current preventive measures. In IncidentResponseSim we need to change the following information (compared to the baseline scenario):

– Infection Rate, $P_{IR} = 0.02$
– Conditional Probability of Prevention, $P_P = 0.6$

The Simple Random Sampling of Number of Defrauded Customers results in 171 defrauded customers at the 95 percentile, an EF of 3,352,588 SEK, with an FL standard deviation of 114,013 SEK. In 95% of all iterations the defrauded money did not exceed 3,545,783 SEK, which is our conditional fraud VaR.

5   Trojan Strategies Versus Transaction Limits

In this simulation, we model the direct economic effects of various banking trojan strategies using "Simple Random Sampling of Direct Economic Consequences". The number of defrauded customers is set to 24 in all simulations, changing only the trojan strategy and the daily transaction limit (Figure 3).

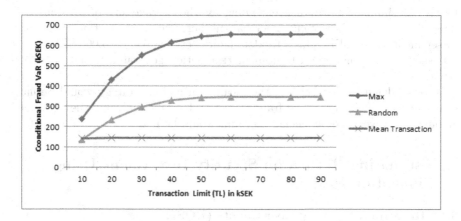

Fig. 3. Conditional fraud VaR (at the 95th percentile) for different trojan strategies (specified in the text), given a specific online channel.

5.1   Max

In this simulation, we simulate a trojan agent going for the account balance, up to the daily transaction limit. In Figure 3, we can see that the curve rises sharply and then levels off. The reason for this is the distribution of wealth among the channel customers (Section 3), with only a few customers with account balances "in the right tail". This implies that a transaction limit above 50,000 SEK makes little sense for this scenario. Thus, the effect of the transaction limit is dependent on both the distribution of wealth in the channel, and the expected fraud scenario.

From a defender perspective, this strategy would be easy to detect using fraud detection.

5.2   Random

In this simulation, we change the odds a bit and simulate a trojan agent going for a random uniformly distributed amount between 0 and the minimum of the account balance and the daily transaction limit. As expected, conditional fraud VaR is much lower than for the previous strategy, although the general form of the curve is the same.

From a defender perspective, the random strategy would be a bit harder to detect using behavior-based fraud detection. However, some fraudulent transactions will be high, and may attract attention from fraud detection and also be easily spotted by customers.

5.3   Mean Transaction

Lastly, we simulate a trojan agent going for the average size of previous customer transactions. Every customer has his/her "mean transaction" simulated by setting it to 500 SEK, plus a random figure between 0 and 10,000 SEK. Using this strategy, the maximum fraudulent transaction generated would be 10,500 SEK.

From a defender perspective, the mean transaction strategy would be hard to detect using behavior-based fraud detection by only analyzing the defrauded amounts; however, the beneficiary account would be new.

6   Estimating Return on Security Investment Using Simulation Results

6.1   Return on Security Investments (ROSI)

In this section, we will evaluate different security investments using a framework that is used within the information security domain called Return on Security Investment (ROSI) [22]. In this framework, $ROSI$ is defined as:

$$ROSI = \frac{MLR - COS}{COS} \qquad (4)$$

where MLR is defined as monetary loss reduction, and COS is defined as cost of solution. These values are discounted, when needed, and $ROSI$ should be positive for the investment to be profitable.

To calculate the monetary loss reduction, an Annual Loss Expectancy (ALE) is first calculated as the product of the Annual Rate of Occurrence (ARO) and the Single Loss Expectancy (SLE).

$$ALE = ARO \cdot SLE \qquad (5)$$

Then, either a modified ALE ($mALE$) is calculated, or a mitigation ratio is estimated (including the potential benefits of the implemented solution, i.e., the countermeasures). Thus, we have:

$$MLR = ALE - mALE \qquad (6)$$

or

$$MLR = ALE \cdot MR \qquad (7)$$

where MR is defined as the mitigation ratio.

6.2 Simplified Example

We can imagine a chief information security officer (CISO) deciding if, and how, to mitigate a probable threat (Section 4.1). The CISO has four different mitigating actions in mind: adding 10% prevention, 5% detection, or 5% response, or doing nothing.

In this simplified example, we can see that by adding preventive measures we get the highest $ROSI$, i.e., 0.15 (Table 1).

Table 1. ROSI analysis using IRTs and conditional fraud VaR calculated by Incident-ResponseSim (at the 95th percentile).

Action	COS	#Frauds	Cost	MLR	$ROSI$
Do nothing	0	48	1,042,431	0	N/A
Add prevention (+0.1)	400,000	26	581,281	461,150	0.15
Add detection (+0.05)	300,000	38	826,431	215,999	-0.28
Add response (+0.05)	200,000	38	826,431	215,999	0.08

7   Discussion

Admittedly, the basic IRT implemented in this simulation is simple. However, it is possible to elaborate on the IRT so that it better represents the actual risk situation and the countermeasures applied, assuming that necessary data is available. Ways to do this include, for example, separating response into automatic and manual response, or allowing for more than binary outcomes. In [11], we argued that the simplicity of the basic IRT suits the work effort needed during an active attack using banking trojans. In the same article, we argued that event tree analysis, which IRTs are making use of, is made possible by low under-reporting, i.e., IRTs need "good enough" frequency statistics to accurately document the quality of the different parts of countermeasures. For different reasons, there will be under-reporting, but ways to minimize the problem exist, like reimbursing customers who report fraud, or if governing bodies legislate that retail and corporate customers must report when being defrauded. Furthermore, it is possible to back-test for non-reported transfers to known mule accounts. This can be used to both adjust frequency counts, and to estimate the quality of the current reporting practices by calculating the ratio of reported versus non-reported fraud.

The method for calculating conditional fraud VaR is partly inspired by credit risk methodology. We use simple random sampling to create the distribution of FL.

In this article, we have presented several different use cases, or scenarios, which are relevant to a fraud prevention manager either during the design of new online channels, or during risk management of existing ones. The presented scenarios are still quite simple, but the underlying simulation platform makes it possible to include more complex behavior with regard to the agents when needed.

Additionally, we have presented a simple example using simulation results together with $ROSI$ calculations. We have opted for using conditional fraud VaR in our calculations, to be on the conservative side. One reason for this is that it is hard to measure the indirect costs of fraud.

8   Conclusions

IncidentResponseSim makes it possible to simulate the effects of active attacks using impersonation, like banking trojans. The simulation platform can, for example, be used during the design phase of online banking services, during active attacks, and during stress testing. Initially, IncidentResponseSim will be most valuable for financial institutions which are able collect the necessary statistics from their own incident response process.

In this article, we presented how to generate a set of plausible scenarios using IncidentResponseSim, including estimating risks pertaining to newly entered markets, single points of failure, and emerging threat landscapes. Additionally, we presented how to evaluate security investments using our proposed conditional fraud VaR model together with $ROSI$, to be able to support decisions about future security investments.

We argue that IncidentResponseSim can be a valuable tool for risk management of online financial services. However, further investigation and experimentation using real data are needed, and the results need to be validated by subject matter experts.

Future work includes adding functionality to IncidentResponseSim, like social network analysis for the analysis of the effects of different ways to warn customers about ongoing attacks, and potentially adding expert knowledge using Bayes, or more dynamic models like game theory. It would also be interesting to directly integrate more detailed models than ROSI.

Acknowledgments. I would like to thank Lars-Göran Mattsson, Per Näsman, and Torbjörn Thedéen at KTH Royal Institute of Technology, Stockholm, Sweden, and Stefan Axelsson at Blekinge Institute of Technology, BTH, Sweden, for feedback while writing this article.

References

1. ENISA: Methodologies for the identification of critical infrastructure assets (2015)
2. ECB: Recommendations for the Security of Internet Payments (2013)
3. ENISA: ENISA Threat Landscape (2014)
4. FFIEC: Supplement to Authentication in an Internet Banking Environment (2011)
5. Schneier, B.: Secrets & Lies: Digital Security in a Networked World, pp. 318–333. John Wiley & Sons, New York (2000)

6. Mauw, S., Oostdijk, M.: Foundations of attack trees. In: Won, D.H., Kim, S. (eds.) ICISC 2005. LNCS, vol. 3935, pp. 186–198. Springer, Heidelberg (2006)

7. Edge, K.S., Dalton II, G.C., Raines, R.A., Mills, R.F.: Using attack and protection trees to analyze threats and defenses to homeland security. In: MILCOM. IEEE (2006)

8. Edge, K.S., Raines, R.A., Grimaila, M., Baldwin, R., Bennington, R., Reuter, C.: The use of protection trees to analyze security for an online banking system. In: The Proceedings of the 40th Hawaii International Conference on System Sciences (2006)

9. Kordy, B., Mauw, S., Radomirović, S., Schweitzer, P.: Foundations of attack–defense trees. In: Degano, P., Etalle, S., Guttman, J. (eds.) FAST 2010. LNCS, vol. 6561, pp. 80–95. Springer, Heidelberg (2011)

10. Pat-Cornell, M.E.: Fault trees vs. event trees in reliability analysis. Journal of Risk Analysis 4(3), 177–186 (1984)

11. Gorton, D.: Using Incident Response Trees as a Tool for Risk Management of Online Financial Services. Journal of Risk Analysis 34(9), 1763–1774 (2014)

12. Gorton, D.: Modeling fraud prevention of online services using incident response trees and value at risk. In: The Proceedings of the International Conference on Availability, Reliability and Security (ARES) (2015)

13. Wikipedia: Online banking. http://en.wikipedia.org/wiki/Online_banking (Accessed: August 30, 2015)

14. Julisch, K.: Risk-Based Payment Fraud Detection. Research Report, IBM Research, Zurich (2010)

15. Kaspersky: The Great Bank Robbery: Carbanak cybergang steals $1bn from 100 financial institutions worldwide. http://www.kaspersky.com/about/news/virus/2015/Carbanak-cybergang-steals-1-bn-USD-from-100-financial-institutions-worldwide (Accessed: August 30, 2015)

16. Florncio, D., Cormac, H.: Phishing and money mules. In: IEEE International Workshop on Information Forensics and Security, pp. 1–5 (2010)

17. Bank For International Settlements: An Explanatory Note on the Basel II IRB Risk Weight Function (2005)

18. Wikipedia: Agent-based Models. http://en.wikipedia.org/wiki/Agent-based_model (Accessed: August 30, 2015)

19. Luke, S., Cioffi-Revilla, C., Panait, L., Sullivan, K., Balan, G.: MASON: A Multi-agent Simulation Environment. Simulation, 517–527 (2005)

20. Lopez-Rojas, E.A., Gorton, D., Axelsson, S.: Using the RetSim Simulator for Fraud Detection Research. Int. Journal of Simulation and Process Modeling, 144–155 (2015)

21. Lopez-Rojas, E.A., Axelsson, S.: BankSim: a bank payment simulation for fraud detection research. In: The 26th European Modeling and Simulation Symposium (EMSS), pp. 144–152 (2014)

22. ENISA: Introduction to Return on Security Investment (2012)

23. PandaLabs: PandaLabs Annual Report 2012 Summary (2013)

Network and Software Security

Challenges in Managing Firewalls

Artem Voronkov[✉], Stefan Lindskog, and Leonardo A. Martucci

Karlstad University, Karlstad, Sweden
{artem.voronkov,stefan.lindskog,leonardo.martucci}@kau.se

Abstract. Firewalls are essential security devices that can provide protection against network attacks. To be effective, a firewall must be properly configured to ensure consistency with the security policy. However, configuring is a complex and error-prone process. This work tries to identify the reasons behind firewall misconfigurations. To achieve our goal, we conducted a series of semi-structured interviews with system administrators that manage access control lists in networks of different sizes. The paper discusses our interview results and describes future work.

1 Introduction

Network security is essential for all types of organizations. Making sure that the network's perimeter is properly defended is an important measure to prevent leakage of sensitive information. One common solution to mitigate attacks is a firewall. The main function of firewalls is to inspect the network traffic and prevent unauthorized access from outside the organization's secure domain. However, configuring a firewall has proven to be an error-prone task [4,5].

Firewall filtering actions, such as accepting or rejecting packets, are performed according to a set of static configuration rules that use only information contained in the packet, such as source and destination network addresses, port and protocol. The constant growth of networks forces firewall rule sets to expand over time. These rule sets can be tangled, and this complicates their readability and finding the right place for a new rule in case of policy expansion.

This paper investigates the complexity of the process of configuring firewalls. We address the question: what are the main difficulties network security specialists deal with? The answer to this question will significantly help in further research on firewall usability.

The remainder of the paper discusses related work in Sect. 2. The methodology used and an outline of the conducted interviews are given in Sect. 3. In Sect. 4 we describe the data obtained from our semi-structured interviews and discuss the outcome. Concluding remarks are given in Sect. 5.

The work was partially funded by the High Quality Networked Services in a Mobile World (HITS), a research project of the Knowledge Foundation of Sweden.

The authors would like to thank Zeeshan Afzal for his time and input to this work.

S. Buchegger and M. Dam (Eds.): NordSec 2015, LNCS 9417, pp. 191–196, 2015.
DOI: 10.1007/978-3-319-26502-5_13

2   Related Work

Over the past few year, several studies have focused on a firewall configuring process and some other related topics. Wool [4,5] gives an overview of the most common firewall misconfigurations among system administrators and, according to him, most misconfigurations belong to inbound traffic. This is the worst case scenario, because filtering incoming traffic is the main function of firewalls. For that reason, research on firewall misconfiguration detection, such as [2], have been conducted. There are no studies however on understanding the reasons for misconfigurations.

Access Control Policy Management was studied by Bauer et al. [1]. Access control professionals were divided into two groups: policy makers and policy implementers. Policy makers design access control rule sets and policy implementers are responsible for realizing them. By conducting semi-structured interviews, Bauer et al. identified three factors that lead to unmanageable access control rule sets: (1) policies are made by several people, (2) policy makers and policy implementers are different people, and (3) current access control systems can not always implement the desired policy. In contrast to the work of Bauer et al., we focus on firewall misconfigurations and understanding the reasons behind them.

3   Methodology and Interview Details

To identify problems in configuring firewalls, real data must be obtained directly from system administrators, since the literature does not provide an answer to our research question. We considered two possible alternatives: a quantitative method (questionnaire) and a qualitative method (interviews). An advantage of a questionnaire is mainly the low cost of data collection and processing. However, using semi-structured interviews, we get much more information and do not need so many respondents. Since it was not easy to recruit system administrators for the user study, we decided to use semi-structured interviews as a main approach for obtaining the data. Interviews allow us to focus on primary questions and gives the opportunity for multiple comments about the problem from the respondents. Nevertheless, a questionnaire was designed to identify the main difficulties specialists in network security deal with on a daily basis. The questionnaire will be used as a subsidiary method to include people who lack the time to take part in our ordinary interviews.

3.1   Semi-structured Interviews

We designed our questions not only to explore our topics of interest but also to encourage the respondents to elaborate on specific problems they encounter. While conducting the interviews, we followed the best practices and recommendations found in the literature [3]. The interviews were audio recorded and later used to produce the transcripts for data analysis. The interviews focus on the following topics:

- Overview of the respondent's experience of working with firewalls.
- Efforts to maintain firewalls.
- Solutions used to provide protection to the network.
- Difficulties they face in the process of configuring/maintaining firewalls.
- Interaction within the groups of system administrators.
- Security incidents that have happened in the organization.
- Formal and informal procedures for simplifying the management of rule sets.

3.2 Respondents

Six system administrators (all males) from different organizations who are responsible for networks of different sizes were recruited. They voluntarily agreed to take part in our research. The interviews lasted 40 minutes approximately. It is worth noting that all the respondents are independent from our research group and no financial compensation was offered. All the answers in the interview are anonymous and the respondents are identified by numbers #{1–6}. Table 1 shows participants, their experience of working with firewalls, network size that they manage, effort for support and type of organization they work in.

It should be mentioned that this is a pilot study. To validate our initial results, additional interviews will be conducted with respondents from different organizations including people that also are involved in education on firewall configurations.

Table 1. List of respondents

Respondent	Experience	Network size	Effort	Organization
#1	12 years	≈50 nodes	1 hour/week	Institute
#2	8 years	≈400 nodes	2 hours/week	Institute
#3	19 years	≈850 nodes	0.5 hour/week	University
#4	17 years	≈450 nodes	9 hours/week	Enterprise
#5	3 years	≈70 nodes	1 hour/week	University
#6	20 years	≈500 nodes	0.5 hour/week	University

The responsibilities of all system administrators interviewed are almost identical: they administrate security devices, such as firewalls and intrusion detection systems, and quite often also switches and routers. All have extensive experience of managing firewalls and have created configuration files on their own. The "Effort" column in Table 1 represents the average amount of time spent by these professionals on maintaining firewalls. All the specialists had implemented firewall policies that have been used for a long time. That is the reason why they are nearly static and their maintenance does not require much effort. Another reason why the numbers in this column are low is that five of six system administrators from the list have colleagues they cooperate with. The only exception is respondent #4, who works alone and thus spends a considerable amount of time on managing firewalls.

We conducted interviews with people from three different types of organizations, e.g., universities, international research institutes and enterprises. The size of the organizations varies from 16,000–18,000 faculty, staff and students for universities, 2,500–3,000 staff members for institutes and more than 100 employees in the enterprise.

4   Results and Discussion

This section reports our findings and discusses the results.

4.1   Results of the Semi-structured Interviews

1. **Having more people responsible for security measures is not always beneficial.** Five respondents mentioned that some difficulties occur when there is more than one person responsible for firewalls. It is then necessary to have well adjusted mechanisms of interaction, such as frequent personal communication and good documentation. Nevertheless, almost all our respondents use either the first or the second mechanism of interaction, but not both at the same time. Another issue is that the availability of several system administrators generates the problem of distribution of roles. It does not work properly for four respondents and they have been confronted, at least once, with this issue.
2. **A variety of approaches is used to simplify the process of maintaining firewalls.** All the respondents use different ways to spend less resources on maintenance of security measures. However, the approaches are not equally distributed among the respondents, see Table 2.

Table 2. List of approaches used by respondents

Respondent	Documentation	Comments in configuration files	Firewall management/ testing tools	Revision history	Frequent personal communication
#1	Yes	Yes	No	No	No
#2	Yes	Yes	Yes	No	No
#3	Yes	Yes	No	No	Yes
#4	No	Yes	Yes	Yes	Not applicable
#5	No	Yes	No	No	Yes
#6	No	Yes	No	No	Yes

"Frequent personal communication" means the interaction in one group of system administrators. By "Documentation" we refer to electronically or hand-written security policies and more detailed instructions and procedures for how to handle a particular system. It is worth noting that system administrators that do not yet have a documentation of the configurations and practices mentioned that they will start working on this.

Another issue that needs clarification is why many of our respondents do not use "Firewall management/testing tools" and "Revision history" approaches. For the first approach, most of respondents mentioned that it is too expensive to use it. For instance, respondent #6 answered: "Too expensive, but, to be honest, we do not know the costs of configuration mistakes". For the second approach, two respondents answered that they use configuration management systems, i.e., Ansible[1] and Puppet[2], and they do not need to manually write a "Revision history" separately for firewall configuration files, since such systems have a built-in version control of files. Another respondent answered: "All changes are written in a simple text file, newest on top".

3. **Firewall misconfigurations are still common.** All the respondents have experienced mistakes in firewall configuration files and different types of misconfigurations continue to occur despite the presence of a large number of auxiliary mechanisms. Too strict/permissive, redundant rules and unauthorized access to some nodes were a few reasons given by the respondents. The most common case is too strict rules. However, these misconfigurations usually do not have severe consequences and it does not require much time to figure them out. Since system administrators serve people, they will immediately start receiving complaints from users when this type of misconfiguration occurs. This implies that they will have an opportunity to make changes to the configuration file without prolonged delay. Too permissive rules is far worse in terms of discovery time. Two of our respondents stated that they have dealt with this error and found it out either during a scheduled manual check or from colleagues who discovered it by chance. The main reason for firewall misconfigurations is the human factor. Five respondents encountered the problems when they tried to multitask while configuring firewalls at the same time.

4. **Policy creators and implementers are the same people.** According to our results, among all our respondents there is no one who is responsible for creating security policies. The responsibility for the policy lies solely on the system administrators.

5. **It is easy to configure a firewall.** Only two of six of our respondents answered that it is difficult to configure firewalls. Both of them agreed that the most complicated part is "reading firewall rules" in order to find a suitable position for a new rule to be placed. Four respondents argued that they had no difficulties configuring firewalls. Respondents #3 and #4 stated: "I have been doing it for almost twenty years. For me it is quite straightforward" and "Once you get used to it, you can do pretty much everything", respectively. Respondent #5 answered: "It is not really difficult for use cases we have. We do not do anything fancy and do not use any advanced features".

---

[1] http://www.ansible.com
[2] http://www.puppetlabs.com

4.2   Discussion

The first and third findings reported above correspond to the findings from [1] and [5], respectively. The first finding showed that it is not a good idea to have several people responsible for firewalls. In our pilot study we also had a case with only one professional being responsible for the network. Respondent #4 mentioned that the knowledge of all procedures and configurations is inside his head, since they do not have any kind of formal documentation. From his point of view, it is better to have more people and as a result a good redundancy of the knowledge, despite the fact that it will initially require a lot of work for him. Finding four deviates from what Bauer et al. [1] stated. It seems that committing a security policy creation to firewall configuration implementers is normal practice among system administrators. There are many ways to simplify the process of configuring firewalls, and thus the second result was expected as well.

Unexpectedly, four respondents reported that it is easy to configure firewalls. However, all of them have discovered misconfigurations several times. It would be interesting to investigate where errors come from if it is not the complexity of the process of configuring firewalls. To answer the question "If firewalls are easy to configure, why are there so many misconfigurations?" we need to continue conducting interviews. We believe that it might be easy to manage firewalls when configurations are almost static. Another source of misconfigurations could be some approaches that are used to simplify the process of configuring firewalls. Actually, none of them guarantee that the firewall configuration is fully consistent.

5   Concluding Remarks

We described the ongoing work on understanding the challenges of firewall management. A number of semi-structured interviews with system administrators have been conducted. Both expected and unexpected results were obtained. We were not aware that experienced system administrators claim that it is easy to configure firewalls. In our future work, we are interested in further exploring the issue. Our intention is to propose a concept of a visualization to our respondents and collect their opinions and suggestions on it.

References

1. Bauer, L., Cranor, L.F., Reeder, R.W., Reiter, M.K., Vaniea, K.: Real life challenges in access-control management. In: CHI 2009. ACM (2009)
2. Chao, C.: A flexible and feasible anomaly diagnosis system for internet firewall rules. In: APNOMS 2011. IEEE (2011)
3. Galletta, A.: Mastering the Semi-Structured Interview and Beyond: From Research Design to Analysis and Publication (Qualitative Studies in Psychology). NYU Press (2013)
4. Wool, A.: A quantitative study of firewall configuration errors. Computer **37**(6), 62–67 (2004)
5. Wool, A.: Trends in firewall configuration errors: Measuring the holes in swiss cheese. IEEE Internet Computing **14**(4), 58–65 (2010)

Multi-layer Access Control
for SDN-Based Telco Clouds

Bernd Jäger[1], Christian Röpke[2]([✉]), Iris Adam[1], and Thorsten Holz[2]

[1] Nokia Networks, Munich, Germany
{bernd.jaeger,iris.adam}@nokia.com
[2] Ruhr-University Bochum, Bochum, Germany
{christian.roepke,thorsten.holz}@rub.de

Abstract. The telecom industry has recently started to adapt the emerging paradigm of *Software-Defined Networking* (SDN) in combination with cloud computing to the telecommunication world. Both technologies enable a high degree of automation and flexibility for existing and novel networks. As this combination can reduce costs and enables the development of new business opportunities, telecom providers build so-called *telco clouds* leveraging SDN for operating the underlying network infrastructure. In this context, a major concern is to maintain security once network functions and SDN controllers run virtualized inside the telco clouds. In particular, compromised cloud applications and SDN controllers may disturb correct functioning such that costs increase, security deteriorates or reputation degrades. Therefore, we propose a multi-layer access control system to mitigate such adverse consequences and, thereby, focus on securing both SDN's application layer as well as its control layer.

Keywords: Software-defined networking · SDN controller security · SDN application containment · Telco cloud

1 Introduction

During the last decade, cloud computing has revolutionized the IT industry. Based on the separation of software from hardware, data centers became virtualized and IT services could be provisioned in a flexible and cost-efficient way. The telecom industry has recently started to adapt virtualization techniques to the telecommunication world focusing on the emerging technology of *Network Function Virtualization* (NFV). NFV aims at separating so-called *Virtual Network Functions* (VNF) such as signaling servers and conferencing servers from proprietary, thus, expensive hardware. Complementary to NFV, *Software-Defined Networking* (SDN) has evolved as a second major trend which fundamentally changes the telecom industry. SDN decouples network control programs such as packet forwarding from network devices in a way network control runs logically centralized while forwarding hardware remains distributed. By converging cloud computing and NFV with SDN, telecom providers can benefit from automation

© Springer International Publishing Switzerland 2015
S. Buchegger and M. Dam (Eds.): NordSec 2015, LNCS 9417, pp. 197–204, 2015.
DOI: 10.1007/978-3-319-26502-5_14

and flexibility which, on the one hand, is promising to reduce costs and, on the other hand, enables to develop new business opportunities. Inside a telco cloud, however, providers face two main problems. First, cloud applications can get compromised, thus, may perform malicious actions while remaining correctly authorized. Second, compromised SDN controllers could maliciously re-program the underlying SDN-based network or manipulate the cloud applications' instructions. To mitigate adverse consequences, we propose a multi-layer access control system. The basic idea is to restrict the set of instructions a telco cloud component is allowed to perform. As this enables to reduce the set of critical instructions to a minimum, we can mitigate malicious behavior such as privilege escalation and malicious network re-programming. Since we consider manipulations on multiple layers (i.e., on the application layer and the control layer), we present an access control system taking these layer's specifics into account.

2 Background

Figure 1 depicts a simplified example of a telco cloud which runs a conference service for end users. Inside this telco cloud, various VNFs (also called cloud applications) provide communication services whereas a management system and a SDN controller orchestrate these VNFs and the underlying SDN-based network, respectively. User Equipment (UE), such as mobile phones, and computers connect to the telco cloud, for example, via a SDN-based access network or the Internet. Considering a conference call between a mobile network user and an Internet user, signaling (dashed line) via the Session Initiation Protocol (SIP) terminates in a so-called Call Session Control Function (CSCF). During signaling, the CSCF is able to detect non-conforming SIP UEs and to block them for a certain amount of time by blacklisting (BL) functionality inside the SDN switch, e.g., to avoid Denial-of-Service (DoS) attacks. After connection setup, a Policy and Charging Enforcement Function (PCEF) controls the data traffic

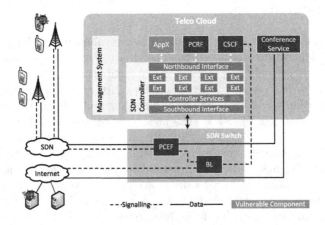

Fig. 1. Simplified Telco Cloud

of end users at runtime to enforce telco cloud specific policies, e. g., to block traffic of users who have exceeded the data volume limit or have not paid their invoice yet. This function is managed by the cloud application called Policy and Charging Rules Function (PCRF) which in real-time decides on, for example, quality and billing parameters. At this point, the two end users can exchange data (solid line) by utilizing the cloud application called conference service.

As indicated before, this example includes the cloud applications PCRF and CSCF which, in contrast to the conference service, interact with the SDN controller. Therefore, we also denote them as *SDN applications*. Inside the SDN controller, controller services provide interfaces towards such SDN applications (called *northbound interface*) and towards SDN switches (called *southbound interface*). Furthermore, many SDN controllers provide services such as a topology manager, a statistic manager and a flow programmer in order to view and modify the current network state. Since such basic services alone may not meet the customer's needs, often third-party software running inside the SDN controller is needed to extend this basic functionality. Such *SDN controller extensions* could, for example, extend the northbound and southbound interface or provide additional features such as network protocol specific packet processing. In the literature, such extensions are also called *SDN kernel applications* [1], *kernel modules* [2] or *network services* [3].

Figure 1 also illustrates our attacker model. On the one hand, we consider infected end user systems which, for example, exploit vulnerabilities in cloud applications or SDN controllers. On the other hand, we consider intentionally or unintentionally misbehaving cloud applications, e. g., from other tenants as well as SDN controller components (e. g., extensions) presenting flaws or vulnerabilities. Considering this, attackers may impersonate cloud applications, connected to the SDN controller's northbound interface and misuse the set of operations in order to perform malicious actions on the SDN end user traffic. Attackers could also send specially crafted packets to a SDN switch triggering it to delegate this packet to the SDN controller. If vulnerable, the SDN controller could be exploited, for example, resulting in crashes during packet parsing[1] or code execution depending on the vulnerability. As a result of such attacks, legitimate end user traffic as well as cloud application data could be dropped or deleted, manipulated and copied. In particular, denial-of-service and eavesdropping attacks can significantly compromise the telco cloud's correct functioning.

3   System Design

Our system is illustrated in Figure 2 and extends a SDN-based telco cloud by various components. Inside the cloud management system, a descriptor allows to define application-specific policies. Furthermore, the SDN controller is extended by a Policy Enforcement (PE) unit, a modified northbound interface, a SDN-specific interface for controller extensions and a corresponding service which provides this interface. Since attacks can be launched by SDN applications as well

---

[1] https://wiki.onosproject.org/display/ONOS/Security+advisories

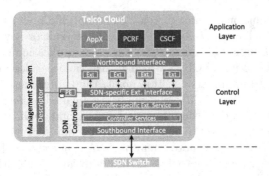

Fig. 2. System Design

as via SDN controller components, we control the critical instructions invoked on both the application layer and the control layer.

3.1 Application Layer Access Control

Gruschka *et al.* [4] show that cloud applications are exposed to manifold attacks, for example, by end users or via the cloud management interface. In worst case, cloud applications that are connected to a SDN controller, can get compromised and, thus, may send malicious instructions. Therefore, we propose an access control mechanism that supplies a policy enforcement unit in a SDN controller configurable through an application-specific profile. The profile is provided by a descriptor from an independent management system. Thus, a SDN controller is enabled to restrict the instruction set of a cloud application according to the specified application profile. SDN controllers translate such high-level instructions on the northbound interface into forwarding rules which are finally added to Forwarding Tables (FT) in a SDN switch. Such a forwarding table provides a mask used for matching of end user packets, e.g., packet headers. Packet headers enable to prove whether instructions match, for example, the specified end user address range, the specified source/destination addresses according to the defined network topology, or the specified protocols/ports to be processed by the corresponding cloud application. The descriptor-based application profile also enables influence on the allowed actions of matching packets like, for example, dropping or forwarding as well as on allowed modifications of the packet header.

Figure 3 shows the descriptor for a simplified application profile for the example network (shown in Figure 1). The PCRF/PSCF usually forward nearly the entire user traffic but allow to block/blacklist individual misbehaving end-users. As a first security measure, the PCRF as well as the CSCF are assigned to its own forwarding table preventing mutual modification of forwarding rules. But that increases security only to a certain extent as at least SIP signaling passes both forwarding tables and can, therefore, be influenced by both the PCRF and the CSCF. One possible attack would be a DoS attack, where a compromised

Method: Application Profile provided by Pseudo Descriptor for Multiple Pipelined Forwarding Tables				
Source Address	Prot.	Prio	Action	Sink Addr.
Application: PCRF, assign Forwarding Table 1 (FT1)				
Tardy Payer 1 of SIP-user address range (1ϵ)	SIP/Voice	Prio2	drop	-
Tardy Payer i of SIP-user address range (1ϵ)	SIP/Voice	Prio2	drop	-
All other users of SIP-user address range (all ϵ)	SIP	Prio1	goto FT2	-
All other users of SIP-user address range (all ϵ)	Voice	Prio1	forward	Conf. Server
Application: CSCF, assign Forwarding Table 2 (FT2)				
Malicious User 1 of SIP-user address range (1ϵ)	SIP	Prio2	drop+error	-
Malicious User j of SIP-user address range (1ϵ)	SIP	Prio2	drop+error	-
All other users of SIP-user address range (all ϵ)	SIP	Prio1	forward	CSCF

(1ϵ):   means that only one element of the whole user address space (a single user) can be blocked
(all ϵ): means that a complete user address space (using *) can be forwarded

Fig. 3. Application Profile Example

PCRF tries dropping all voice and SIP traffic of priority 1 instead of forwarding it. That is not accepted by the SDN controller's PE unit because the application profile explicitly states that only forwarding to the specified destinations (FT2, Conf Server) is possible. If not allowed to drop the complete traffic, the compromised PCRF could try to block as many individual end users (tardy payers) as possible. But for the "blocking"-action the application profile specifies that only individual end users (1ε) and not complete address ranges (all ε) can be blocked. In case of excessive end user blocking, an alarm is raised once a configurable threshold is exceeded.

Telco networks facilitate such precautions as their topology and their behavior is usually quite well defined. Also the information for the application profile such as user address spaces, protocols, destination addresses and so on is already available in management systems. When thinking of virtualized telco networks according to ETSI NFV [5] in conjunction with SDN, quite a few management and orchestration systems will be involved. But their interworking is well specified. It may be necessary to add a management entity like an SDN orchestrator. As all these management and orchestration entities are specified to support a large grade of automation, also an automated update of the application profile is imaginable, e.g., if the network topology changes due to scaling. An advantage of the descriptor-based method is enabling the network service provider to increase the security of the SDN end user traffic from a telco network architecture and functionality point of view without the necessity to be familiar with SDN controller specifics.

3.2 Control Layer Access Control

On the control layer, we witness third-party SDN controller extensions which necessarily extend basic SDN controller functions in order to meet network operators' needs. Such extensions can significantly harm SDN controllers either unintentionally (e. g., through bugs or vulnerabilities) or intentionally (e. g., through malicious logic) [1,3]. Moreover, end user systems can compromise correct functioning, for example, by launching DoS attacks [6] or by exploiting vulnerabilities in SDN controllers[23]. Because of security and robustness considerations, we therefore extend access control to the control layer and provide restrictions on SDN controller components (especially third-party extensions) with high-level permissions in a SDN controller independent fashion.

High-Level Permissions. Current sandbox systems are based on low-level permissions, i. e., system calls [1] and Java/OSGi permissions [3]. Considering that 50% to 80% of network outages are caused by human errors[4], we believe that sandbox misconfiguration is likely to happen in practice or that operators simply grant all permissions to each third-party extension. High-level permissions such as *readTopology* or *addForwardingTableEntry* are easy to understand by operators and can help to configure sandboxes correctly. Thereby, the sandbox configurations can remain with a reduced set of allowed permissions. As a consequence, vulnerable and compromised third-party SDN controller extensions are limited to a minimum set of critical operations which enables to counter various attacks. Taking a load balancer extension as an example, such a service must at least receive packet-in messages, read the topology and view statistics in order to determine both to which backend server and by what path a network client should reach a determined backend server. Furthermore, it needs to add and remove forwarding rules in order to program the determined path which may change over time. But allowing this extension to use aforementioned critical operations without any restriction, if exploitable, an attacker may be able to misuse that set of operations. For such a case, our system allows restricting that set of critical operations, for example, in the way that a load balancer is only able to read a certain part of the topology or to write only forwarding rules containing IP destination addresses of one of the backend servers. If restricted like this, an attacker cannot, for example, view or re-program the entire network anymore.

Considering that large companies such as Cisco and HP as well as the industry's leading open source OpenDaylight controllers are built upon Java and OSGi, we utilize Java security services in order to create high-level and SDN-specific permissions which are used to control the access to corresponding critical operations. In fact, access control on the control layer is built upon previous work [3] which already benefits from Java security services. By using this, all SDN controller components (including third-party extensions) run in a separate sandbox while access to critical and low-level operations can be effectively controlled. We extend previous work and add a new set of high-level permissions. The following permissions serve as a basis for this set but our design is not limited to these permissions: *readTopology, readStatistics, addForwardingTableEntry,*

[2] https://wiki.opendaylight.org/view/Security_Advisories

[3] https://wiki.onosproject.org/display/ONOS/Security+advisories

[4] http://www-935.ibm.com/services/au/gts/pdf/200249.pdf

delForwardingTableEntry, recvDataPkt and *sendDataPkt*. This set of permissions allows to control access to critical SDN controller resources such as the global network view, network statistics, the forwarding tables inside of SDN switches, the ability to process data packets which are sent to the controller as well as the ability to reply on such packet forwarding delegation requests. For example, we extend Java's set of low-level permissions by the high-level and SDN-specific permission *readTopology*. This permission is easy to understand by operators and enables access control to a valuable SDN resource, i.e., the global network view. Since we extend Java's standard permissions, policy enforcement is achieved by leveraging Java's sandbox capabilities. In particular, we use the Java security manager as well as the OSGi conditional permission admin service to enforce each SDN controller extension to perform only the associated set of allowed critical operations. In case of policy violations, the corresponding extension is stopped while all other SDN controller components remain unaffected.

SDN Controller Independence. Due to the fact that extensions are closely tied to the SDN controller's implementation today, we design access control on the control layer independently from the SDN controller's implementation. Thereby, we support applying our proposal to a wide range of existing SDN controllers (i.e., SDN controllers which are based on Java and OSGi). In particular, we connect the vendor-specific part of a SDN controller with our system by a controller-specific extension service, which allows implementing of high-level critical operations in a controller-specific way, thus, taking the SDN controller's specifics into account. On top, we provide a standard interface to aforementioned SDN-specific critical operations such that developers of SDN controller extensions must not implement complex network functions for each SDN controller individually. Beside making the development of extensions easier, SDN controller independence also enables deployment of diverse SDN controllers in the same setup. With respect to security, this reduces the overall attack surface based on the idea that similar functionality (e.g., SDN services) provided by different systems (e.g., SDN controllers from different vendors) have only few intersecting vulnerabilities. For example, if a compromised extension is able to exploit a vulnerability in SDN controller C_A, a copy of that extension running on SDN controller C_B is not necessarily able to harm this SDN controller in the same way.

4   Related Work

Porras *et al.* [7] introduced a security kernel focussing on assigning certain authorization priorities to SDN applications in order to prefer applications with high authorization over ones with low authorization. In contrast to our work, Fort-NOX does not consider restricting the set of possible instructions to mitigate massive misusing in case an authorized SDN application gets compromised. Wen *et al.* [2] discussed a controller-independent system called PermOF which benefits from high-level and OpenFlow-specific permissions and focuses on SDN applications. To the contrary, we focus on both SDN applications and SDN controller extensions as well as cloud application-specific permissions. Open Network Operation System (ONOS)[5] intends to be a carrier-grade SDN controller which benefits from high-level permissions and Java security services while the permission system is not yet completely implemented. Similar to our system, it may be suitable for controlling SDN controller extensions as well, but, unlike our system, ONOS aims at a SDN controller-specific solution. Shin *et al.* [1] and Röpke *et al.* [3] propose a sandbox system for SDN controllers which considers both SDN applications and SDN controller extensions. However, these systems depend on low-level permissions whereas our proposal benefits from high-level permissions which are much easier to understand for operators.

5 Conclusion

Telecom providers started to build telco clouds based on the emerging technologies of NFV and SDN. Leaving cloud applications and SDN controller extensions with unlimited access to critical operations can result in the adverse misuse of such operations, if they can exploit an appropriate vulnerability. The security of SDN end user traffic can be significantly improved by the proposed access control system restricting affected telco cloud applications and the SDN controller to access only a reduced set of critical operations. Important advantages of the proposed solution are controller independence and high-level configuration.

References

1. Shin, S., Song, Y., Lee, T., Lee, S., Chung, J., Porras, P., Yegneswaran, V., Noh, J., Kang, B.B.: Rosemary: a robust, secure, and high-performance network operating system. In: ACM SIGSAC Conference on Computer and Communications Security (2014)
2. Wen, X., Chen, Y., Hu, C., Shi, C., Wang, Y.: Towards a secure controller platform for openflow applications. In: ACM SIGCOMM Workshop on Hot Topics in Software Defined Networking (2013)
3. Röpke, C., Holz, T.: Retaining control over SDN network services. In: International Conference on Networked Systems (2015)
4. Gruschka, N., Jensen, M.: Attack surfaces: a taxonomy for attacks on cloud services. In: 2010 IEEE 3rd International Conference on Cloud Computing. IEEE (2010)
5. Chiosi, M., Clarke, D., Willis, P., Reid, A., Feger, J., et al.: Network functions virtualisation: an introduction, benefits, enablers, challenges and call for action. In: SDN and OpenFlow World Congress (2012)
6. Shin, S., Yegneswaran, V., Porras, P., Gu, G.: AVANT-GUARD: scalable and vigilant switch flow management in software-defined networks. In: ACM Conference on Computer and Communications Security (2013)
7. Porras, P., Shin, S., Yegneswaran, V., Fong, M., Tyson, M., Gu, G.: A security enforcement kernel for openflow networks. In: ACM SIGCOMM Workshop on Hot Topics in Software Defined Networking (2012)

---

[5] https://onosproject.org

Guaranteeing Dependency Enforcement in Software Updates

Luigi Catuogno[1], Clemente Galdi[2(✉)], and Giuseppe Persiano[3]

[1] Dip. di Informatica, Università di Salerno, Fisciano (SA), Italy
[2] Dip. di Ing. Elet. e Tecnologie dell'Informazione, Università di Napoli Federico II,
Napoli, Italy
clemente.galdi@unina.it
[3] Dip. di Scienze Aziendali - Management & Innovation System,
Università di Salerno, Fisciano (SA), Italy

Abstract. In this paper we consider the problem of enforcing dependencies during software distribution process. We consider a model in which *multiple independent* vendors encrypt their software and distribute it by means of untrusted mirror repositories. The decryption of each package is executed on the user side and it is possible *if and only if* the target device satisfies the dependency requirements posed by the vendor. Once a package is decrypted, the protocol *non-interactively* updates the key material on the target device so that the decryption of future packages requiring the newly installed package can be executed.

We further present a variant of the protocol in which also the vendor-defined installation policy can be partially hidden from unauthorized users.

1 Introduction

Software deployment is a critical activity within the life cycle of computer systems. The tasks of distribution, installation, and update of software components require to be carefully designed and managed in order to keep the whole system safe throughout their accomplishment. A fault occurring during any of the above tasks might prejudice the system integrity and trustworthiness.

Distribution facilities are required to disseminate wellformed and uncorrupted components. At the same time deployment agents are required to install/update a component on the system if and only if its installation requirements are met. For example, an application might come with the list of those required libraries that should be already present on the system, as well as the system could enforce any kind of software updates policy concerning of version, freshness, provenance and so on. Generally, such properties and requirements are referred to as *dependencies*. Recent studies [9] identify dependencies breaking (during component deployment tasks) as a major cause of systems malfunctioning.

This work has been partially supported by the Italian POR project *"WISCH, Work Into Shaping Campania's Home"*.

S. Buchegger and M. Dam (Eds.): NordSec 2015, LNCS 9417, pp. 205–212, 2015.
DOI: 10.1007/978-3-319-26502-5_15

In this paper we present a comprehensive mechanism for security and reliability in software deployment, focusing the attention on the scenario depicted by *Package Management Systems* as a special case of software deployment systems.

We consider the case in which *multiple independent* software vendors provide encrypted software packages along with their installation policies. Our system guarantees on one hand the confidentiality, integrity, freshness and authenticity properties of the packages. On the other hand, it allows a *strong enforcement* of dependencies in the sense that if the target device is missing any of the packages required for the installation, the software package cannot be decrypted and, thus, it cannot be installed. Each new package contains a *random secret package key* that is used to encrypt every future package that depends on the current one. In this respect, this protocol provides a *non-interactive* procedure that allows each device to update the set of secret package keys associated to the installed packages. We also present an extension of our protocol in which the installation policy itself can be partially hidden from the user.

Our protocols constitute a sharp improvement with respect to previous solutions in which either package security and dependencies are *managed separately*, or software vendors have to cooperate to generate packages keys, i.e., software vendors *cannot be independent*, or the user and the vendor have to run an interactive protocol that is either *inefficient* or *leaks the device profile*, i.e., the list of installed packages.

2   Related Works

One of the first papers addressing security issues in software deployment via Internet is [14], where the author suggests to introduce a trusted third party certifier who creates digital certificates for software vendors/developers. Nevertheless, it has been shown in [4,15] that it is potentially prone to a number of vulnerabilities due to the improper use of cryptographic primitives. In [2] the authors show that several major package management systems are vulnerable to *man-in-the-middle* attacks. In particular, [1,3,4] highlights the threat of malicious mirrors and third-party components in the distribution network (*e.g.*, HTTP proxies) and address the issue of confidentiality of software updates.

A secure software distribution infrastructure, leveraging run-time application integrity verification (*code signing*), is envised in [5]. Weaker notions of authentication have been deployed in Microsoft Windows (Authenticode) and Android OS partially inherited from the Java framework. However in [16] authors warn about the weak or non-existent resilience of some of such solutions to possible key disclosure and the lack of "trust revocation" mechanisms.

Several works highlight that package dependencies remains a major matter of concern [8,11,13].

In [1] the author face the problem of achieving software confidentiality in cache-enabled network. Each device is characterized by a set of (essentially) static attributes (*e.g.*, processor, OS, ...). Software packages are encrypted by using Ciphertext-Policy Attribute-Based Encryption (CP-ABE) schemes where, informally, device attributes are seen as keys.

3   System Model and Requirements

We consider a model in which we distinguish three different players. Our model resembles the current Linux software distribution system. We will also describe the security requirements guaranteed by our system.

System Model. Software distribution/updates are carried out by means of a Distribution Server (DS) and possibly a set of Mirror Server (MS). The role of the DS is to generate properly formatted and encrypted software packages, containing the actual software to be installed, the installation policy and, possibly, the software metadata. Furthermore, the DS has to manage the timely and efficient distribution of the encrypted packages to the set of Mirrors. The DS is managed by the software vendor and it will be considered *trusted*. The role of the Mirror Servers is to answer requests sent by users and provide the required packages. Since MSes are typically managed by third parties they will be considered to be *untrusted*. Finally, the Users can query either one MS or the DS directly.

Security Requirements. Our system guarantees the following security properties.
   Confidentiality. We will only focus on the protection of software confidentiality over the communication channel. Indeed, once the software is decrypted on the device, it might be maliciously distributed at will.
   Authenticity and Integrity. The proposed solution will allow each user to *locally* verify that the software that she has downloaded meets such properties.
   Freshness. Software freshness is crucial in many application scenarios, e.g., virus definitions.Typically a new *fresh* package outdates all its previous versions/releases.
   Strong dependencies enforcement. We require that an adversary is not able to force the installation of a software on a system that does not meet all the prerequisites.
   Clearly some of the above properties are already (in some cases optionally) provided by currently available package managers. Since the solution we propose in this paper does not rely on any other software component, we need to design a system that is able to guarantee all the above requirements at once.

Adversary Model. As in [1], we consider a Dolev-Yao [7] adversary that models the following:

- A user tries to install a software package on a device on which some of the prerequisites are missing.
- Network adversaries who try to get confidential information on the updates or try to corrupt the legitimate updates that are being transferred through the network.

In our model, the user *does not* have the complete control of the device as we assume that the device is able to securely run a trusted service that manages some private information. Such an assumption is not so strong if we consider that nowadays, the majority of platforms and devices features an isolated environment that allows to securely run applications and manage secure storage [10].

The Network Adversary has complete access to the communication network, i.e., she can manipulate, create or duplicate legitimate messages.

4 The Protocol

In this section we describe the proposed protocols. Our system consists of two procedures. The first one, executed by the Distribution Server, is used by the software vendor to create an encrypted and signed package E and its associated metadata M_E. Such a package will be then distributed to the software mirrors. A second procedure, executed by the user, takes as input the package E and its metadata and either installs the software therein contained or rejects it.

4.1 The Protocol: An Informal Description

As stated in the previous sections, whenever a new software package is installed on a given system, we can consider the new capability as a new *attribute* of the system. Following the idea underlying ABE schemes, the new attribute should be used to modify the *secret key* of the system in order to extend the set of ciphertexts that can be decrypted by the system.

In our proposal, the set of ciphertexts that have to be decrypted consists of the set of encrypted software packages. A system should be able to decrypt a given package only if it holds all the necessary *attributes* that are needed to execute the software therein contained. Furthermore, the package itself should contain some information that allows the modification of the private key. Such a modification should be done *non-interactively*.

In our solution, each package p is identified by a unique name n and contains a random key k_p which we call the *package key*. Every other package p' that depends on p should be encrypted with a random *encryption key* r that can be reconstructed if and only if the package key k_p is known.

Informally, the distribution protocol works as follows. Consider, for example, a package p that depends on packages $p_1, \ldots, p_m$ named $n_1, \ldots, n_m$, i.e., all the packages in $\mathcal{N} = \{n_1, \ldots, n_m\}$ are prerequisite for the installation of p. Let us denote by k_i the package keys *contained* in the software package p_i. The vendor generates a random encryption key $r = r_1 + \ldots + r_m$ and computes $e_i = \text{ENCRYPT}_{k_i}(r_i)$. In other words she encrypts the random subkey r_i of the *encryption key* r for package p with the *package key* of package p_i. The vendor builds a software package p by putting together the software, all the necessary metadata, a randomly generated package key k_p. This package is encrypted with the key encryption key r. The vendor publishes the encrypted package along with $e_1, \ldots, e_m$, i.e., $E = (e_1, \ldots, e_m, \text{ENCRYPT}_r(p))$.

When the package p needs to be installed, the user downloads E. In this case, if the user holds all the package keys $k_1, \ldots, k_m$, associated to all the required packages, she can (a) decrypt every e_i, (b) reconstruct the key r and (c) properly decrypt $E_r(p)$. If the system is missing any of the prerequisite, she will not be able to execute the decryption and, thus she will not be able to install the package.

4.2 A Protocol for Monotone Formulae

The protocol described in the previous section solves the problem of enforcing prerequisite matching in software installation whenever the installation policy requires *all the packages in the set* $\mathcal{N} = \{n_1, \ldots, n_m\}$, i.e., the installation policy can be described by a single-clause DNF formula $\phi = (n_1 \wedge \ldots \wedge n_m)$.

Clearly this type of formula is not expressive enough to describe arbitrary installation policies. As an example it cannot express an installation policy that requires the presence of package p_i in one to its allowed versions $v_1, \ldots, v_m$, i.e., $n_{i,v_1} \vee \ldots \vee n_{i,v_m}$.

Our generalized protocol uses secret sharing schemes [6,12,17] that consist of a pair of efficient algorithms: the distribution algorithm takes as input an *access structure*, a monotone collection $\mathcal{A} \subseteq 2^P$ and a secret s and outputs a set of shares $S = (s_1, \ldots, s_{|P|})$, one for each player in P; the reconstruction algorithm takes as input the access structure $\mathcal{A}$ and the set $\hat{S} \subset S$ of shares held by the players in $\hat{P} \subset P$. If $\hat{P} \in \mathcal{A}$ than the reconstruction algorithm outputs the secret s otherwise it output a special symbol $\perp$.

Let p be a software package and let ϕ its installation policy. In the following we will assume that ϕ be described by a *monotone* boolean formula. The formula can be seen an access structure $\mathcal{A}_\phi$ defined over $\mathcal{N} = \{n_1, \ldots, n_m\}$.

Notice that, from the practical point of view, if a package $\hat{p} \in P$ is required for the installation of package p, it has to be the case that the vendor has already installed $\hat{p}$ otherwise she could not have tested its own software. We can thus safely assume that the software vendor knows the package key $k_{\hat{p}}$.

The software vendor generates a random encryption key r and shares it among the packages in N by using an efficient secret sharing scheme for $\mathcal{A}_\phi$. In this way, each package $n_i \in N$ will have an associated share s_i. Each such share is then encrypted with the package key k_i, i.e., $e_i = \text{ENCRYPT}_{k_i}(s_i)$. The sequence $R = (n_1, e_1), \ldots, (n_m, e_m)$ will be included in package. Intuitively, each device holding the package keys of all the packages required by some set in the installation policy will be able to recover r, otherwise it will obtain no information about it.

The vendor then generates a random package key k, a timestamp t and creates a package containing the software s, the software name n, the package key k, the timestamp t, a freshness interval length Δ, the software metadata M_s. This package is encrypted by using the encryption key r. The encrypted package, along with the encrypted shares R and the installation policy $\mathcal{A}_\phi$ are packed together to obtain the E.

The vendor creates metadata information for E by including the package name n, the timestamp t, the software metadata M_s and other required information for E, e.g., size, hash value, creation date, extra information, etc. Notice that once the package is encrypted, the package name, the timestamp and metadata M_s are bound to the software but, at the same time, they are not accessible without decrypting it. Since such information are also needed in clear in order to speedup integrity checks, we add them both the E and M_E. Finally, the vendor signs separately E and M_E and sends them to the Mirrors.

The installation procedure is executed by the user. The user obtains the signed metadata (M_E, σ_M) either from the Distribution Server or from one Mirror Server along with the signed package (E, σ_E), possibly from a different mirror.

As a preliminary step, the user checks the signatures on these packages by using the verification key of the software vendor. The user checks that the bundle E matches the metadata information contained in M_E. Furthermore, depending on the local and on the vendor policy, she checks the freshness of the package. If any of the above checks fails, the installation is rejected. Otherwise the user extracts from the bundle E the sequence $R = (n_1, e_1), \ldots, (n_m, e_m)$ and the installation policy $\mathcal{A}_\phi$. She decrypts all the shares she can by using the package keys contained in the local package inventory and, if possible, reconstruct the encryption key r. If this operation is successful, she decrypts E, extracts the software metadata M_s from M_E and verifies their correspondence. If all tests pass, she installs the software and adds the pair (package name, package key) to the local package inventory.

The management of package removal, software upgrades and updates can be executed by means of appropriate deletions and insertions of information from the local inventory.

Security Analysis. In this section we provide a security analysis w.r.t. the security requirements presented in Section 3.

Confidentiality. The confidentiality of the software in the encrypted package is guaranteed by means of a symmetric encryption scheme. Since we assume that such a scheme is secure, the confidentiality of package relies on the impossibility of extracting the package key k from the encrypted shares $\langle (n_1, e_1), \ldots, (n_m, e_m) \rangle$. Here, again, the security of each share is guaranteed by the security of the symmetric encryption scheme used to encrypt it. Furthermore, for every set $A \subseteq N$ such that $A \notin \mathcal{A}_\phi$, since secret sharing scheme is perfect, the user can obtain no information on the decryption key given all the decrypted shares associated to the packages in A. This means that the user can obtain the encryption key if and only if she holds all the packages keys associated to required packages.

Authenticity and Integrity. Software integrity is guaranteed by the use of secure hash functions in the generation of the metadata associated to the software and for the one associated to the encrypted package E. Secure signature schemes are used to guarantee the authenticity of the information that the Distribution Server sends to the Mirror Servers and that these ones forward to the Users.

Freshness. The encrypted package E and its associated metadata M_E both include a timestamp t generated by the Distribution Server along with the length of the validity period Δ. From the point of view of the issuer the package has to be intended to be fresh in the interval $[t, t + \Delta]$. On the other hand the freshness of a package can be influenced by the installation policy of the user. For example, an administrator may use the following policy: *Install security packages immediately but install other packages only when the version is stable.* Clearly every newly released software is considered *fresh* by the issuer and, in principle, outdates its previous versions. But, under the above policy, the same *fresh* package might not be installed by the administrator that keeps considering the previous versions *fresh.* For this reason we do not bind the freshness to the issuer-generated freshness interval but we allow the user to override this interval whenever its local policy requires to. As observed in [4], the presence of the freshness interval in E and M_E and the possibility of downloading such information from different sources increase the security of the installation procedure.

Strong dependencies enforcement. The user installation procedure guarantees the correct dependency enforcement as the user is not enabled to decrypt any downloaded package unless she meets the issuer-defined installation policy (*i.e.*, she has got all package keys related to the required pre-installed packages). This statement relies on the assumption that the user is not enabled to modify the local package inventory by adding surreptitiously any key to the database. We stress that if we start from a safe system, the strong dependency enforcement guarantees that the installation does not bring the device in an unsafe state that, in turn, guarantees the inventory integrity.

A (Partial) Policy-Hiding Protocol. The protocol presented in the previous section assumes that the installation policy is public. Our idea underlying the protection of the policy is to invert the importance of policy security and solution efficiency. In other words we allow a less efficient solution in favour of a more secure one. More specifically, it is possible to use a *standardised* access structure defined over a set of *anonimized* package names. Intuitively, standardised access structure do not allow to use secret sharing scheme designed for specific classes of access structures. At the same time, anonymised package names do require a linear search in the package inventory for retrieving the package key, in place of the direct access given the package name. Due to space limitations, the description of this variant of the protocol is not included in this paper.

5 Conclusions and Open Problems

In this paper we have presented a protocol for guaranteeing strong dependency enforcement during the software installation process. Each package is considered as an *attribute* for the device that can be used to widen the set of packages that can be installed on it. Our protocol improves over previous solutions for a number of reasons as (a) we explicitly consider multiple independent (and non-interacting) software issuers (b) software package can only decrypted if and only if the device meets the issuer-defined dependency policy and (c) the update of the device's key material is executed locally without any interaction with the issuer.

At this stage, our solution does not handle package conflicts. We are planning to investigate such issues in a future work. Finally we are currently working on the implementation of our protocols in order to measure its performance.

References

1. Ambrosin, M., Busold, C., Conti, M., Sadeghi, A.-R., Schunter, M.: Updaticator: updating billions of devices by an efficient, scalable and secure software update distribution over untrusted cache-enabled networks. In: ESORICS (2014), pp. 76–93 (2014)
2. Bellissimo, A., Burgess, J., Fu, K.: Secure software updates: disappointments and new challenges. In: HotSec (2006)
3. Cappos, J.: Avoiding theoretical optimality to efficiently and privately retrieve security updates. In: Sadeghi, A.-R. (ed.) FC 2013. LNCS, vol. 7859, pp. 386–394. Springer, Heidelberg (2013)
4. Cappos, J., Samuel, J., Baker, S., Hartman, J.H.: A look in the mirror: attacks on package managers. In: Proceedings of the 15th ACM Conference on Computer and Communications Security, pp. 565–574. ACM (2008)
5. Catuogno, L., Gassirà, R., Masullo, M., Visconti, I.: Smartk: Smart cards in operating systems at kernel level. Information Security Technical Report 17(3), 93–104 (2013). Security and Privacy for Digital Ecosystems
6. Di Crescenzo, G., Galdi, C.: Hypergraph decomposition and secret sharing. Discrete Applied Mathematics 157(5), 928–946 (2009)
7. Dolev, D., Yao, A.C.: On the security of public key protocols. IEEE Transactions on Information Theory 29(2), 198–208 (1983)
8. Dolstra, E., De Jonge, M., Visser, E.: Nix: a safe and policy-free system for software deployment. In: LISA, vol. 4, pp. 79–92 (2004)
9. Dumitraş, T., Kavulya, S., Narasimhan, P.: A fault model for upgrades in distributed systems (cmu-pdl-08-115). CMU-PDL-08-115 (2008)
10. GlobalPlatform. TEE system architecture v1.0. http://globalplatform.org
11. Hart, J., D'Amelia, J.: An analysis of RPM validation drift. In: LISA, vol. 2, pp. 155–166 (2002)
12. Ito, M., Saito, A., Nishizeki, T.: Secret sharing scheme realizing general access structure. Electronics and Communications in Japan (Part III: Fundamental Electronic Science 72(9), 56–64 (1989)
13. Neuhaus, S., Zimmermann, T.: The beauty and the beast: vulnerabilities in red Hat's packages. In: USENIX Annual Technical Conference (2009)
14. Rubin, A.D.: Trusted distribution of software over the internet. In: 1995 Symposium on Network and Distributed System Security, (S)NDSS 1995, San Diego, California, February 16–17, 1995, pp. 47–53 (1995)
15. Samuel, J., Cappos, J.: Package managers still vulnerable: How to protect your systems. login: Usenix Magazine 34(1), 7–15 (2009)
16. Samuel, J., Mathewson, N., Cappos, J., Dingledine, R.: Survivable key compromise in software update systems. In: Proceedings of the 17th ACM Conference on Computer and Communications Security, pp. 61–72. ACM (2010)
17. Shamir, A.: How to share a secret. Communications of the ACM 22(11), 612–613 (1979)

Electronic Citizen Identities and Strong Authentication

Sanna Suoranta$^{(\boxtimes)}$, Lari Haataja, and Tuomas Aura

Department of Computer Science, Aalto University, Espoo, Finland
`sanna.suoranta@aalto.fi`

Abstract. Both public and commercial services in most countries depend on government-issued identity documents for citizen authentication. Traditionally such documents have been fairly uniform around the world, i.e. identity cards and passports. The dawn of strong electronic authentication, however, has created a much more diverse situation. New technologies such as tamper-proof microchips and cryptographic authentication are used in different ways for both offline and online authentication. Countries have made quite different choices in what kind of security or privacy they prioritize and what services are supported. This paper attempts to form an overall picture of electronic citizen-identity and strong-authentication technologies and of the management of electronic citizen identities around the world. Understanding of the global state of the art is necessary because Internet services are often global and accessed across national borders, and because there sometimes is a need to bootstrap the user identity from the government issued or sanctioned credentials. This survey provides background information both for the selection of authentication technologies and for research on strong authentication.

1 Introduction

In modern society, most services are electronic, partly implemented in servers on the Internet, and most authentication is based on prudent data management practices or cryptographic techniques. However, citizen identity documents are still very much physical, such as security-printed passports and identity cards. Such documents are becoming obsolete as services move to the Internet or, even in physical everyday situations, require linking of the person to online accounts and database entries. Thus, governments around the world see the need for electronic citizen identity. The first smart-card-based electronic identification card was published in Finland in 1999 [1], [2] and many others were conceived during the Internet boom. However, the wide-spread deployment of strong electronic authentication has taken much longer than initially expected and most countries have their particular solutions that arise from the local culture and history. In this article, we describe authentication services used all around the world. The technologies behind the services are often quite similar, but the methods of credential provisioning and supported services vary.

S. Buchegger and M. Dam (Eds.): NordSec 2015, LNCS 9417, pp. 213–230, 2015.
DOI: 10.1007/978-3-319-26502-5_16

Table 1. Summary of authentication services. (M in policy field means that country has mandatory identity card, V that the card is voluntary, and the word "none" that there is no identity card (Wikipedia: List of national identity card policies by country, http://en.wikipedia.org/wiki/List_of_national_identity_card_policies_by_country, Referred 7.9.2015). Electronic identity cards are marked with (e-ID) if the system does not have a well-known name.)

Country	Policy	Service Name	Technology
Argentina	M	DNI (e-ID)	Smart Card
Australia	none	Smart card	Smart Card
Austria	V	(e-ID)	Smart Card
Belgium	M	(e-ID)	Smart Card
Brazil	M	RIC (e-ID)	Smart Card
Canada	V	CRA login	password
		e-Banking	Bank Credentials
China	M	(e-ID)	Smart Card
Estonia	M	(e-ID)	Smart Card
		e-Banking	Bank Credentials
		DigiDoc Mobile ID	Mobile Certificate
Finland	V	TUPAS	Bank Credentials
		Mobile ID	Mobile Certificate
		FINEID (e-ID)	Smart Card
France	V	(e-ID)	Smart Card
Germany	M	(e-ID)	Smart Card, RFID
India	none	e-Pramaan	Hybrid
Indonesia	M	e-KTP	Smart Card
Italy	V	CIE (e-ID)	Smart Card
Japan	V	(e-ID)	Smart Card
Lithuania	V	e-Banking	Bank Credentials
Mexico	V	(e-ID)	Smart Card
New Zealand	none	RealMe	Online Credentials
Portugal	M	Citizen Card	Smart Card
Russia	M	(e-ID)	Smart Card
Saudi Arabia	M	(e-ID)	Password
Slovenia	M	e-ID (passport)	Smart Card
South Africa	M	(e-ID)	Smart Card
South Korea	M	I-PIN	Password
		public key certificate	Public Key
		SMS verification	Mobile Device
Spain	M	DNIe (e-ID)	Smart Card
Sweden	V	BankID	Bank Credentials
Switzerland	V	SuisseID	USB Token
		SuisseID	Smart Card
Turkey	M	(e-ID)	Smart Card
UK	none	-	-
USA	V	-	PKI, SAML

One important but rather poorly defined concept is *strong authentication*. The traditional government-issued identity documents are somehow seen to provide strong, or legally accepted, proof of the credential holder's identity. Depending on the country, this strength arises from the one-to-one mapping of physical persons to identifiers or database entries in the resident register, or from decentralized but consistent track record of being known by the same identity throughout one's life. In the electronic world, strong online or offline authentication intuitively means achieving a similar level of security as with the traditional paper-based identity documents. This is often translated to technical requirements on the initial identity verification (identity proofing) and on the authentication methods. For example, initial registration in person may be required, which is a clear difference to most Internet-based services with ad-hoc registration. Also, simple password-based authentication is usually seen as weak, and the strong authentication should use two factors, preferably a physical token combined with either a memorized secret code or biometric verification. In practice, not all national systems conform strictly to such requirements.

This study covers the G20 countries and selected others with particularly interesting authentication solutions. Table 1 summarizes the authentication systems investigated in this article. We have organized the discussion based on the authentication technology. Some countries are mentioned several times through the article because they use multiple methods for authenticating their citizens.

The rest of the article is organized as follows. We start by discussing the most common technologies used in government-issued credentials: passwords in Section 2 and smart card tokens in Section 3. Official identity credentials issued by non-govermental agencies are considered in Section 4, hybric systems combining several technologies in Section 5, and countries with no official citizen identity technologies in Section 6. Section 7 discusses the overall picture of strong electronic authentication and, finally, Section 8 concludes the article.

2   Password-Based Systems

Passwords are widely used in authentication even though they are not considered to be a strong method. Their advantages are familiarity for users, low cost for service providers, and relatively easy deployment. However, good passwords are hard to remember and creating separate high-entropy passwords for different services is a burden to the users. Since passwords are prone to leaking, uses need to update them periodically. Single sign-on (SSO) systems and password safes can help users to cope with password fatigue but they do not fully eliminate the problems of using passwords. For these reasons, passwords are not considered to provide strong authentication and they are seldom used as the sole method of citizen authentication. Some countries, however, do also offer password authentication. We will discuss the examples from several countries.

In South Korea, many web-based services require users to authenticate themselves with their real identity, for example, even for reserving a movie ticket. A few years ago, most of the web services still used the person's name as the username and resident registration number as the secret password. However, all the services did not protect their user databases properly, and almost half of the resident registration numbers were leaked in various attacks making identity theft possible [3]. Obviously, the system had to be changed. Nowadays, users have an I-PIN ID string as the username and a separate password, and these are certified by visiting a service point where the user's identity is verified. The I-PIN ID can be changed if the credentials are leaked. The user can choose the I-PIN ID but it must be unique. [4]. In addition to the password-based I-PIN system, South Koreans have mobile-phone-based authentication using SMS (cellular text messages) and electronic authentication certificates, which are mostly used for Internet banking [5].

India has a similar system, called e-Pramaan [6], that offers four levels of authentication. Password-based authentication is the level-1 authentication mechanism that can be used by itself or combined with the other authentication levels that are based on one-time-passwords, hardware or software tokens, or biometrics. During registration, physical identity document of a user is checked. Nevertheless, self-registration is also possible, in which case the password is delivered through SMS or postal service.

New Zealand began its identity management system in 2000 [7]. Currently, the system is known as RealMe, and it provides single sign-on with high-entropy passwords. A password must be composed of of letters, numbers and special characters [8]. Anyone living in New Zealand can open a RealMe account provided that they verify their identity at a local post office where a photo of the user is taken and attached to their account. In case if the user is not a citizen of New Zealand, the user must provide visa or other documents. However, a user can also create an unverified account that can only be used with services that do not require strong authentication. RealMe also provides stronger two-factor authentication that will be described later. In addition to authentication, the user of RealMe can add other verified information, for example her address, to the account, and the online services can then use the information if the user gives permission. This makes registration for additional services easier and faster since the user does not need to fill in all her personal information.

Saudi Arabia controls tightly the use of Internet. All the traffic goes through a national content filtering system that is strictly monitored by the government [9]. Prior to access any e-services, users are required to verify their identity at an eID verification office where they receive a username and password. The password recovery system is based on answers of the reminder questions given in the registration phase. [10] Saudi Arabia has also started deploying a smart-card-based eID where the electronic chips is primarily used to protect against forgery and to detect fingerprints rather than online authentication.

3   Smart-Card-Based Systems

In this section, we discuss smart-card-based citizen authentication systems. A prime example is Estonia, which has managed to establish a working electronic identity among the first in the world. The identity is based on e-ID cards that were launched in 2002. In the early days, the main online authentication tool was online bank credentials, which the e-ID has gradually replaced. Nowadays, 90% of Estonians have active e-ID cards that can be used, for example, for digital signatures, for online voting in all elections, and as public transport ticket in the two biggest cities, Tallinn and Tartu [11]. It is worth noting that during 2011 parlament election, 24,3% Estonians cast their vote online [12].

A smart card consists of a computing chip that is capable of processing and storing sensitive information. This chip can be embedded in various plastic cards: bank cards, identification cards, student cards, loyalty cards etc. Typically, a smart card provides one of the two communication interfaces: contact and contactless. Some smart card may provide both the interfaces. A contact card requires physical contacts to communicate and these cards are inserted into a card reader. On the other hand, contactless card can be accessed wirelessly within a short range using electromagnetic induction technologies such as RFID or NFC [13]. Smart cards provide a tamper-resistant environment for storing security-sensitive information e.g. user credentials. Similarly, user details such as photo, name, identification number, date of birth etc. can be printed on the card surface. Therefore smart card can be used both as a physical token as well as a secure storage for the user credentials.

Many countries have mandatory identity cards [13] and, nowadays, many of them incorporate the smart card feature. Thus, citizens do not need to carry an additional e-ID card in their pockets. Most of the systems are based on contact cards but some of the latest ones are contactless. The advantage of the smart cards in comparison to passwords is that the user only needs to remember a short secret PIN number, and that the secret together with the possession of the physical card form two-method authentication. However, the main purpose of the chip is usually to increase the security of the cards against forgery and to enable storage of additional information, such as biometric data, for offline use. Only some of these cards are actively used for online authentication in Internet-based service. The technical reason is that the card alone is not sufficient for online authentication: a national public-key infrastructure (PKI) or a single sign-on system (SSO) is needed to enable the use of the same card in all online services [14].

Many countries, for example Australia, Portugal, and Switzerland, use smart-card-based authentication. In Europe, several countries started to develop electronic identification when European Union Parliament enacted the directive of digital signatures [15] in 1999. However, there have been many debates and discussions, and only now, 15 years later, the authentication systems start to be widely deployed. Next, we give examples of countries using smart card technology for citizen authentication.

Germany has an electronic identity card as the mandatory official identification technology. It is based on NFC technology and was taken into use in 2010. It contains a digital biometric passport photo for offline authentication and a digital certificate for online authentication and digital signatures. The system offers two security levels for card readers and software that can be used, for example, for digitally signing email [16]. Vulnerabilities, such as malware recording PIN codes, have been discovered, but they all require the card to be present in the card reader during the misuse. The digital signature is protected with a separate PIN and signing requires a reader with integrated keyboard [17]. In addition to the electronic identity card, many counties have other smart cards that are used to identify citizens. Germany, for example, has digital health cards that contain patient data [13]. Such cards are not combined together with the identity card for historical reasons, because of administrative boundaries between government departments, or for perceived privacy reasons.

Italy has also an electronic identity card, called Carta d'identità Elettronica (CIE), which contains a digital version of the card holder's photo but no other information by default. Due to Italian legislation, the CIE card is issued by municipalities, but the Certification Authority of Ministry of Internal Affairs can issue a digital certificate that is stored on the card [18]. In addition to CIE cards, Italy has another system called National Service Card (CNS) for accessing electronic government services. The CNS consists of certificates that can be used for authentication and digital signatures. However, it is not an official identity card because it has no photo and only municipalities can issue identification cards [19]. In addition to the above, Italy is planning to introduce in 2015 an online system called SPID that acts as a SAMLv2 identity provider for citizens and public and private services. The above-mentioned cards can be used as authentication tokens in this system [20].

France has also decided to deploy electronic identification based on smart card technology. The card would include biometric identification information in the form of two fingerprints and a photograph, and other information such as marital status [21]. However, the system has encountered resistance because people are afraid that the biometric data will leak to outsiders and the privacy of the users will be compromised. This resistance has postponed the electronic identification for several years, first from 2006 to 2008 [13] and its publication date was not scheduled in 2012 [22].

Spanish Documento Nacional de Identidad electrnico (DNIe) is also based on a smart card that contains an X.509 certificate for authentication and digital signatures and photograph of the citizen and his/her signature [23]. Applying for the card requires going to an office of the National Police where the applicant is authenticated. Information in the card is protected by a PIN code.

Electronic identity cards are becoming popular also in Asian countries. In Japan, municipalities issue Resident Registration Cards that have a chip with RSA keys certified by the government. The cards can be used for authenticating to online services and for signing digital documents. Also foreign residents can get this card [24]. Furthermore, Indonesia, one of the world's most populous countries, is creating smart-card-based electronic identification system called e-KTP. The deployment is motivated by identity fraud in previous elections [25]. The e-KTP is based on a contactless card that contains face and iris photos and fingerprints as biometric information [26]. However, the Indonesian cards currently contain no credentials for online use.

China is starting to deploy third-generation identity cards with a smart chip. The cards contain fingerprints as biometric identification [27]. The identity card is used frequently compared to western countries: for example, it has to be presented when buying travel tickets or using services of Internet cafes. The Internet-user authentication, however, can only be used to trace offenders and not for pro-active online authentication to services.

The Turkish electronic identity system uses smart cards that contain a certificate and biometric information such as fingerprints or finger-veins, and a picture of the card holder. A standard smart card reader can access only part of the information stored on the card, i.e. the name of the card holder and the certificate. Biometric information is protected with a PIN code and should be accessed only with trusted card readers. [28] The system has been piloted in recent years and, in 2014, the citizens should be able to get their electronic identity cards with digital signature certificates [29].

South American countries are also using smart card technology, mostly for offline authentication. In Brazil, the first electronic Registry of Civil Identity (RIC) card was issued to their then-president Lula da Silva in end of December, 2010 [30]. The card contains biometric information in the form of fingerprints, and it offers both contactless and contact-based reading methods [31]. Similar to the European counterparts, the Brazilian identity card can be used as a travel document in Mercosur states. Chilean identity card contains certificates for digital signatures and authentication, as well as fingerprint and facial photographs [32]. In Argentina, the compulsory national identity card (DNI) holds, for example, biometric information in the form of fingerprints and facial photo, social security information, medical and public transportation history — this has terrified those who care about privacy and know Argentinian history [33], [34]. Mexico started issuing electronic identity cards first to minors. The card contains iris images, fingerprints and a photo as biometric information [35].

In Russia, identity has been verified with an Internal Passport in offline services. These will be replaced with a smart card that contains a digital signature certificate [36]. Also, South Africa is renewing its Identity book, a passport-like identity document [37], to a smart-card-based identity card in the next few years [38].

As the long list of countries above shows, smart-card-based solutions are popular among countries that have or are developing electronic identity for their citizens. Overall, the trend is towards integration of smart-card-based authentication into national identity cards. The major differences are in how much non-identity information the card itself holds, and whether there are keys and infrastructure for online authentication to public and commercial Internet services. Countries with comprehensive Internet coverage naturally put more emphasis on online authentication and less on on-card data storage.

4   Non-governmental Identity Providers

In many countries, the electronic citizen identity provider is not the state itself but some other entity that has gained a trusted role. This section looks at examples from the surveyed countries and explains how such systems arise.

4.1   Post Offices

In most countries, the postal service has been a monopoly of the state, and, even though competition has reached the transportation of mail, the post offices are still seen as some kind of trusted government agents. Moreover, the postal service performs the critical task of delivering registered letters, including official ones, to the right persons, and thus needs processes and trained personnel for verifying the identity of any citizen. This background makes post offices one possible agency for offering electronic identity credentials.

For example in Switzerland, the Swiss Post provides digital identity and signature credentials that are stored either on a smart card or a USB stick [39]. The token is ordered using an online form, but it must be fetched in person from a post office where the identity of the recipient is verified from an identity card or passport. The user can decide the PIN code that protects the information on the card or in the USB device. The smart card requires a separate card reader but almost all computers can access the USB stick without installing other new hardware. The user instructions list many security threats and risks against the software system, for example typing in the PIN on a computer that has been compromised, but also countermeasures for them [39].

Nowadays many users prefer mobile devices to a personal computer. The SuisseID Mobile Service allows user to activate the SuisseID authentication for mobile devices [39]. The system supports iPad and iPhone, Google Nexus, Samsung Galaxy and Nokia/Microsoft Lumia. Clearly the diversity of the mobile devices is a challenge to mobile identity systems that aim to reach the entire population.

4.2   Bank Credentials

Another group of relatively trusted non-governmental agencies is the banks. The experience of dealing with high-value transactions has taught banks to be careful when authenticating their customers. Many of the banks' security procedures implement national or international standards, and compliance is critical for the banks to avoid unnecessary liability. they also monitor continuously the level of fraud. Moreover, anti-money-laundering legislation creates stringent requirements for the banks to authenticate and know their customers.

Banks have their own secure electronic identity implementations that are still sometimes based on passwords, but increasingly on smart cards. [40] Bank cards with a smart-card chip can be used as authentication tokens if the customer also has a computer with a card reader. Some banks provide special stand-alone readers to their customers for chip-and-PIN-based login that follows the

Chip Authentication Program (CAP) specification. Another strong authentication method that the banks use is a list of one-time-passwords (OTP), which has the advantage of being low-tech and inexpensive. In order to get the credentials, a customer must go to a branch office of a bank, establish a customer relationship, and show her passport or other official identification to the bank officer. This initial authentication forms the basis for the future online authentication with the bank-issued credentials.

As the banks have working online authentication systems, it is natural to extend their use to other services. This applies particularly to regions that have developed electronic banking, such as many Northern European countries. To become generic identity providers, the banks had to define common APIs for authentication for third parties. For example, nine Swedish banks have a service called BankID and all Finnish banks have a joint service APIs called TUPAS [41] defined by the Federation of Finnish Financial Services. Also many governmental services in these countries accept online bank authentication. For example, the Lithuanian Government Electronic Gates portal uses online banking authentication. [40]

One way in which the role of the banks as generic authentication services has evolved is that, when there is an online payment method that binds the identity of the online customer strongly to the payment made, that can be reused (or misused) for authentication purposes. For example, the Finnish TUPAS authentication is architecturally very close to a national online payment method and uses the same OTP credentials.

As said, the bank-provided authentication has the advantage that the banks are relatively trusted entities and that they are in any case required to strongly verify the identities of their customers. For the customers, the credentials are familiar and their use has no visible cost. For the banks themselves, authentication provides only a minor revenue stream; however the authentication service locks the customers of consumer banking to the established banks that are accepted by most businesses as identity providers. A major disadvantage is that if a person does not have a supported bank account, authentication becomes impossible. A familiar example of this are international students who need to authenticate in order to register to the university, yet need to register before they can get a bank account. Another disadvantage is that, as the use of bank credentials becomes more frequent, the security of the online banking may suffer.

4.3 Mobile-Phone-Based Systems

In addition to banks, nowadays also mobile operators offer electronic authentication in many countries. The Mobile Certificate is based on cryptographic keys stored on a subscriber identity module (SIM) card, which is the small smart card that binds a mobile phone to the operator and subscriber account. The keys can be used for authenticating the user, encrypting and verifying data, and confirming transactions [13]. In the authentication process, a user receives a confirmation message to the phone and types in a PIN code. The network operator acts as a trusted party and notifies the service if the authentication was successful [42].

The details can vary slightly from country to country but the basic protocol is the same. Mobile certificates are in use for example in Austria, Finland, Estonia, Lithuania, the Netherlands, Norway, Poland, Slovenia and Turkey [40].

Mobile certificates are easy to use for the citizen that is accustomed to using a mobile phone. The PIN code and 24-hour customer service of the mobile operators makes the system relatively secure. If the mobile phone or its SIM card gets stolen, the credentials can be revoked immediately. However, the after revocation, the user must change the SIM card to a new one [40]. The authentication can be cumbersome for those who are not comfortable using mobile phones. For example, in Finland, the price for a user is 0,17 euros per authentication, which is considered quite high, at least compared to bank credentials whose costs are hidden in the monthly service changes. The service providers that rely on the authentication pay also a similar fee for each authentication event.

The Generic Bootstrapping Architecture (GBA) [43] is another phone-based system that reuses the credentials and infrastructure of the mobile network for user authentication to third parties. However, this standard has not been widely deployed and pilots have targeted specific applications rather than broad citizen authentication.

Yet another way to use mobile phones is two-factor authentication where the phone acts as a trusted communication channel. For example, the RealMe authentication system in New Zealand uses two-factor authentication when extra security is needed. In the authentication, the service sends a verification code to the user's mobile phone, and she enters the code manually into the online service in order to confirm the login [8]. The two-factor authentication is usually considered to be more secure because stealing the username and password is not enough to gain access and the physical mobile device (or more accurately, the SIM card) is also needed. The user is much more likely to detect if her mobile phone is stolen than if her password is stolen.

One recent concern about using the phone as the trusted channel is that malware or untrusted apps can compromise the messages received on a smart phone [44]. Trusted computing technologies that isolate the credentials from the rest of the software running on the device may provide a technical solution by hosting eIDs [45] or deploying new architecture for eIDs [46], but such systems have not yet been deployed. At the moment, the diversity of mobile platforms limits their use for general citizen authentication, but if standards evolve, that may well be next direction of electronic citizen identity.

5   Hybrid Systems

Many of the above mentioned systems could be seen as hybrid systems in two ways: either one technical system combines two or more authentication methods, or multiple systems with different methods operate side by side as part of the overall national infrastructure.

The multi-method authentication schemes typically use some combination of a physical token (smart card), PIN code, and biometric authentication.

Software-based credentials and SMS are common choices as a second authentication channel in commercial systems but have not seen similar wide deployment in citizen authentication. The multi-method authentication systems can support several security levels by allowing the use of a single method for some services. For example, the Indian e-Pramaan provides several levels of authentication [47].

Many countries have added biometric information also to their passport in the form of a facial photo or fingerprint. For example, the Japanese passport has RFID tag containing a digital photograph [48] and European Union member states that belong to the Schengen region have to have both a photo and a fingerprint stored on a passport [49]. Many airports have automatic passport control where the holder of a biometric passport can verify her identity: the passport is shown to a machine that compares the photo stored on the passport to a current photo taken by the machine itself. The reading of the data from the chip embedded in the passport does not require any actions from the passport holder. However, the passports are generally not used for authentication to online services.

One example of multiple systems operating side by side comes from Finland where smart-card-based PKI, bank credentials with one-time passwords, and SIM-card-based mobile certificates are all accepted, with no official preference of one technology over the others. This hybrid system is the result of failed deployment of the smart cards as the primary method of strong authentication as citizens preferred existing or more convenient methods.

6   Countries Without Citizen Authentication

Many countries are still in the pilot or development phase in their online citizen authentication projects. However, in some counties, there is strong ideological opposition from people and politicians against identity cards, especially if their deployment requires a central register of all citizens or if owning or carrying the card would be mandatory. This may even be seen as an assault on the liberty of the citizens. Nevertheless, development of public and commercial online services is important target in these countries, too.

For example, in United Kingdom, the parliament enacted the Identity Cards Act in 2006 that introduced identity cards that could be used to travel within the European Union. The biometric information collected to a database would have included fingerprints, iris scans, and facial photos. Later, the act was overturned, mainly due concerns about the safety of the database, and those who had already purchased the card had to obtain passports instead [50]. The new Identity Documents Act from 2010 required the destruction of the collected personal data stored in the National Identity Register [51]. In the UK, many use their driving licenses as identity documents, and there exists also a CitizenCard that young people can use as a proof of age, but these cards are not smart cards [52]. However, UK has a Government Gateway that acts as a portal to online government services [53]. It offers two authentication methods: passwords that are send by mail after the registration, and digital certificates that are no longer issued.

In the United States of America, the government published guidelines for agencies to use electronic authentication for services in order to reduce the use of paper and to speed up administrative processes [54]. Instead of a centralized governmental service, USA decided to allow citizens to access governmental services by choosing the authentication provider among private sector industry partners whose credentials they already have [55], [56]. In practice, no single system has seen broad use and different government agencies make use of service-specific passwords or commercial smart-card solutions. Canada, on the other hand, relies on private sector services such as banks to provide access to governmental services such as revenue agency in addition to agency-specific password login [57]. Australia offers plethora of solutions listed by Department of Finance [58].

7   Discussion

Smart cards embedded in the national identification cards appear to be the favored solution when states replace paper-based identification documents with electronic identity. For offline authentication this is natural choice because the tamper-proof chip and cryptographically signed information increase the difficulty of copying and falsifying identity cards. Moreover, PIN code or biometric identification information on the chip provides two-factor authentication in one physical package. For example in India, 23% of the citizens had registered to the e-Pramaan system by 2013 [2]. It is estimated that over 2,2 billion people (33% of world's population) have an electronic identity card in 2009, and over 900 million of the cards have biometric information such as facial or fingerprint images [59].

There is, however, a divide between the countries where the cards are used only for offline identity checks and ones where they contain cryptographic credentials for online authentication. In the first group, there are counties where physical security and control over the citizens is a priority, but also ones that have filled the need for online authentication with commercial solutions and risk management and, thus, feel no urgency for new authentication technology. In the second group, it is easy to spot examples of countries that have high Internet penetration, and rapidly developing countries that are making aggressive use of new technologies for improving their public services.

In many countries, the government is considered the natural electronic identity provider for the citizens because it issues birth certificates and passports and because it needs to identify the citizens for taxes and benefits. Government agencies have databases for storing sensitive information about the citizens, and electronic identification can be built on the existing infrastructure. Furthermore, the companies that rely on government-provided authentication do not need to spend money to create their own separate customer authentication solutions [2]. Estonian prime minister said that digital signatures save time and money when he and the Finnish prime minister signed digitally the first intergovernmental agreement in 2013 [60]. Estonia is now offering its electronic identity to others than Estonian citizens, which encourages establishing new businesses in the country [61].

Nevertheless, authentication to online services with the electronic identification cards has not taken off even in all the countries where the technology has been deployed – citizens have not bought card readers. For example in Spain, 27 % of the citizens had the DNIe card but only 2% had the card reader and less than 5% had used it to authenticate for online services in 2010 [62].. According to OECD [63], the lack of mature digital identities delays the development of Internet economy across the world. However, the factors that determine the success or failure of new citizen identity technologies seem to be local to each country, and technical factors cannot explain the popularity of a technology in one country and lack of interest in another.

One commonly stated reason for resisting electronic identity provided by a state is the fear of loosing privacy and liberty. Such fears arise from two sources: Firstly, storing information about the citizens in one central database is seen risky because it would attract attackers or could be misused by the government. Secondly, the identity provider is able to track the uses of the electronic identity and, thus, follow the moves of the citizens both online and in the physical world. The Electronic Frontier Foundation sees two problems with state provided e-ID [34]: If the national identity card is mandatory, it can be used to discriminate people, and if it contains biometric information, the system gives false assumption about security, since biometric information cannot be reissued if it is compromised. The attitudes to such issues vary between countries for cultural and historical reasons; some nations put more trust into their governments than others, and some prefer private services to governmental ones. Most of the countries we evaluated are considered to be democracies, and only China, Russia and Saudi Arabia are considered to be autoriatarian regimes and Turkey as hybrid regime [64].

From the global perspective, some of the fears are clearly justified: for example, identity cards have been used to identify victims for genocide in Ruanda where the information about tribe was listed on the cards [59]. Totalitarian regimes are also known for tracking the online activities of their citizens, and the availability of strong electronic identity helps them in establishing such controls. In UK and USA, the above arguments have lead to discontinuation of governmental projects to provide electronic identity. Instead, these countries prefer service-specific or commercial authentication systems. Such political opposition is likely to hinder the adoption of any global or regional standards, such as the European ones [40].

8 Conclusion

Electronic authentication, both online and offline, is often seen as a key building block of secure public services and moving them to the Internet. However, the technical and ideological approaches to citizen authentication vary between countries. In this article, we have surveyed the landscape of citizen identities and strong authentication across the world. The solutions can be roughly divided to two categories: state provided electronic identity cards with or without biometric information and with or without cryptographic credentials for online access, and outsourced authentication solutions where companies from trusted industries provide authentication that is approved by law as equivalent to signature or verifying identity from a passport. In general, the chosen technical solutions are conservative and stand apart from the innovative developments seen in in open Internet services, such as the use of social networks or mobile applications and payment methods. Some of the development processes have been long and unfruitful and many are still under work. Outcomes of some countries have frightened those who feel greater need for privacy. International recognition of strongly verified identities is still a long way off, and the reasons seem to have little to do with the technology.

Acknowledgment. This work was supported partially by TEKES as part of the Cyber Trust program of DIGILE (the Finnish Strategic Center for Science, Technology and Innovation in the field of ICT and digital business).

References

1. Rissanen, T.: Electronic identity in finland: Id cards vs. bank ids. Identity in the Information Society **3**(1), 175–194 (2010)
2. The Economist: Which firms will profit from providing your identity online? February 9, 2013. http://www.economist.com/news/international/21571418-which-firms-will-profit-proving-your-identity-online-voucher-business (referred March 25, 2015)
3. Oh, Y., Obi, T., Lee, J.S., Suzuki, H., Ohyama, N.: Empirical analysis of internet identity misuse: case study of south Korean real name system. In: Proceedings of the 6th ACM Workshop on Digital Identity Management, DIM 2010, pp. 27–34. ACM, New York (2010)
4. Ministry of Security and Public Administration: What is public I-PIN? (2009). http://www.g-pin.go.kr/center/pic/sub_01.gpin (referred February 3, 2015)
5. K4E consulting: Real name rule on korean websites, October 2012. http://www.korea4expats.com/article-id-requirement-access-korean-websites.html (referred February 3, 2015)
6. Department of Electronics and Information Technology (DeitY): e-Pramaan: Framework for e-authentication. Framework, Ministry of Communications & Information Technology, Government of India (GoI) (2012)
7. Tu, Y.C., Thomborson, C.: Preliminary security specification for new zealand's igovt system. In: 7th Australasian Information Security Conference (AISC 2009), Australian Computer Society, Inc. (2009)
8. Department of Internal Affairs, New Zealand: Realme for logging in. https://www.realme.govt.nz/about-realme/realme-for-logging-in/ (referred January 29, 2015)
9. Internet Service Unit, King Abdulaziz city for Science & Technology: Introduction to content filtering (2006). http://www.isu.net.sa/saudi-internet/contenet-filtring/filtring.htm (referred March 26, 2015)

10. Saudi: National e-government portal, frequence asked questions (2015). http://www.saudi.gov.sa/wps/portal/yesserRoot/faq (referred March 26, 2015)
11. e-estonia.com, the digital society: Electronic id card. https://e-estonia.com/component/electronic-id-card/ (referred March 25, 2015)
12. Kitsing, M.: Online participation in Estonia: active voting, low engagement. In: Proceedings of the 5th International Conference on Theory and Practice of Electronic Governance, ICEGOV 2011, pp. 20–26. ACM, New York (2011)
13. Fioravanti, F., Nardelli, E.: Identity management for e-government services. In: Digital Government. Integrated Series in Information Systems, vol. 17, pp. 331–352. Springer US (2008)
14. Paul, C.L., Morse, E., Zhang, A., Choong, Y.-Y., Theofanos, M.: A field study of user behavior and perceptions in smartcard authentication. In: Campos, P., Graham, N., Jorge, J., Nunes, N., Palanque, P., Winckler, M. (eds.) INTERACT 2011, Part IV. LNCS, vol. 6949, pp. 1–17. Springer, Heidelberg (2011)
15. European Parliament: Directive 1999/93/ec of the european parliament and of the council of 13 december 1999 on a community framework for electronic signatures (1999). http://eur-lex.europa.eu/legal-content/EN/ALL/?uri=CELEX:31999L0093 (referred March 12, 2015)
16. Bundesdruckerei GmbH: Id card - id document for the real and digital world (2015). https://www.bundesdruckerei.de/en/714-new-german-id-card (referred February 23, 2015)
17. djwm: CCC reveals security problems with German electronic IDs. The H Security, September 22, 2010. http://www.h-online.com/security/news/item/CCC-reveals-security-problems-with-German-electronic-IDs-1094577.html (referred March 26, 2015)
18. Graux, H., Inte, F., Majava, J., Meyvis, E.: eiD interoperability for pegs: Update of country profiles study italian country profile. Technical report, IDABC European eGovernment Services, August 2009. http://ec.europa.eu/idabc/servlets/Docea18.pdf?id=32311 (referred February 23, 2015)
19. Agenzia per l'Italia Digitale, Presidenza del Consiglio dei Ministri: Specifiche tecniche, March 2, 2015. http://www.agid.gov.it/agenda-digitale/infrastrutture-architetture/carta-nazionale-servizi/specifiche-tecniche (referred March 11, 2015)
20. per l'Italia Digitale, A.: Sistema pubblico per la gestione dell'identit digitale, March 10, 2015. http://www.agid.gov.it/agenda-digitale/infrastrutture-architetture/spid (referred March 11, 2015)
21. Le Conseil Constitutionel, France: Loi relative la protection de l'identit, March 2012. http://www.conseil-constitutionnel.fr/decision/2012/2012-652-dc/decision-n-2012-652-dc-du-22-mars-2012.105165.html. Dcision n 2012-652 DC du 22 mars 2012
22. Snat: Projet de loi de finances pour 2014: Adminstration territoriale, February 16, 2015. http://www.senat.fr/rap/a13-162-1/a13-162-15.html
23. DGPGC: DNI electrnico gua de referencia bsica, July 4, 2014. http://www.dnielectronico.es/PDFs/Guia_de_referencia_basica_v1_4.pdf (referred March 13, 2015)
24. Ministry of Internal Affairs and Communications: Basic resident registration card (2009). http://www.soumu.go.jp/main_sosiki/jichi_gyousei/c-gyousei/zairyu/english/basic_resident_registration_card.html (referred February 4, 2015)

25. Messmer, E.: Indonesia advances world's most ambitious biometric-based national identity card project. NetworkWorld, September 20, 2012. http://www.networkworld.com/article/2160047/access-control/indonesia-advances-world-s-most-ambitious-biometric-based-national-identity-card-proj.html (referred March 25, 2015)

26. Priyanto, U.: National electronic id card (e-KTP) programme in indonesia. ID World, Abu Dhabi, slides, March 18–19, 2012. http://www.mesago.de/download/IDA/5_Presentations/Powerpoint_Presentation/Conference_room1/Day1/Session1/1_Priyanto_Unggul.pdf (referred March 25, 2015)

27. ChinaNews: Harbin first third-generation ID card contains fingerprint anti-counterfeiting, January 23, 2014. http://www.chinanews.com/sh/2014/01-23/5770899.shtml (referred March 26, 2015)

28. Mutlugün, M., Adalier, O.: Turkish national electronic identity card. In: Proceedings of the 2nd International Conference on Security of Information and Networks, SIN 2009, pp. 14–18. ACM, New York (2009)

29. Information Technologies and Communications Authority: Electronic certificate service providers. http://www.btk.gov.tr/bilgi_teknolojileri/elektronik_imza/eshs.php (referred February 5, 2015)

30. Soares, E.: Brazil: New national ID card launched, January 4, 2011. http://www.loc.gov/lawweb/servlet/lloc_news?disp3_l205402458_text (referred March 25, 2015)

31. Giesecke & Devrient: G&D becomes first manufacturer to gain ITI certification for new eID cards in Brazil. Press Release, April 18, 2012. http://www.gi-de.com/en/about_g_d/press/press_releases/G%26D-Becomes-First-Manufacturer-to-Gain-ITI-Certification-for-New-eID-Cards-in-Brazil-g19648.jsp (referred March 26, 2015)

32. Indra: Indra awarded the implementation of the electronic identity card ans passport in chile, July 19, 2010. http://www.indracompany.com/en/noticia/indra-awarded-the-implementation-of-the-electronic-identity-card-and-passport-in-chile (referred March 26, 2015)

33. Marty, B.: Argentina's national ID cards to store sensitive data. Panam Post, July 1, 2014. http://panampost.com/belen-marty/2014/07/01/argentinas-national-id-cards-to-store-sensitive-data/ (referred March 26, 2015)

34. Electronic Frontier Foundation: Mandatory national IDs and biometric databases (2014) (referred March 26, 2015)

35. Pys.org: Mexico to pioneer iris technology on ID cards, January 21, 2011. http://phys.org/news/2011-01-mexico-iris-technology-id-cards.html (referred March 26, 2015)

36. Voronov, A., Dementieva, X.: Russians to get plastic digital identity cards. Russia & India Report, September 5, 2013. http://in.rbth.com/society/2013/09/05/russians_to_get_plastic_digital_identity_cards_29081.html (referred March 26, 2015)

37. Department of Home Affairs, Republic of South Affica: General information about south african identity books / identity documents (2015). http://www.dha.gov.za/index.php/civic-services/identity-documents (referred March 26, 2015)

38. South African Government: Identity document (2015). http://www.gov.za/services/personal-identification/identity-document (referred March 26, 2015)

39. Swiss Post: SuisseID (2015). https://postsuisseid.ch/en/suisseid (referred March 27, 2015)

40. Fleurus, C., van der Peijl, S., Zuuren, E.V., Wauters, P., Whitehouse, D.: Towards a trusted and sustainable European federated eID system. Final report, European Commission, Information Society and Media Directorate-General (2011)

41. Finnish Bankers' Association: Tupas identification service, April 19, 2011. http://www.fkl.fi/en/themes/e-services/tupas/Pages/default.aspx (referred March 25, 2015)

42. Mobile certificate (in finnish), April 15, 2011. http://www.mobiilivarmenne.fi/documents/Mobiiliasiointivarmenne-Varmennepolitiikka.pdf (referred April 20, 2015)

43. 3GPP: Generic authentication architecture GAA; generic bootstrapping architecture GBA. Technical report, 3GPP (2014). http://www.3gpp.org/DynaReport/33220.htm (referred April 20, 2015)

44. Schneier, B.: Two-factor authentication: Too little, too late. Commun. ACM **48**(4), 136 (2005)

45. Nyman, T., Ekberg, J.E., Asokan, N.: Citizen electronic identities using TPM 2.0. In: TrustED 2014. ACM, November 3, 2014

46. Tamrakar, S., Ekberg, J.E., Laitinen, P.: On rehoming the electronic id to TEEs. In: Trustcom 2015, August 2015

47. First Post India: Three new online aadhaar services to authenticate your identity, May 24, 2013. http://www.firstpost.com/india/three-new-online-aadhaar-services-to-authenticate-your-identity-812451.html (referred February 4, 2015)

48. Collins, J.: Japan issues e-passports. RFID journal, March 28, 2006. http://www.rfidjournal.com/articles/view?2224 (referred February 5, 2015)

49. European Union: Council regulation on standards for security features and biometrics in passports and travel documents issued by member states, December 13, 2004. http://eur-lex.europa.eu/LexUriServ/LexUriServ.do?uri=OJ:L:2004:385:0001:0006:EN:PDF. No 2252/2004

50. Porter, A., Kirkup, J.: ID card scheme will be scrapped with no refund to holders. The Telegraph newspaper, May 24, 2010. http://www.telegraph.co.uk/news/politics/7757720/ID-card-scheme-will-be-scrapped-with-no-refund-to-holders.html (referred March 25, 2015)

51. Mathieson, S.: Minister destroys national identity register. Kaple, government computing, February 10, 2011. http://central-government.governmentcomputing.com/news/2011/feb/10/minister-destroys-national-identity-register (referred March 25, 2015)

52. Citizencard: Citizencard (2014). http://www.citizencard.com/ (referred March 25, 2015)

53. Government Gateway: Welcome to the government gateway (2015). http://www.gateway.gov.uk/ (referred March 28, 2015)

54. Bolten, J.B.: E-authentication guidance for federal agencies, December 16, 2003. https://www.whitehouse.gov/sites/default/files/omb/memoranda/fy04/m04-04.pdf (referred September 7, 2015)

55. Wagner, M.: E-gov (a speech in the U.S house of representatives, March 24, 2004. http://www.gsa.gov/portal/content/101464 (referred March 28, 2015)

56. NIST: National strategy for trusted identities in cyperspace (NSTIC). http://www.nist.gov/nstic/ (referred March 31, 2015)

57. Canada Revenue Agency: My account for individuals, March 5, 2015. http://www.cra-arc.gc.ca/myaccount/ (referred March 28, 2015)

58. Australian Government, Department of Finance: Authentication and identity management (2008). http://www.finance.gov.au/policy-guides-procurement/authentication-and-identity-management/ (referred March 28, 2015)

59. Allonby, N.: ID cards - a world view. GlobalResearch, August 31, 2009. http://www.globalresearch.ca/id-cards-a-world-view/14992 (referred March 25, 2015)

60. Estonian World: Estonia and finland become first in the world to digitally sign international agreement, December 23, 2013. http://estonianworld.com/technology/estonia-finland-become-first-world-digitally-sign-international-agreement/ (referred March 29, 2015)
61. The Economist: Estonia takes the plunge, June 26, 2014. http://www.economist.com/news/international/21605923-national-identity-scheme-goes-global-estonia-takes-plunge (referred March 26, 2015)
62. Kitsing, M.: Online participation in Estonia: active voting, low engagement. In: Proceedings of the 5th International Conference on Theory and Practice of Electronic Governance, ICEGOV 2011, pp. 20–26. ACM, New York (2011)
63. OECD: Digital identity management, enabling innovation and trust in the internet economy. Technical report, OECD (2011) http://www.oecd.org/sti/ieconomy/49338380.pdf (referred March 30, 2015)
64. The Economist Intelligence Unit: Democracy index 2012: Democracy at a standstill, March 2013. http://pages.eiu.com/rs/eiu2/images/Democracy-Index-2012.pdf (referred June 18, 2015)

Author Index

Printed in the United States
By Bookmasters